100 THINGS
PENN STATE FANS
SHOULD KNOW & DO
BEFORE THEY DIE

Lou Prato

D1512275

TRIUMPH
BOOKS

Library of Congress Cataloging-in-Publication Data

Prato, Lou.
100 things Penn State fans should know & do before they die / Lou Prato.
    pages cm.
ISBN 978-1-62937-144-3 (paperback)
    1.   Pennsylvania State University—Football—History. 2.   Penn State Nittany Lions (Football team)—History. I. Title. II. Title: One hundred things Penn State fans should know and do before they die.
GV958.P46P7 2015
796.33209748'53—dc23
                                 2015014314

This book is available in quantity at special discounts for your group or organization. For further information, contact:
    Triumph Books LLC
    814 North Franklin Street
    Chicago, Illinois 60610
    (312) 337-0747
    www.triumphbooks.com

Printed in U.S.A.
ISBN: 978-1-62937-144-3
Design by Patricia Frey
Photos courtesy of Penn State University unless otherwise indicated

For all the Penn State fans
of the past, present, and future.
We Are—Penn State!

Contents

Foreword

The first thing anyone should know about Penn State is that there is no place like Penn State. While the storied history of Pennsylvania State University is well-documented, this book provides a magnificent roadmap into the university's past and the future.

Like many others, I grew up watching Penn State football on TV: the plain blue and white uniforms with the black shoes; the coach with the big glasses roaming the sideline as fans erupted in a chant, yelling "We Are—Penn State!" Every Saturday I would tune in for this three-hour sport spectacle and after watching I believed I knew everything about Penn State and Penn State football. Boy was I wrong!

I first visited Penn State during the summer of 1998. I was attending the Penn State Football camp for the very first time. I can vividly remember the drive to campus. It felt like the longest car ride of my life. I recall the open fields, mountains, more open fields, more mountains, and then I noticed a huge stadium rising in the horizon. There it was, Beaver Stadium, the place I had seen on TV so many times in the past, the place where history had been made, the meeting place for over 100,000 Penn Staters every other Fall Saturday.

As we pulled up to East Halls, I opened the car door, looked around, and wondered to myself, *Is this the place they really call Happy Valley?*! It was summer, so there weren't many students around. The dorms were rather empty, and the thousands of fans were nowhere to be found. As soon as my parents dropped me off I felt a sudden wave of homesickness rush over me. I wasn't sure Penn State was the place for me, but I decided to stick it out for a week and give football camp a shot.

Fortunately, I had a good week of camp and at the end I was told someone wanted to spend a few minutes with me before I headed home. As I walked into the small conference room, I immediately noticed the figure sitting at the table. It was the coach I had watched on TV growing up—Coach Paterno, Joe Pa, the best coach in college football—and he wanted to say hello to me! I was excited, nervous, and thrilled all at the same time but I played it cool. I shook his hand and introduced myself. I told him my name, Adam Taliaferro, and Coach Paterno replied, "Yes, I know who you are. You're the cornerback with the fine Italian last name." Coach Paterno then told me about the educational opportunities at Penn State and the opportunity to play big-time college football. I decided to commit to Penn State, and thus my Penn State journey began.

I tell you my story because the day I committed to Penn State was the first time I felt "Penn State Pride." The word "pride" is defined as "a feeling of deep pleasure or satisfaction derived from one's own achievements, the achievements of those with whom one is closely associated, or from qualities or possessions that are widely admired." The word "pride" is also defined as "a group of lions forming a social unit."

As you read through the *100 Things* you will undoubtedly come across numerous instances in Penn State's history that will stir your Penn State Pride. You will read about moments where the Nittany Lions came together as a unit to make history. Most importantly, you will better understand why Penn State is such a special place to so many people.

I would not be the person I am today without many of the individuals and moments mentioned in this book. In September, 2000, I sustained a spinal cord injury during my freshman season while playing in a game against Ohio State. I was given only a small chance of ever walking again and my life was forever changed. At the lowest point of my life, the entire Penn State community was there to pick me up. Coach Paterno; the coaching staff; Dr. Sebastianelli; George Salvaterra and the training staff; JT (Jeremy); Spider (Kirk); Don Ferrell (TK); teammates; former lettermen; alumni; and Penn State fans across the country supported me throughout my journey to walk again. Through my eight months of recovery, a day did not pass where I wouldn't hear from someone connected to Penn State. Whether it was Sue Paterno driving three hours to bring me cookies in the hospital or receiving a letter of well wishes from a Penn Stater I never met, I will in no way ever forget how Penn State helped me and my family through my greatest adversity.

Penn State is truly a special place. If you have walked the campus, strolled downtown, or experienced a football weekend, you know exactly what I am talking about. If you have not visited Penn State, this book is a great starting point. Please enjoy this journey celebrating Penn State's past, present, future, and all the fantastic moments that make Penn State what is today. Penn State's outlook is brighter than ever and I look forward to many more wonderful memories as coach James Franklin leads our Nittany Lions into the future! We Are!

—Adam Taliaferro

Acknowledgments

If not for Mitch Rogatz and Tom Bast at Triumph Books, I would not have written this book. This is my fourth book for Triumph and, once again, Tom in acquisitions gave me this opportunity. I can't thank him enough for all he has done for me since that first book in 2006 that I co-wrote with Scott Brown, *What It Means to Be a Nittany Lion.*

I know Mitch has to approve all books published by Triumph because he is the president and publisher. I thank him once again for trusting me with writing another book for his company. Book publishing is a tough business, particularly in this era of the Internet and eBooks. Authors like me who concentrate on books about sports, particularly those of regional interest, owe Mitch a debt of gratitude for keeping this genre of books alive.

I'm sure Tom and Mitch consulted with others at Triumph in making their decision to let me be part of this popular series of *100 Things* books. So I thank them, too.

I also need to thank Adam Motin, Triumph's managing editor, and the editor he assigned to work with me, Michelle Bruton. Adam was one of my editors for *Game Changers: The Greatest Plays in Penn State Football History,* along with Laine Morreau. After his promotion in 2012, Adam assigned Laine to be my editor for *We Are Penn State: The Remarkable Journey of the 2012 Nittany Lions,* and that worked out well. Adam did it again with Michelle, who not only corrected all my grammatical, punctuation, and style mistakes but offered encouragement throughout my tight writing deadline and the editing process.

Outside of Triumph, no one deserves more thanks than my wife and best friend, Carole. Without her support I would never have written any books, and this one required super understanding and patience because of a personal situation. She has been the love of my life almost from the day we met more than 60 years ago and she has tolerated my mistress—writing—through courtship and marriage.

It's a good thing for me that Carole was a big Penn State football fan even before I met her, and she continues to be passionate about Penn State's athletic teams, especially football, basketball, ice hockey, wrestling, and women's volleyball. She is neither a journalist nor a professional writer, but reads all my copy before I submit it and has saved me from numerous errors over the years, including in this book.

I also need to thank my mother, Florence, who passed away before she could see and read the books I have written about Penn State football. She didn't know much about football, but if she had not shipped me off to Penn State decades ago, I certainly wouldn't be writing this book.

I owe a big thanks to Adam Taliaferro for writing the foreword. He epitomizes the heart and soul of Nittany Lion football players and, as you will read, Adam's "miracle" is part of Penn State's memorable history.

Because of the scope of this book, there are hundreds of people who indirectly helped me in researching and writing the articles and books that were sources for me this time. There are far too many to identify but I thank them, and if they read this book they'll know they are in this group.

There are several special people who need to be singled out for this project, and some of them are quoted and identified in various chapters. Mike Poorman is one. He gave me great advice on the overall content and rankings of the book as well as editorial suggestions on a few specific chapters that required his expertise. I thank Mike for his help and his continued friendship.

Before we became friends, Mike was the editor of *Town and Gown* magazine, a popular monthly publication in the State

College–Penn State community. Several chapters in this book actually originated with assignments for *Town and Gown* and its sister preseason football and basketball annuals, first by Mike and in recent years by one of his successors, Dave Pencek.

I also owe great thanks to Phil Grosz and Matt Herb of *Blue White Illustrated* (*BWI*) and Mark Brennan of *Fight On State* magazine. Both magazines and their websites are read by the most dedicated of Penn State sports fans. Phil is the owner-publisher of *BWI* and Mark was once his editor before setting up his own website and magazine. It was under Mark's direction shortly after the publishing of my first book that I became a regular contributor for *BWI* and I continue to write for *BWI* and *Fight On State*. Matt is now the *BWI* editor. Many chapters in this book had their genesis with articles I wrote for *BWI* and *Fight On State*. Thanks, guys. You made it easier to organize and write this book.

As with all my previous books, two Penn State departments were helpful in the gathering of photographs. So a special thanks to Jeff Nelson and Barry Jones from Athletic Communications and Jackie Esposito and Paul Dzyak of the Penn State University Sports Archives.

I also want to thank Ken Hickman, the director of the Penn State All-Sports Museum, and two legendary football broadcasters, Fran Fisher and Steve Jones, for their assistance along the way. Unfortunately, Fran passed away before this book was published. He was a great friend and will be missed.

Some of the others who helped in my research of specific chapters over the years include Marty Adams, Jesse Arnelle, Horace Ashenfelter, Joe Battisa, John Black, Charlie Blockson, John Bove, Ned Book, Benny Bronstein, Ted Brown, Dick Bundy, Spider Caldwell, John Cappelletti, Mike Corcoran, Roger Corey, John Coyle, Tim Curley, Kirk Diehl, John Duda, Della Durant, Michelene Franzetta, Dave Joyner, Bob Krimmel, Bud Meredith, Ron Moehler, Lenny Moore, Jon Nese, Thomas Palchak, Charlie

Pittman, Hank Opperman, Dan Radakovich, Wally Richardson, Dave Robinson, Pete Rohrer, Jason Rupp, Jack Sherry, Michael Signora, Sam Stellatella, Bill Summers, Jeff Tarman, Carolyn Todd, Wally Triplett, Michael Weinrab, and Roger Williams.

Lastly, thanks to all the Penn State fans out there who keep being interested in what I write. You make it all worthwhile.

Introduction

Selecting the "100 Things to Know and Do" for this book was much easier than ranking them.

First, as you will read, I cheated. Yes, there are 100 chapters of such things Penn State fans need to know and do, but even within some of those chapters, I combined pertinent facts that might have been in separate chapters if I had more room. There also are 36 sidebars that contain additional information, plus a chapter near the end with several quick hits that didn't make it into the chapters or sidebars.

You also need to know that this is primarily a book for football fans. That's natural because Penn State's No. 1 sport is football. However, in discussion with my publisher, we decided to include several chapters highlighting other varsity sports. Choosing which of those sports to include was not too difficult based on my criteria, although readers may disagree with my choices.

The criteria I used for all the chapters and sidebars was the same. My fundamental benchmark was history and the significance of a historical figure, event, or team to the evolution of football and the entire athletic program. This is not a chronological listing but one that considers the impact of the past on Penn State's athletic environment and the university in 2015.

Someone else writing this book might have a totally different perspective on what to include in it. My version is based on history because I have been deeply involved with the university's sports history since 2000, when I began helping the athletic department with the development of the Penn State All-Sports Museum. I became the first director of the museum in 2001, and although I retired as the director at the end of 2005, I continue to serve on the museum's advisory board.

My work with the museum reignited my interest in Penn State's athletic history, particularly football, and I have written several books and a multitude of newspaper, magazine, and Internet articles about that illustrious history. Many of the chapters and sidebars in this book originated with my research for those books and articles.

The story behind the creation of the famous cheer "We Are— Penn State!" was known only by a few cheerleaders until I began writing about it in the late 1990s. No one knew how Penn State became Linebacker U until my articles started appearing in 2005 traced it all back to former Lions linebacker Dan Radakovich in the mid-1950s who became the team's first linebackers coach.

Then there was the naming of Beaver Stadium. It has been well publicized that the stadium is named after James Beaver, one of the most important men in the history of the university. I discovered that the Penn State student body had seriously considered another Penn State benefactor in 1892 before voting to name the athletic grounds, including the football playing field, after Beaver. That one even surprised a few longtime Penn State historians.

No one knew when tailgating started until I found out while researching my first book, *The Penn State Football Encyclopedia*. Nor was there much known about the roots of the now-popular Blue-White game that ends spring practice until I first wrote about it in 2010.

I give you this insight not to boast about it. I want readers to understand the research and diligence that went into each chapter and sidebar of this book.

That insight also involved personal experience, because I have been involved in many of the "things" in this book—sometimes as a fan and sometimes as a reporter—going back to my freshman year at Penn State in 1955.

I was there when Lenny Moore and Jim Brown dueled in the Penn State–Syracuse game in 1955 and when a 12-men-on-the-field penalty helped Penn State beat Kansas in the 1969 Orange Bowl. I was at the New Orleans Sugar Bowl on January 1, 1979, when Penn State lost the National Championship Game to Alabama, and again on January 1, 1983, when Penn State beat Georgia to win its first national title. And I was there at many other times, far too many to mention here.

Over the years I have become an acquaintance or friend to many people who are in this book. Those relationships have enabled me to tell their stories from a different perspective. Some of them are quoted in this book, others are not. But they were all helpful in my understanding what each of them meant to Penn State's athletic legacy.

I have tried to make each chapter not only informative but as lively and entertaining as it could be in such concise form. Whether I succeeded even 50 percent of the time will be up to you.

The rankings are another matter. People who know me will tell you I do not like to do rankings of any type or make predictions, especially on the outcome of football games. It's just not my nature. I only do rankings and predictions when forced. Thus, if I didn't do them for this book, you would be reading the words of another author and not mine.

Rankings depend on subjective criteria, and even with strict guidelines one view can differ vastly from another. What's normal for anyone doing rankings is to favor the more familiar or the latest. That is why all-time teams are so heavily based on the modern players. So keep in mind my rankings lean in the other direction—history.

When I began this project, my editors at Triumph gave me some advice: concentrate on your first 10 rankings because they are the most important. They were right. I did my first rankings on December 8, 2014. My first five have not changed. The next five include three from my original top 10 list but moved around slightly.

Basically, after chapters 1–15, the rankings are almost like a crapshoot at the gambling tables. Before I did my final rankings, I moved chapters up and down continually as my thought process did cartwheels. As I write this, I am satisfied with the final rankings in the book. But I just know I will be kicking myself when you read this, wondering if I should have moved this one up and that one down.

As I wrote earlier, my insertion of the non-football chapters is also based on history and the impact of the event or person on Penn State today. That's why "The Creamery" is No. 9 in this book and the second non-football chapter, "Play Days," about the beginning of Penn State's women's varsity sports, is next, at No. 24.

The information in each chapter is condensed. There is much more behind the narrative. Anyone interested in reading more about a particular event or person should start with the source material listed at the end of this book. You can also contact me through my publisher.

Finally, one reason for Triumph to publish books in this series is to stimulate fan interest. I hope I will stimulate yours. I expect you to let me know how your rankings differ from mine, and why. Talk to me at a book signing or at a football game. Or visit the Penn State All-Sports Museum and leave me a message.

We Are—Penn State! I just know there are 100 *more* things we Penn State Fans need to know and do before we die!

1 Cheer "We Are—Penn State!"

A grey-haired American tourist wearing an old leather air force flying jacket and a blue baseball cap with the words "Nittany Lions" in white on the front stood on a wooden platform on a mountain above the town of Zermatt, Switzerland, and gazed across the chasm at the world-famous Matterhorn. At first, he didn't notice the young couple in their twenties walking out of the gift shop.

The woman was wearing a white hoodie with the words "Penn State" on the front. Just as the couple passed, the old man turned, spotted the young lady's hoodie, and smiled.

"We Are—," the old man shouted. Several other tourists looked at the man and probably wondered what he was yelling about.

The young couple turned toward the old man and immediately saw his blue cap. Almost in unison they yelled back, "Penn State!"

The terse tableau must have seemed strange to the dozens of international tourists, including fellow Americans, who had witnessed the perplexing verbal exchange between the old man and the young couple. They had never seen each other before, but they had a common bond instantly in four words. That's what frequently happens whenever Penn State fans encounter each other, no matter the location or the circumstances. It could be a crowded restaurant in Los Angeles or a ferry boat in Hong Kong. Or maybe on the streets of New York City or at a campground near Yellowstone Park.

"We Are—Penn State!"

It is one of the most famous and familiar sports cheers in college football, instantly identifying the people who yell it as dedicated Penn State fans.

Although there are other college cheers that rival Penn State's in familiarity—such as Alabama's "Roll Tide!" and Texas' "Hook 'em Horns"—none involve the participants in such a unique way because at least two people must be involved. One person or more yell the first part, "We Are—," and a second soulmate or more responds with "Penn State!" It can be uttered just once or several times in succession. And when concluding a quick series of the cheer, a tagline is also added, with the people who started it all off shouting, "Thank you," and the respondents yelling back, "You're welcome!"

As one might expect, the cheer has spawned many copycats. Marshall University fans believe the cheer was invented at their

The Suhey-Triplett Myth

In recent years, Penn State's famed cheer has been credited to Steve Suhey, an All-American guard on the 1946 and 1947 football teams. At a team meeting late in the 1946 season, the players voted unanimously not to play a scheduled game at segregated Miami when told they had to leave their two black teammates at home. With the two black players still on the team a year later, Penn State was invited to play in the Cotton Bowl in segregated Dallas. Wally Triplett, recognized as Penn State's first African American varsity player, was a standout wingback on those teams.

According to one variation of the story that Triplett began relating a few years ago, a player or two asked aloud sometime after the 1946 Miami team meeting if they would have to vote again if another such racial instance occurred. Another version has players wondering about another meeting before the Cotton Bowl invitation was accepted in 1947. Either way, Triplett says Suhey, the co-captain of the 1947 team, strongly asserted publicly to several players there would be no meetings because, he said, "We're Penn State."

Suhey probably used those words. He was a passionate leader and one of the players behind the team's decision not to play Miami. Penn State fans can accept the mythology the next time they holler the cheer, but be sure to remember those diligent cheerleaders who created it.

school. That myth stems from a 2006 popular inspirational movie, *We Are Marshall*, depicting the true story of a 1970 charter plane crash that killed 75 people, virtually wiping out Marshall's football team and devastating the college town of Huntingdon. However, an article in the *Huntingdon News* in January 2007 pointed out the Marshall version was heard for the first time in 1988, several years after the creation of Penn State's cheer.

Actually, the Penn State cheerleaders who crafted the cheer in the mid-1970s did borrow from the cheers of three other colleges—Ohio State, Southern Cal, and Kentucky—to create their own unique one. It started in 1975.

"The only cheer everyone in the stadium knew was 'N-I... Double-T...A-N...Y...Roar, Lions, Roar,' because the Blue Band would do it before the game with their hats to get the crowd going," remembered former cheerleader Bob Krimmel, then the group's advisor. The cheerleaders wanted to devise a new cheer to revitalize the crowd.

They found parts of what they were seeking in Penn State's third game of the season at Ohio State and a couple weeks later while watching a televised game from USC. They took the traditional "O-H-I-O" that rolls back and forth around Ohio Stadium and the "We Are SC! We Are SC!" shouted rapidly without pause by USC, and turned it into a cheer where everyone yells the same words: "We Are Penn State," but without the deliberate pause.

The cheerleaders tried out the new cheer in the student section at Beaver Stadium, then in the north end zone seating area, during the first three home games that opened the 1976 season. "It went nowhere," said Krimmel.

When Penn State played its first away game, at night against Kentucky in Lexington, they found the golden key. "There was this unbelievable roar back and forth across the stadium, with one half yelling 'Blue' and the other half screaming, 'White,'" said Krimmel. "We knew that would work for us."

Still, it took more than five years to fully succeed, first with the students—who had been moved near the south end zone in a major Beaver Stadium expansion before the 1978 season—and then with the rest of the fans. I vividly remember shouting the cheer as a spectator at the 1979 Sugar Bowl in the New Orleans Superdome, but it still had not caught on with the Penn State football nation.

A September 1981 game at Nebraska regenerated the cheerleaders when they heard the home fans yelling in unison, "Go…Big Red" throughout the game. They intensified their teaching process, and by the end of that year, the Penn State crowd was cheering it without prompting from the cheerleaders. Somewhere along the way, the "Thank you" and "You're welcome" were added.

The cheer is now immortalized with a 12-foot sculpture installed the summer of 2014 on a prominent and busy corner at University Drive and Curtin Road close to Beaver Stadium, Pegula Arena, and the Bryce Jordan Center. The words "We Are" in large shining steel letters stand permanently on a concrete foundation for all to see, a gift by Penn State's Senior Class of 2013.

So, there you have it—the birth of the illustrious four words that all Penn State fans must cheer and opponents hate to hear.

"We Are—Penn State!"

2 The Grand Experiment

Even before he became Penn State's head coach in 1966, Joe Paterno began thinking about the kind of football team he wanted. Paterno believed he could build an outstanding football team composed of superior athletes who also were superior students. He wanted to recruit the sons of ordinary farmers, mill hands, and other working-class families who were smart, diligent, and persevering and who could not only win football games, but would go on to be major contributors to society.

Paterno had nothing but disdain for the "dumb jock" syndrome, a conviction held by much of the public—especially those in academics—that most athletes would not be in college if not for their physical abilities and skills. Even many coaches and administrators steered players toward degrees in physical education rather than the more demanding engineering, premedical, and business curriculums.

Penn State had its share of borderline students in past decades, but in the early 1950s, the university implemented new entrance rules for scholarship athletes to conform to NCAA standards. The thrust of the rules was that athletes would be admitted to Penn State under the same qualifications as non-athletes. Furthermore, the student-athlete "must maintain normal progress with his class and maintain a term cumulative scholastic average which would keep him off probation." In conjunction with the new rules, assistant coaches were assigned to monitor the classroom work of the athletes and provide tutoring when needed.

By the latter years of the Rip Engle tenure, Penn State was recruiting better students who were also good athletes. Tackle Joe Bellas, an accounting major with a 3.5 GPA, and linebacker John Runnels, a pre-law major with a near-perfect 4.0 GPA, not only made All-East but became Penn State's first two first-team Academic All-Americans. They also were among the first student-athletes in the nation to receive $7,500 NCAA postgraduate scholarships

In the fall of his second season, Paterno started to talk openly about his philosophy. He wanted the kids to have a full college life, to socialize and to live among the students. There would be no false promises, no cheating, no special privileges, and no bending of the rules. And if they didn't study and go to class, they were out.

Sportswriters started hearing Paterno expound on his credo at the small, informal Friday night media receptions before home games. In October 1967, Paterno's seemingly radical idea appeared in public for the first time in a *Philadelphia Daily News* article by beat writer Bill Conlin. Conlin gave Paterno's idea an official name by capitalizing the two words Paterno had used to define it.

"I'm thinking in terms of a Grand Experiment," Conlin quoted Paterno. "It sounds a little corny, I know, but it's that kind of thing for us because we intend doing it with people who belong at Penn State. Everybody assumes if you have a great football team there have to be sacrifices in the area of [academic] standards. People tell me it can't be done without sacrificing standards. They tell me I'm daydreaming...."

Conlin wrote that Paterno wanted to prove Penn State could "play good football in the best league possible, with people who belong in college, and who kept things in perspective. Look, I want these kids to enjoy football. But I also want them to enjoy college. I want them to learn art and literature and music and all the other things college has to offer."

There was another facet to the Grand Experiment that Paterno told Ridge Riley, creator of the popular football newsletter for alumni. "What's needed is about 40 good football players, 15 excellent ones, and four or five great ones," Paterno said. "They must all have pride and enthusiasm. Among the superstars, there should be a breakaway runner, a great kicker, a versatile quarterback and so on.... Sure, there are only a dozen or so schools in the country which will come up with these standards year after year. Penn State can do it if everyone gets behind us. Eventually we should have this kind of team."

When word of Paterno's Grand Experiment started making the rounds of the coaches' fraternity, most of them thought he was

From Onkotz and Pittman to Urschel

All-Americans Dennis Onkotz and Charlie Pittman were the first to prove the Grand Experiment worked. They were in Paterno's first recruiting class and became Academic All-Americans in 1969 as well as first team All-Americans on the field.

Onkotz was a consensus All-American linebacker in 1968 and 1969 while studying biophysics. He made national news when it became known he went to class on Saturday mornings before the afternoon games because that was so rare for college football players.

"We were the symbols of what Joe was pushing, the scholar-athlete," Onkotz wrote in the book *What It Means to Be a Nittany Lion*. "We went to class, we graduated, we did all those things you're supposed to do."

The teams Onkotz and Pittman played on were undefeated in 1968 and 1969, and from the fourth game of the 1967 season, they never lost a game.

Pittman was the rushing leader all three seasons, but the records he set have all been surpassed by the likes of Hall of Famers Lydell Mitchell and Curt Warner. Pittman was a business major, and encouraged by Paterno, he later earned an MBA. Tony Pittman followed his dad to Penn State and was a defensive starter on another undefeated team in 1994. He not only was an Academic All-American like his father but also received an $18,000 fellowship as a Hall of Fame scholar-athlete.

Decades later in the 2000s, the Grand Experiment was still working with first-team All-Americans linebacker Paul Posluszny and offensive guard Stefen Wisniewski, who also were Hall of Fame scholar athletes, as well as math genius and third-team All-American guard John Urschel.

Onkotz has spent most of his life as a financial consultant and Pittman is vice president of a major media company.

"I am who I am today because of Joe Paterno's Grand Experiment and Penn State," Pittman said. Onkotz and many others would certainly agree.

crazy or a hypocrite. Many predicted Paterno would be a flop both on the field and off it. They were all wrong.

Since Bellas and Runnells through 2014, 29 other Nittany Lions have earned first-team Academic All-American honors and 13 of them were selected first-, second-, or third-team All-Americans on the field. Seventeen scholar-athletes, including five who were first-team All-Americans on the field, have received $18,000 postgraduate fellowships from the College Football Hall of Fame. Eighteen players have received $7,500 postgraduate scholarships from the NCAA, and four players earned $5,000 postgraduate scholarships from the National Association of Collegiate Athletic Directors.

The graduation rates of Paterno's players have been among the best in the nation. Since the NCAA began releasing annual graduation rates in 1990, Penn State football players have averaged more than 80 percent and as high as 93 percent. Those figures are consistently among the top in the Football Bowl Subdivision and higher than the average of the Penn State student body.

Equally significant, the players of the Grand Experiment are now successful doctors, lawyers, business owners, educators, financial consultants, stockbrokers, authors—you name it—first-class citizens who are major contributors to society.

Perhaps the Grand Experiment can be summed up by attorney Harry Hamilton, a third-team All-American defensive back and a two-time Academic All-American in 1982 and 1983 who also won a $7,500 NCAA postgraduate scholarship.

"Joe always told us his all-time team is going to be the players that played for him that contributed the most to society," said Hamilton.

That's the ultimate result of the Grand Experiment and it is Joe Paterno's lasting legacy.

The Football Culture

The only reason this chapter is not ranked No. 1 in this book is because it is incomplete. I believe everyone needs to know about the claims made during the summer of 2012 that a corrupt football culture at Penn State allowed a respected assistant coach to roam freely for years without exposing him as an alleged pedophile. He has been convicted and is now in prison. This is not about the case itself or—with one significant exception—about the controversy that continues in many judicial and public venues.

That exception is the assertion in an internal investigative report by former FBI Director Louie Freeh that an immoral, self-serving destructive "culture of football" at Penn State was at the root of the entire matter. Freeh's report commissioned by the school's board of trustees for $6.5 million is still being debated inside and outside the courtroom. The alleged facts and conclusions by Freeh and his investigators and the flaws and dubious assumptions condemned by their critics are too detailed to get into here.

I have examined the Freeh Report in depth and found multiple flaws, instances of hearsay, and outright untruths, none more prominent than the ludicrous insistence that Penn State's academics were perverted by the "culture of football."

In the 106-year history of the NCAA between 1906 and 2012, Penn State never had one major violation of NCAA rules, and just a few self-reported and mostly inadvertent secondary violations. The university has a well-documented history of stressing academics in athletics, dating back to the days of the so-called "tramp athletes" in the early 1900s. Since then, the academic requirements for athletes have been no different than the rest of the student body, and often tougher when it came to maintaining eligibility. In a period from 1928 to 1948, Penn State eliminated all financial aid for athletes. During that time and in the decades since, the university has restructured the athletic department several times to emphasize academic control.

In the Joe Paterno coaching era, he pushed academics to its highest level, particularly with his Grand Experiment (see chapter 2) but also throughout the entire university. His challenge to the board of trustees after winning the national championship in 1982 to make the school No. 1 in academics led to an unprecedented fund-raising campaign that helped Penn State become a world-class institution with an enviable academic curriculum, faculty, and facilities.

In January 2004, the then-president of the NCAA, Myles Brand, cited Penn State as the collegiate model for combining academics and athletics. At the conclusion of an extensive two-day on-campus visit where he met with sundry administration, athletic department, and faculty personnel, as well as student-athletes, Brand stated: "Penn State is the poster child for doing it right in college sports."

Brand's assessment has been backed up by the NCAA's own facts from the year it began releasing annual graduation rates in 1990 until 2015. Penn State graduation rates for football players are among the best in the nation, averaging more than 80 percent and as high as 93 percent.

The crown jewel of the athletic department's emphasis on academics is the Morgan Academic Support Center for Student-Athletes, formed in 1986, with a full-time staff nowadays of 18, dozens of part-timers, and two academic counselors and a learning specialist assigned specifically to football. It's a prototype that has been adopted by other colleges. That's significant to note because of an absurd Freeh Report recommendation on page 139 citing the need for the athletic department to "integrate, where feasible, academic support staff, programs and locations for student-athletes."

In another false and sweeping contention on page 139, Freeh claimed that "over several decades the athletic department was permitted to become a closed community...an island, where staff members lived by their own rules." Earlier, on page 127 in a section titled "The Penn State Culture," Freeh states, "...there is an over-emphasis on 'The Penn State Way' as an approach to decision-making, a resistance to seeking outside perspectives, and an excessive focus on athletics that, if not recognized, negatively impact the University's reputation as a progressive institution."

Yet nowhere is there anything in his 267-page report to support these inflammatory charges, except for a couple of nebulous remarks and one particular vague footnote from unidentified people who were interviewed.

As I wrote in a column for *Blue White Illustrated* in December 2012, "Thirty former past chairs of the Faculty Senate, from various academic backgrounds and disciplines, felt so strongly about all these culture accusations that they issued an angry public defense and criticism of both the Freeh report and NCAA sanctions. 'Not only are these assertions about the Penn State culture unproven,' they wrote, 'we declare them to be false. As faculty members with a cumulative tenure at Penn State in the hundred years, and as former Faculty Senate chairs with intimate knowledge of the University stretching back decades, these assertions do not describe the culture with which we are so very familiar...And we have taken pride in an institutional culture that values honesty, decency, integrity, and fairness."

Readers need to keep in mind that none of the more than 430 individuals that Freeh investigators specified they interviewed were under oath, nor were they identified in the report. Several people told me they were harassed and bullied, particularly if their responses to questions did not please the interrogator.

Neither Freeh nor any of his investigators have testified in a courtroom or in legal depositions, nor has Freeh been asked to defend his accusations in public or even privately before the board of trustees. At least two lawsuits—one by the Paterno family and another by three senior university administrators accused of a cover-up by Freeh with questionable evidence—are slowly meandering through the judicial system. There are also documents from another now-settled court case that show Freeh was apparently in cahoots with the NCAA and certain members of the board of trustees to punish Penn State football, Paterno, and the three administrators.

Unfortunately, the media hasn't waited and has done little to investigate the claims of the Freeh Report and his alleged collusion with the NCAA and certain Penn State trustees. One story after another since November 2011, often quoting a disgruntled and controversial former administrator, helped feed the overwhelming public perception that continues of a supposedly corrupt football culture and a cover-up.

As the famous 18th-century author Sir Walter Scott wrote so many decades ago, "Oh, what a tangled web we weave...when first we practice to deceive."

4 Breaking the Color Line

Penn State was not among the first trickle of college football teams to have African American football players, but when it did, the school did more for civil rights than most of its peers.

African American athletes at Penn State go back to 1910–11 with sophomore Cumberland Posey playing varsity basketball. Posey is one of the most significant African American sports figures of all time, best known for his 35 years as a player and then as the owner of baseball's famous Homestead Grays. However, Posey returned home to Pittsburgh after that one season and it was decades before another African American player was on the basketball team.

As Posey was leaving, Jim Piner was arriving from Devon, near Norristown. In his freshman year of 1911–12, Piner became the first African American to win a varsity letter as a star sprinter on the track team. Sometime before or during his junior year, Piner also left school and never returned.

It would be 25 years before another African American athlete would become a star on the track team, and Barney Ewell turned out to be a great one. He set several collegiate records, and despite a career interrupted by World War I1, he won an Olympic gold medal in the 400 meter relay race in 1948.

There were just a couple of other African Americans on varsity teams between Piner and Ewell, including a reserve boxer named Theodore Elkton Gilbert in 1925, but they are virtually unknown.

Ewell was on campus when the first two African American football players were recruited. Triple-threat tailback Dave Alston and his older brother Harry of Midland were the stars of the 1941 freshman team. Just why no African American players had been on the team before them is not known. Perhaps it was racism; it certainly was a product of the time.

In the late 1930s, the star of one of Penn State's biggest rivals, Syracuse, was a tailback named Wilmeth Sidat-Singh. On the West Coast, the 1939 UCLA team was making headlines with three standout African American players: Kenny Washington, Jackie Robinson, and future movie actor Woody Strode.

Dave Alston had such a sensational freshman year that national sportswriters predicted he would be a collegiate star on par with the UCLA trio. Unfortunately, Dave died unexpectedly in August 1942 from complications in a routine tonsillectomy surgery, and his brother Harry quit school.

Stardom was predicted for Dave Alston, Penn State's first African American player, after a great freshman season. However, he died unexpectedly before he could play in a varsity game.

At least one African American player, Denny Hoggard from west Philadelphia, is known to have worked out with the football team after Alston's death. He didn't play until 1946, after returning from the armed services. By that time, sophomore wingback Wally Triplett had made history by becoming the first African American to start a game in 1945. Hoggard didn't earn a letter in 1946 but Triplett did, making history again.

Near the end of that 1946 season the nearly all-white Penn State football team crashed through the color line by refusing to play a scheduled game at segregated Miami without Triplett and Hoggard. That was just the beginning of what Penn State would do for the civil rights of African Americans.

In late September 1947, the athletic department rejected an invitation to the Penn State boxing team to participate in a match at the Sugar Bowl carnival in segregated New Orleans in late December, even though there were no African Americans on the Lions team. "It is the policy of the College (sic) to compete only in circumstances which will permit the playing of any and all members of its athletic teams," stated athletics director Carl Schott.

About three months later, Triplett and Hoggard became the first African Americans to play in the Cotton Bowl in segregated Dallas, thanks not only to their teammates but to their all-white opponent, SMU. But more needed to be done.

Soon after Rip Engle became Penn State's head coach in 1950, he opened the door wider for more African Americans. Lenny Moore, Rosey Grier, Jesse Arnelle, and Charlie Blockson would break down several racial barriers, including the integration of college football in Fort Worth in 1954.

"We weren't necessarily concentrating on recruiting black players, we just made an effort to get the best football players," Paterno, then an assistant, remembered later.

In the 1959 Liberty Bowl in Philadelphia, tackle Charlie Janerette, a Philadelphia native, was the first African American to play against all-white Alabama. Two years later, All-American end Dave Robinson integrated the Gator Bowl. The next year, when the Penn State charter plane was diverted to Orlando on the way back to the Gator Bowl, the entire team and coaches walked out of the airport restaurant when Robinson was denied service.

Still, it would be Paterno who would intensify the recruitment of African American players after becoming head coach in 1966. "I identified strongly with black kids," Paterno wrote in his autobiography, *Paterno: By the Book*, because of the open prejudice against Italians he experienced growing up in Brooklyn.

In 1969 several African American players led by All-American halfback Charlie Pittman asked the team to reject an invitation to the Cotton Bowl game in Dallas because of the racist environment. The team voted to support their African American teammates and decided to return to Miami's Orange Bowl, missing what turned out to be a chance to win the national championship.

As the years passed, Paterno and his assistants brought more and more of the best African American high school players to Penn State.

"I never went after a black kid just because he was black," Paterno told me a few years ago. "I wanted the best player, whether he was white or black. I don't think we've ever gotten the publicity we deserve for the environment that's been created here and the opportunities that have been created for the kids, regardless of whether they're African American."

It may not have been that way for African American football players more than a half century ago, but there is no doubt what Penn State did helped break down the barriers of that color line.

5 Linebacker U

Penn State was destined to become famous as Linebacker U since 1906, even though the substance and texture that defined the school's plethora of outstanding linebackers that led to the nickname didn't occur until the mid-to-late 1970s.

Penn State's initial first-team All-American in 1906, William "Mother" Dunn, was a linebacker. So was the Lions' eighth one in 1940, Leon Gajecki. There might have been more between 1906 and 1939—when three halfbacks, two guards, and one end were selected in a stretch from 1915 to 1923—if not for the de-emphasis of all Penn State athletics from 1928 to 1948.

After scholarships resumed in 1949, the first player selected as first-team All-American was linebacker Sam Valentine in 1956. Furthermore, two linebackers who came out of that 20-year dark period went on to make their names in the NFL: Chuck Cherundolo with the Steelers and Eagles and Chuck Drazenovich of the Redskins.

What's pertinent about Cherundolo and Drazenovich's bloodlines from Linebacker U to the NFL is that the illustrious nickname evolved primarily because of all the Penn State linebackers that were playing in the NFL in the late 1960s and the 1970s.

Penn State didn't have a linebackers coach until Dan Radakovich, a Lions linebacker from 1954 to 1956, was added to the staff by Rip Engle as a graduate assistant to coach linebackers in 1958. After one of his linebackers, sophomore Jay Huffman, was the MVP of the Lions' 7–0 victory over Alabama in the 1959 Liberty Bowl, Radakovich was promoted to full-time.

Radakovich is the true "Father of Linebacker U." Among early linebackers he sent to the NFL were Bill Saul (with four teams from

1962 to 1970) and Ralph Baker of the New York Jets (1964–74). Radakovich coached Penn State's first two-time All-American linebacker Dennis Onkotz in 1968–69 and the player considered the Nittany Lions' greatest linebacker of all time, Jack Ham, in 1968–70.

Who Created the Nickname Linebacker U?

No one seems to know who bestowed the distinguished nickname Linebacker U on Penn State.

Dan Radakovich, the team's first linebackers coach, thinks sportscaster Howard Cosell may have done it. Radakovich cites a 1974 Cosell radio broadcast that praised the former's coaching, then with the Pittsburgh Steelers, as "the man who turned out all those great linebackers" at Penn State. Although Linebacker U was not mentioned in that commentary, it's possible Cosell conceived of the term later.

The first use of the term by Penn State's sports information office was in a news release the week of September 2–9, 1978, before the second game of the season against Rutgers. Buried in the 19th paragraph of the release was this sentence about defensive tackle Bruce Clark: "Instead of a graduate of 'Linebacker U,' he has become a defensive tackle in the tradition of Mike Reid, Mike Hartenstine, and Randy Crowder." From that point, the next mention of the nickname in an SIO news release was an October 26, 1980, account about fiery linebacker Chet Parlavecchio.

John Morris, the SIO in 1978, died several years ago and no one else connected with the athletic department in those years remembers if he or someone else coined the phrase.

Ronnie Christ, who covered Penn State for the *Harrisburg Patriot-News* at the time, recalls using the nickname on December 31, 1978, prior to the National Championship Game against Alabama in the Sugar Bowl the next day. The headline on his story blared: "Penn State Hasn't Lost Its Linebacker U Reputation."

If the creator of the famous name is ever determined, a plaque should be displayed in his or her honor at the Penn State All-Sports Museum. That's the least Penn State could do for its well-earned reputation as Linebacker U.

"He was by far the best technique coach I ever saw and I am indebted to him," Ham wrote in the foreword to Radakovich's 2012 autobiography, *Bad Rad: Football Nomad*. "I have more respect for Rad as a coach than anybody I've been around, and I've been around a lot of them."

After Ham's junior year, Radakovich left Penn State to go to law school and be an assistant at the University of Cincinnati. Before his departure, he taught an offensive line coach, the now-disgraced Jerry Sandusky, how to coach linebackers, and Sandusky proceed to send a bunch of linebackers into the NFL.

In a November 28, 1978, article in the official NFL magazine *PRO*, Glen Sheeley, a onetime sports editor of the Penn State student newspaper, delved into the history of Penn State linebackers in the NFL:

> To observers of NFL linebackers it must seem as if someone at Penn State has discovered the secret of cloning.
>
> This season, if all goes true to form, at least a dozen Penn State Alumni will be playing linebacker in Pro Football—Jack Ham (Pittsburgh), Ed O'Neil and Ron Crosby (Detroit), John Skorupan (Giants), Jim Laslavic (San Diego), Chris Devlin (Cincinnati), Kurt Allerman (St. Louis), Greg Buttle (New York Jets), Dave Graf (Cleveland) and new draftees Randy Sidler (Jets), Ron Hostetler (Los Angeles), and Tom DePaso (Cincinnati).
>
> Should you desire further proof of the popularity of the Penn State linebackers—or Nittany Lions that played standup defensive end in college and were drafted as linebackers—you can add former modern day NFL players Chuck Drazenovich, Dave Robinson, Ralph Baker, John Ebersole, Bruce Bannon, Tom Hull, and Dennis Onkotz. Another ex-Penn State linebacker, Charlie Zapiec, is considered one of the best defensive players in the Canadian Football League.

Sheeley's list didn't include other pro linebackers before 1978 like Steve Smear, Doug Allen, John Ebersole, and Bob Mitinger. Matt Millen, Lance Mehl, Scott Radeic, Shane Conlan, Walker Lee Ashley, Andre Collins, Brandon Short, LaVar Arrington, and others would be added to the list by the end of the 20th century. Then, in the 2000s, another great group from Linebacker U coached by Ron Vanderlinden would make their names in the NFL: Paul Posluszny, Dan Connor, Sean Lee, and NaVorro Bowman, as well as defensive linemen-turned-linebackers Tamba Hali and Cameron Wake.

Sheely did not mention the now-famous nickname in his 1978 article, but that is around the time Linebacker U was just catching on.

Over the years, other colleges have challenged Penn State's reputation, particularly USC, Miami, and Ohio State.

In 2012, Rivals.com declared Miami should have the title based on the number of linebackers Miami had in the NFL that year—eight compared to Penn State's seven and USC's six. A little petty, perhaps?

A writer for NFL.com bestowed the honor on Florida State in July 2014, dismissing Penn State as no better than No. 5 after FSU, Miami, USC, and Georgia, based primarily on NFL draft picks for the last 25 years. The writer didn't disclose he was a 1985 Florida graduate whose journalism career has been spent mostly covering Florida and Georgia.

Only one other team equals Penn State with three linebackers in the College Football Hall of Fame, and that's Alabama. Ohio State and Tennessee have two. Miami and USC? Zero.

The pretenders and wannabes will always be there. But Penn State has the legacy. Yes, We Are—Linebacker U!

The First Game: 1881 or 1887?

No matter what you've been told, read, heard, or seen, the first Penn State football game was definitely not in 1887.

Yes, the game on November 12, 1887, at Bucknell is cited as the official start of the Penn State football program. But on that same day, six years earlier, a team from Penn State also played at Bucknell—known as the University of Lewisburg until 1896. Penn State won both games, too, 9–0 in the cold, sleet, and drizzle of 1881, and 54–0 in the cold, but no rain, of 1887.

That wasn't all. The 1881 players are credited with originating Penn State's now-famous blue-and-white uniforms, with "togs" made by Billy Hoover of Shingletown Gap. There was no way, the players said, they would have chosen pink and black as the 1887 team did with its 12 Canton flannel pants and canvas jerseys from Schaffer and Sons of State College.

Student Ivan P. McCreary set up the 1881 game and managed the team. Later research determined they played under an amalgam of rules that were part rugby and part American football. Little is known about what happened, except McCreary also umpired the game. At the end he sent word of the outcome back to campus, 50 miles away, by telegraph that read: "We have met the enemy and they are ours, nine to nothing."

Years later, Penn State researchers found more evidence in a long account of the game in the January 1882 edition of the *University of Lewisburg Mirror*, which read in part: "The State College team was well uniformed and disciplined, whereas our boys...were not up to their dodges."

When George "Lucy" Linsz and Charlie Hildebrand organized a team in 1887, no one on campus or in town remembered the

1881 team, probably because the '81 group never played another game.

Unlike the team in 1881, which was loosely organized without faculty knowledge or interest, the 1887 team had the full support and encouragement of college president George Atherton and the faculty. Atherton had approved a student-run Penn State Athletic Association and the 1887 team became part of the new Football Department.

Utilizing an official *American Football Rule Book*, the team started practicing. Bucknell, which already had a team, challenged Penn State, and the teams worked out a home-and-away agreement, with each team paying its own expenses for the 55-mile trip.

With 12 Penn State fans watching, the Bucknell players tried to intimidate the visitors on the first play by ripping off the tassels of the ski caps they were wearing as "helmets." That must have really made the Penn State guys mad. The final score was 54–0.

The December (and sixth) issue of the new monthly student newspaper, the *Free Lance*, is one of the rare sources with some details about the game. "It is a fact worth mentioning that our boys made their first 'touch down' within two minutes after the game had [started]," the newspaper reported. "The teams were well match [sic] in size and strength. Neither side could gain anything by what is called rough playing, and all the points scored were made by the skillful playing of 'tricks,' the best of which was one of the ones so frequently played by our halfbacks." (*Tricks* meant the actual plays the team ran.)

In the return game played on the Old Main Lawn, Penn State won 24–0, making the 1887 players the first of Penn State's 13 undefeated teams through 127 years. That's acknowledged today with the year prominently displayed alongside other undefeated or championship teams on the wall below the suites at Beaver Stadium—but not the 1881 pioneers.

It wasn't until 1922 that anyone remembered the 1881 team outside of the surviving players. On the eve of the first-ever game against Syracuse at New York's Polo Grounds that year, the 1887 players were honored officially as "the First Penn State Team" at a big party at a Manhattan hotel. When Ivan McCreary heard about it he began a campaign to set the record straight.

It took McCreary and his supporters more than a decade to succeed. At the height of the controversy in the mid-1930s, Penn State formally recognized the 1881 team "as the real pioneers…for playing Penn State's first intercollegiate contest, however informal, and for selecting the blue and white worn ever since by Lion teams except for one season.…"

On October 6, 1936, McCreary and three other surviving members were given gold-plated footballs and varsity *S* letters to mark their achievement, and their deceased nine teammates were honored posthumously.

Unfortunately, over the years, even that recognition has disappeared from Penn State's official history and record books. There's no mention of the 1881 team anywhere, including the All-Sports Museum. And that's just not right!

7 1982: National Champions at Last

Nothing describes the euphoria, satisfaction, and relief of the Penn State fandom when Penn State won its first national championship than the succinct words and emotion of legendary broadcaster Fran Fisher at the end of the 1983 Sugar Bowl in the Superdome on New Year's Night.

The thousands of Penn State fans in the record crowd of 78,124 had to wait until later to hear what Fisher said instantly from deep in his heart, but the fans listening to the Penn State radio network coverage of the game knew what it meant to them. The emotion and joy in his voice perfectly captured the release of nearly a century of frustration.

"Penn State's national champion!" Fisher shouted in the din of the Superdome. "Penn State is the national champion. Penn State has won the ball game 27–23!"

Maybe readers who have never heard Fisher's passionate outburst may not appreciate what those benign few words meant to the Nittany Lions' ardent followers more than 30 years ago. But it was not just the words themselves but the happiness in the voice of the man who said them—a fan since he saw his first game as a 10-year-old in 1932, a freshman in the Blue Band in 1942, and a broadcaster on the radio network since 1966. No one in the Penn State football nation had endured more frustration in his lifetime than Fran Fisher.

Fisher had lived through the de-emphasis decade of the 1930s and early '40s. He watched two undefeated Paterno teams in 1968 and 1969 finish No. 2 in the final rankings and another in 1973 be relegated to No. 5. He was at the microphone in this same Superdome for the 1979 Sugar Bowl when Alabama upset then–No. 1 Penn State on an exasperating goal-line stand to lose its only actual previous championship game. He also remembered two other Paterno teams that lost one game and four with 10–2 seasons that for one reason or another never had a chance at the championship game. And then there was one of his favorite all-time teams in 1947 that went undefeated and set several NCAA records, but was only ranked No. 4.

Of course, it was Coach Joe Paterno; his assistant coaches; and the players, led by quarterback Todd Blackledge, who made the win over Georgia happen. Blackledge was the MVP of the game, and it was his 47-yard pass and Greg Garrity's diving catch in the end zone early in the fourth quarter that was the key play of the game. A *Sports Illustrated* cover photo of Garrity and teammates celebrating the touchdown is still displayed prominently in the homes and offices of Lions fans.

Todd Blackledge

Younger Penn State fans are surprised when they discover one of the team's outstanding quarterbacks, Todd Blackledge, was never more than an honorable-mention All-American.

Blackledge won the Davey O'Brien Award as the nation's best quarterback in 1982 when he led Penn State to its first national championship. He certainly fit the criteria of the O'Brien Award that includes "academic standing and scholarship, leadership qualities and the ability to inspire others, [and] dedication to team success."

Blackledge, an Academic All-American and Phi Beta Kappa with a 3.80 GPA in the classroom, wasn't even one of the four co-captains of that 1982 team because he was a redshirt junior. But there was no doubt who was in charge of the 1980–82 offenses when the Lions lost just five games in three years. In his final game before giving up his final year of eligibility, Blackledge was the Most Valuable Player of the national championship win over Georgia in the Sugar Bowl.

Blackledge is still ninth in Penn State's career passing yardage as of 2015 with 4,812 yards and 41 touchdowns on 341 completions in 658 attempts, and 12th in single-season yardage (1982) with 2,218 yards and 22 touchdowns (second in the records) during a period long before the aerial onslaughts of the 2000s.

He also still holds the dubious team record of 41 interceptions in a career and is just one interception short of the record for one season and one game.

No matter. As Blackledge once said, "I expected to win every game I played."

Although his pro career fell short of what he had expected, Blackledge has become renowned as one the foremost television analysts in college football. In 2009, he was honored with Penn State's highest award as a distinguished alumni, and that's worth more than being an All-American.

Yet Penn State almost didn't make it to the National Championship Game after following up a last-minute 27–24 win over powerful Nebraska in late September that vaulted them to No. 3 in the rankings with a loss two weeks later at No. 4 Alabama, 42–21. The team later credited reserve running back Joel Coles for a fiery post-Alabama locker room speech for re-motivating them.

"Joel just got everyone together and started yelling and screaming at us, basically telling us, 'We're better than that. Just don't hang your head,'" Garrity remembered 30 years later. "He gave everyone a kind of kick in the butt that we needed."

The team rebounded with six straight victories that moved Penn State back up to No. 3 when the bowl matchups were made before the last two games of the regular season. Undefeated No. 2 SMU was obligated to the Cotton Bowl and undefeated No. 1 Georgia to the Sugar Bowl, so a National Championship Game seemed out of the question. Both bowls were interested in Penn State.

Paterno and the team had made it clear they wanted to play the highest-ranked team. On Penn State's off week, SMU had to settle for a 17–17 tie with Arkansas. The next weekend, Georgia beat state rival Georgia Tech 38–18 and headed to the Sugar Bowl. At Beaver Stadium, the Lions beat Pitt 19–10. Penn State moved up to No. 2 and New Orleans had its championship game, although SMU still had a shot if Penn State lost or didn't win convincingly and SMU defeated its Cotton Bowl opponent, Pitt.

Georgia featured the Heisman Trophy winner—junior tailback Herschel Walker, who already owned 10 NCAA and 15 SEC records—and a ball-hawking defense. Penn State's attacking defense would be the match for Walker and would combine with an explosive offense, the first one in team history to gain more yards passing than running, to win the game.

Penn State, favored by 3–4 points, jumped off to a 20–3 lead, but Georgia came back with seven points before halftime and a touchdown early in the third quarter. Blackledge's pivotal touchdown pass to Garrity gave the Lions the cushion they needed when Georgia rallied to pull within three points with less than five minutes left. But the Penn State defense went into shutdown mode.

As the happy players carried Paterno off the field on their shoulders, he pointed his index finger up in the air and the delirious Penn State fans chanted "We're number one!" over and over.

A crowd of nearly 8,000, including Governor Dick Thornburgh, greeted the team at the Harrisburg airport the next day. As the team made the 100-mile trip to State College through the small towns in the central Pennsylvania mountains, thousands of well-wishers lined up along the road cheering and honking car horns.

"I learned as never before how much this team and its success are the expression of so many people," Paterno would later write in his book. "I never saw such love between people who didn't know each other."

Inside one of the team buses, Fran Fisher was smiling, waving back at the fans, and thinking contently *Penn State is the national champion.*

1986: Class Beats Crass for the National Championship

"Class beats crass," blared the headline above a Joe Gilmartin column in the *Phoenix Gazette* after Penn State had shocked Miami in a thrilling, down-to-the-last minute 14–10 upset at the Fiesta Bowl the night before to win its second national championship.

The cocky Miami team led by coach Jimmy Johnson and Heisman Trophy quarterback Vinny Testaverde had rumbled into Arizona a week before the January 2 showdown like an army commando unit on liberty. A dozen players, including Testaverde, stepped off the plane in camouflage fatigues, caps, combat boots, and sunglasses. "That was a great idea," Johnson boasted to the *Gazette*. "I wish I had thought of it."

Some of the Hurricanes players continued wearing the combat fatigues and talking about war throughout the week, perhaps as psychological inspiration. They were also trying to intimidate the Penn State players, well-known for wearing coats and ties in public appearances under the dictates of their coach. It got out of hand the night after Miami's arrival during the entertainment segment of a steak dinner for both teams.

When three Miami players stepped onstage, they stripped down to the fatigues under their clothes. All-American tackle Jerome Brown grabbed the microphone and shouted, "Did the Japanese have dinner at Pearl Harbor before they bombed it? Let's go." The stunned crowd watched as Brown led the entire team out of the room to the team bus.

In the momentary silence, Penn State punter John Bruno—who would become a key player in the outcome of the game—jumped up on the stage. He cracked a joke about Miami players having to "go film *Rambo III*," then returned with a line that has become part of the Penn State football legend. "Excuse me," said Bruno, "but didn't the Japanese lose?" and the crowd of some 1,000 roared with laughter.

"After the major-league tacky stunt, a member of the Miami coaching staff explained it away as, 'That's the way they feel. They're here on a mission,'" wrote Gail Tabor in the *Arizona Republic*. "If there's any justice in the world, the Miami Hurricanes will leave here Saturday with a championship. For rudeness, not football."

Miami's boorish behavior clashed with the quiet, good-natured demeanor of the PSU players and their no-nonsense coach, who had been honored a month earlier by *Sports Illustrated* as the magazine's Sportsman of the Year. (As of 2014, Paterno is still the only college football coach to receive that award since its creation in 1954.) The Miami coach got into the act during a joint appearance that week with Paterno when Johnson referred derisively to Paterno as "St. Joe."

The game was billed by the media as Good vs. Evil, and the Hurricanes players continued their brash and intimidating conduct right up to the kickoff. They had their fatigues on again when they arrived at Tempe's Sun Devil Stadium, and they started taunting and shouting epithets at the Penn State players getting off the bus wearing coats and ties. During the pregame warmups, the Hurricanes ran through the Lions formation and zeroed in on State's supposedly small and slow defensive backs. At one point, the Lions' always-feisty linebacker Trey Bauer disobeyed Paterno's orders not to talk back and zipped a ball past the helmet of one Miami player, making sure he knew who had thrown it.

Most of the media did not think Penn State should be playing for the national championship, despite its No. 2 ranking and the return of 19 of its best 22 offensive players, and 18 of the most talented defensive players, from the 1985 team that lost the championship game to Oklahoma 14–0 in the Orange Bowl. The 1986 Lions had been erratic in the regular season with a questionable offense and a bend-but-don't-break defense that made too many games close.

Despite the flamboyant pranks and braggadocio, Miami was an excellent team. The Hurricanes' explosive offense had averaged 38 points a game, and Testaverde had thrown for 26 touchdowns and just nine interceptions in completing 63.4 percent of his passes to a standout corps of receivers. The defense led by Brown had held opponents to less than 13 points a game.

Penn State had its own All-Americans in linebacker Shane Conlan and tailback D. J. Dozier, but the 6½ points that favored Miami seemed a little low.

Miami had preferred to play the game before its home crowd in the Orange Bowl. But the Fiesta Bowl and its corporate sponsor, the Sunkist Citrus Growers, hooked up with NBC for a $2.4 million payoff to both teams, and hyped it as The Duel in the Desert. This was the first network prime-time major bowl game after New Year's, and the 25.1 rating that night is still a record for a college football game.

"They're the best balanced team we've seen in many years," Paterno told sportswriters. "We can't trade touchdowns. If it's that kind of game, we're out of our league. The more it gets into the 20s the worse our chances are."

However, Paterno had a surprise for Miami. Behind closed practices, the Lions defense worked on a radical new technique to fool and confuse Testaverde and disguise pass coverage. Rather than blitz, the defense dropped eight players into the passing zones and gave Conlan the flexibility to roam.

The supposedly weak Lions defensive backs had their special surprise. They immediately began belting Miami's receivers, setting the tone for the night as the Hurricanes receivers dropped seven perfect passes. "Our little, slow guys back there just rocked 'em, and soon they didn't want to catch the ball," said Conlan after the game.

The defense and Bruno's punting kept the game close, and Conlan's 39-yard interception return on a gimpy knee and ankle led to a mid-fourth-quarter touchdown that thrust the Lions into a 14–10 lead. Still, it took a now-famous interception by linebacker Pete Giftopulos in the end zone to end the game after a fierce rally by Miami in the last three minutes.

"It's nice to see nice guys finish first," wrote Gilmartin in the *Phoenix Gazette.* Yes, class beats crass.

Have Peachy Paterno and Raspberry Rose Ice Cream at the Creamery

A stop at the university's celebrated Creamery for a couple scoops of ice cream is a must for every Penn State visitor, not just for Nittany Lions sports fans.

Football weekends, including the Blue-White Game, are among the busiest times at the Creamery. So are graduation weekends and the five-day Central Pennsylvania Arts Festival in mid-July that attracts exhibits and visitors from around the world.

President Bill Clinton stopped by in 1996. Coretta Scott King, Mister Rogers, Martha Stewart, and the cast of Cirque de Soleil also have been there, along with numerous sports figures such as Bob Costas, Bill Cowher, and race car driver Jeff Gordon.

Clinton made history by becoming the only known customer allowed to have two separate flavors in the mandatory two-scoop serving, cone or dish, since that edict was introduced decades ago. "The reason for no mixing is to help move the long lines faster through the salesroom," said manager Tom Palchak. Clinton had Peachy Paterno and Cherry Quist, another hall-of-fame flavor.

Obviously, the peach is named after Joe Paterno, and he was a regular customer. Paterno often strolled in as he walked from his football office a half mile away to his home not far from the Creamery. Students often were surprised to see him sitting alone on a nearby campus bench eating his cone.

Peach was Paterno's favorite flavor, and in 1987, the Creamery named its product after him. "[It] became a regular topic on Penn State's football television broadcasts," Lee Stout wrote in his 2009 coffee-table book, *Ice Cream U: The Story of the Nation's Most Successful Collegiate Creamery.* "The subject really took off when former Pittsburgh Steeler Lynn Swann did an entire feature for a football broadcast from the Creamery plant, where they just happened to be making a special 'Swann Swirl' ice cream flavor for the network crew."

Publicity from such television shows as *Mister Rogers' Neighborhood* and *Good Morning America* (featuring the late syndicated columnist Erma Bombeck) and dozens of newspaper and magazine stories have helped make Penn State's ice cream famous. But so have the praises of its customers. "Incredibly, no marketing genius and no marketing plan are in place at the Creamery," Stout wrote. "It buys no advertising. Word of mouth has a very special meaning when it comes to ice cream at the Creamery."

The Creamery has more than 150 flavors with some 25–30 available at any one time. But only two of its seven hall-of-fame ice creams are named after coaches. In May 2014, the Creamery introduced a new hall-of-fame flavor in honor of women's volleyball coach Russ Rose, the winningest coach in the history of the sport who, later that season, won his record seventh national championship. Raspberry Rose is made with black raspberry puree, whole strawberries, strawberry sauce, red raspberry sauce, and pure Wilbur's chocolate in a vanilla base. Yum.

"Creamery ice cream is so fresh," Stout wrote, "that only four days, on the average, elapse between the cow and your newly dipped cone. This rich ice cream, with a butterfat content of 14.1 percent, contains only the very best ingredients: fresh milk and cream, of course, and pure vanilla from Madagascar. An imported extract flavors the peach ice cream, and fruit and nuts are brought in from the Pacific Northwest."

A reader who has not tasted any Creamery ice cream may be addicted to Ben & Jerry's or perhaps Baskin-Robbins or Häagen-Dazs. Those businesses and others have sent representatives to Penn State to take the Creamery's five-week short course. Actually, Ben Cohen and Jerry Greenfield started their gold-minted ice cream mine in a vacant Vermont gas station after taking a $5 version of the then-10-week short course by correspondence. The Creamery now displays their class work.

The Creamery ice cream dates back to Penn State's roots as an agriculture college, with the original name of Farmers High School when it was created in 1855. The Creamery has been a staple since the turn of the 20th century, and it's had three homes since the early 1900s. The current location, just two blocks west of Beaver Stadium along Curtin Road, opened in 2006, and the Creamery is almost three times the size of its former home down the street.

One can also order Creamery ice cream anywhere in the US, including Hawaii and Alaska.

Peachy Paterno or Raspberry Rose, anyone?

10 Take a Photo with John Cappelletti's Heisman Trophy

No player is more synonymous with Pennsylvania State University than John Cappelletti, the school's only Heisman Trophy winner.

Even people who rarely follow college football or know nothing about Penn State have heard of him.

In September 2013 Cappelletti became the first Penn State athlete in the university's 158-year history to have his or her jersey number—22—officially retired. Yes, the number is still used in the other varsity sports. But the jersey Cappelletti actually wore in 1973 when he also won the Maxwell Award as college football's outstanding player is now on exhibit at the Penn State All-Sports Museum, along with a duplicate of his Heisman Trophy.

The jersey is locked up in the large football display case with other individual trophies and plaques won by illustrious Nittany Lions players. However, the Heisman Trophy is in a prominent spot near the television monitor that features video of Cappelletti on the playing field and his famous Heisman Trophy acceptance speech. Seeing the jersey, viewing the video, and having a photo taken with the trophy is a must-do for every Penn State fan before they die.

Cappelletti's Heisman landed him in the College Football Hall of Fame in 1993. But his emotional few minutes in front of the black-tie crowd with Vice President Gerald Ford on the dais at the Waldorf Astoria New York touched the hearts of America and led to a movie and book that has made him famous around the world. Eighty players have won the prestigious trophy since its inception in 1935, but Cappelletti's tearful acceptance speech is one of the most memorable.

The tears were for his 11-year-old brother Joey, dying from leukemia, who was in the audience, and Cappelletti dedicated the trophy to him.

"If I can dedicate the trophy to him tonight and give him a couple days of happiness, this is worth everything…." Cappelletti said. "A lot of people think I go through a lot on Saturdays during the week as most athletes do…and it's only in the fall. For Joseph, it is all year around and it is a battle that is unending with him and he puts up with more than I will ever put up with and I think this trophy is more his than mine because he has been a great inspiration to me."

The standing ovation lasted for several minutes.

Four years later, Hollywood used that 1973 Heisman speech as the basis for Cappelletti's life story in an NBC made-for-TV movie titled *Something for Joey*. The movie was a hit, and through reviews and word of mouth, it began being shown in elementary and high schools not only in the United States but around the world. The movie became so popular that in 1983 an adaptation of the screenplay was published as a biography with the same title. What started at the dais of a plush New York hotel became an international inspiration for children and their families.

John Cappelletti poses for a photo at the 1973 Heisman Trophy ceremonies with his mother, Ann; father, John; and brother, Joey. In an emotional speech, he dedicated the trophy to his brother Joey, who was battling leukemia.
(Photo courtesy of Cappelletti family)

"You can't believe it, but I still get letters each week," Cappelletti told me. "I'll get a package of 30 or 40 kids from schools around the world—Japan, Mexico, Canada, Pennsylvania—from kids who are just reading the book at this particular time, and the teacher says, 'Well, you guys all write a letter and tell Mr. Cappelletti what you thought of the book and we'll package it up and send it to him.' Reading the letters is kind of an amazing thing because… there's still so many different things that the kids say [were] important to them and why it meant something to them."

Cappelletti's on-field exploits pale in comparison to his impact on ordinary people and their children. He is still 11th in Penn State career rushing as of 2015 with 2,639 yards on 519 carries, and his 29 touchdowns are tied for fifth. He still holds the record for rushing attempts in a season and in one game—against North Carolina State in 1973. Those statistics are even more amazing when you realize he is the only Nittany Lion to make the top 40 list in just two years.

Cappelletti was a linebacker on the scout team as a freshman but wanted to play tailback.

"Joe [Paterno] said they were going to be loaded on offense [with seniors Lydell Mitchell and Franco Harris] and probably a little bit thinner on defense, and would I mind going to the defensive side of the ball with the intention that I would try and come back to the offensive side," Cappelletti remembered.

He also ran back punts and kickoffs in his sophomore year, and although he led the team in punt returns with 28—the most since Penn State began keeping records in 1946—for 274 yards, Cappelletti was mischievously tagged with the dubious nickname of Fumbelletti.

"It was a matter of communication between Ed O'Neil and I and sometimes we made it look like it was an event rather than just a punt return," Cappelletti laughed. "One guy calling it, the other guy going to get it. I don't remember ever practicing punts and kickoffs an awful lot, and I think there was a time or two I fumbled."

Cappelletti went on to be the No. 1 draft pick of the Los Angeles Rams and played nine years in the NFL. In 1993 he was inducted into the College Football Hall of Fame.

The fumbles are long gone, but John Cappelletti, still as humble, gracious, and self-effacing as he has been throughout his life, is the true symbol of what Penn State is all about.

"I think people can identify with me in different ways than they can with other players, whether it's Penn State or other universities," he said. "There was more to it than just the football player and the football player that won the Heisman."

Somewhere in heaven, Joey is smiling.

11 Pink and Black

The uniforms worn by the first official football team in 1887 certainly were colorful, and quite unusual, if not embarrassing, by modern-day standards: pink and black.

Yet there is some documentation that indicates at least two early Penn State athletic teams wore the now-famous traditional plain blue-and-white uniforms before the 1887 team played the first intercollegiate football game at Bucknell.

The team's "jersey" was a tightly laced pink canvas jacket with the initials PSC FB (for Penn State College Foot-Ball) in black across the chest. The rest of the uniform consisted of knee-length Canton flannel pants with long black stockings, tennis shoes, and—don't laugh—black ski caps with tassels, which may have been pink or black. They disappeared after being yanked away by Bucknell players in that historic first game.

Sometime later, some players denied they chose pink uniforms. They claimed the pink was really cerise—a purplish red—that faded to pink and eventually white in the sunlight and after being washed several times, while the black took on a blue texture. That belated justification doesn't quite jibe with the facts.

Pink actually was a popular color in a period now nostalgically referred to as the Gay Nineties. An early school yearbook, *LaVie*, had a pink-and-black cover, and the school newspaper, the *Free Lance*, made a few references to pink and black as the school colors.

As the team was being organized and practicing in October 1887, the fourth issue of the new monthly newspaper reported on a meeting and subsequent vote taken by the 167 students over a choice of school colors. "Of the colors presented the combination dark pink and black was unanimously adopted by the students," the newspaper noted.

On March 1, 1888, the *Free Lance* reported that the school's baseball team, which had worn white uniforms trimmed in light blue since its first game in 1875, would have new uniforms consisting of "a cap of the college colors, a black jersey, a pink belt, white pants and black stockings."

One year later, the March 1889 edition of the newspaper noted, "The college colors, pink and black, show well."

Then, two and a half years after pink and black were voted as the school colors, a small item buried at the bottom of page 16 of 24 pages in the *Free Lance* reported in three pithy sentences on a meeting of the school's Athletic Association on March 18, 1890, for the purpose of choosing new school colors. "The combination finally adopted was navy blue and white," the newspaper stated.

See, it was no big deal after all!

However, it would take a half century before the football uniforms morphed into the plain, simple, no-frills dark blue or white jerseys, white pants, white helmets, and black shoes now synonymous with Penn State.

The canvas jackets gave way to blue sweaters without padding and brown leather helmets in the early 1900s and then to padded dark blue jerseys and pants with no trace of white into the 1920s. In 1929 a bizarre dose of white stripes was added to the blue jersey, but that was abandoned after a losing season, and an all-white jersey was created to match the all-blue jersey.

No Names on Jerseys

Many in the Penn State football nation believe it is sacrosanct to have the last names of the players on the back of their blue-and-white jerseys.

It may seem like this holy Penn State tradition started in 1887, but names never appeared on jerseys in college football until Maryland did it first in 1961 when, surprisingly, the names were on the front of the jerseys rather than the back. Maryland's groundbreaking move came one year after the new American Football League pioneered the use of names on football jerseys.

Coach Joe Paterno believed that no names on the traditional plain blue-and-white jerseys was part of Penn State's decades-long emphasis on the team, not on individual players. Bill O'Brien believed the players who remained at Penn State after the severe NCAA sanctions were issued deserved to be honored with their names on the jerseys for the 2012 season. O'Brien's successor, James Franklin, has kept the names, and unlike the old breed of players that felt the lack of names singled out Penn State above the crowd for all the right reasons, the new generation loves being singled out individually as much as a team.

What most Penn State fans don't know is that the Lions were one of the first teams in the country to have numbers on their jerseys. Penn State's bitterest rival of the past, the University of Pittsburgh, and nearby Washington and Jefferson are both credited with first wearing jerseys in 1908. Sure enough, when Penn State played Pitt on the last game of that 1908 season, the Nittany Lions players also were wearing numbers.

Back to Maryland in 1961. That season, the Terps played Penn State at College Park and with the names on their uniforms beat the Nittany Lions 21–17. That was Maryland's only win in the 38-game series until 2014 when the Terps played against a Penn State team wearing names on their jerseys for the first time and won 20–19.

There must be a curse on those blue-and-white jerseys with names.

It was in the 1930s that the traditional look of Penn State's uniforms took hold, and by 1937 they had the standardized look we know today with a blue or white jersey, white or cream-colored pants and helmet, and black shoes. Shoes had been consistently black since the early 1900s, although the style occasionally changed, such as from wooden cleats to rubber cleats. In 1939 the NCAA mandated that all players wear helmets, and 10 years later Penn State's onetime leather helmets were plastic. That year Penn State added its now-traditional blue stripe to the helmet.

Of course, the uniforms of the 1940s are different from the uniforms of today in style and material. The uniforms have been tweaked often over the years and even some of the smallest changes—like the white-trimmed collar on blue jerseys—have been noticeable to fans.

Numbers were first used on the backs of jerseys in 1908 and mandated by the NCAA for the back in 1916 and front in 1937. Some 20 years later, numbers would also be required for jersey sleeves for television. Penn State also used blue numbers on helmets from 1957 to 1961 and 1966 1974, but no longer.

Two more recent additions have caused a substantial controversy—the iconic Nike swoosh on the front of the jerseys in 1994 and the names on the backs of jerseys in 2012. Nike, which supplies Penn State with its uniforms, insisted on the first addition; Coach Bill O'Brien insisted on the second to honor the 2012 players who remained loyal to Penn State despite the child abuse scandal.

To some diehards in the Nittany Nation, the names on the jerseys may be worse than the pink-and-black uniforms.

12 Sit in the House That Joe Built

When Joe Paterno first learned that the home football field would be moved from the heart of the Penn State campus to a 60-acre cow pasture on the eastern edge of the school's property, the assistant football coach wasn't pleased. He was certain that would destroy the warm, cozy, and convivial atmosphere of game day at New Beaver Field.

Back then, in the 1950s, most fans, including the 12,000–14,000 students, walked to the games because parking on nearby streets and the golf course lot was limited. The games were always played in the afternoon starting at 1:30. Fans could have lunch or a late breakfast at home, a fraternity, or at a local restaurant, particularly the quaint college-owned Nittany Lion Inn just a few steps from the entrance gates. There weren't many season-ticket holders in those days because tickets were usually readily available except for a big game or two. Students basically walked in free as part of their activities card covering many school entertainment events.

Rip Engle was Penn State's head coach, and one day Engle told Paterno and the other assistant coaches, "The president wants to move the stadium because of the fact that he needed that ground for graduate school."

"I said, 'You can't let them do that, Rip, it will ruin Penn State Football,'" Paterno recalled years later, "because we were close to the Nittany Lion Inn and people were used to coming up there. We had a nice parking area across the street, where the golf course was, and the whole bit."

Paterno compared game day at Beaver Field to the laid-back atmosphere of his roots in the Ivy League, where he had been a star quarterback for Brown University. Engle, his coach at Brown, had brought him to Penn State after his graduation in 1950 to help coach Engle's new team for a year before going on to law school. Paterno fell in love with Penn State and decided not to go to law school. He was the team's quarterbacks coach and offensive guru when plans were announced to move the home field after the 1959 season and rechristen it Beaver Stadium.

The next-to-last game at Beaver Field on November 7, 1959, against Syracuse attracted the largest crowd in its 51-year history—initially announced at 32,000 but later revised upward to 34,000. After the Holy Cross game one week later, workers began dismantling the steel-and-aluminum structure piece by piece and moving it about one and a half miles to the selected site where ground preparations had begun a year earlier.

When the first game was played at Beaver Stadium on September 17, 1960, against Boston University, the structure itself looked eerily similar to Beaver Field, just a little bigger. Seating capacity was 46,284. The permanent grandstands formed a horseshoe with temporary bleachers at the south end zone. The press box was higher, at the top of the west stands, and the running track that had circled the playing field of Beaver Field was still there.

There was a major addition the fans couldn't see. Locker rooms for both teams had been built underneath the west stands. The Water Tower dressing room outside Beaver Field's west gate was a thing of the past.

It looked rather barren outside the stadium, which seemed almost like the middle of nowhere. There was plenty of parking on the grass fields surrounding the facility with just a couple two-lane roads leading to it. Access roads, including what is now University Drive and a four-lane bypass highway for alternate Route 322, were still under construction or modification.

With the fall semester classes yet to start for the 16,091 students, the milestone opening game against BU attracted just 22,559 fans. It wasn't until Army visited in the fourth game of

Nighttime whiteouts at Beaver Stadium create an electrifying atmosphere, and this one in 2014 was one of the best as a loud, partisan crowd of 107,895 watched the Nittany Lions almost upset eventual national champion Ohio State in double overtime.

the next season that Beaver Stadium cracked the capacity barrier with a standing-room crowd of 45,306. Then, on November 21, 1964, Penn State defeated archrival Pitt 28–0 with a record crowd of 50,144 watching in the freezing cold and wind that made the 24-degree temperature feel like zero. That record stood for nearly five years until 2,000 seats were added before the 1969 season and 52,713 showed up on October 11, 1969, to see the Nittany Lions again beat another longtime rival, West Virginia, 20–0.

By that time, Joe Paterno was in his fourth year as Penn State's head coach and his team was in the midst of an undefeated team record of 31 games that remains the school record. With the ultra-success of Paterno's Penn State teams over the next several decades, the Nittany Lions established themselves as one of the biggest attractions in college football. As the fan base continued to increase and the university's enrollment exploded—from 26,823 in 1969 to 40,028 in 2001—the need for more seats continued to evolve.

Since 1969, six reconstruction projects have boosted seating capacity at Beaver Stadium with major expansions before the 1978, 1991, and 2001 seasons. In a major engineering feat in 1978 that required hydraulic jacks to move certain sections back and raise others, concrete grandstands were added and the running track eliminated. An upper deck was added in the north end zone in 1991, and the $93.5 million expansion in 2001 included a new two-tier upper deck in the south end zone featuring a private club and new construction with 50 suites above the east grandstands.

With its 106,572 seats, Beaver Stadium entered the 2015 season as the second-largest stadium in the nation, trailing Big Ten conference counterpart Michigan at 109,901. However, future reconstruction and expansion is ahead but not yet in the planning stage.

And what did Joe Paterno think as Beaver Stadium became the House That Joe Built?

Talking about his long-ago displeasure about leaving New Beaver Field for a cow pasture, he said, "Shows you how smart I am. It was a great move. And I think it's worked out obviously very, very well."

13 Joe Mason and the Princeton Tiger

One of the first things a Penn State fan needs to know is how a Penn State baseball player named Joe Mason created the renowned Nittany Lions mascot with a quick-witted retort to a smart-aleck Princeton sophomore in 1904.

Mason was a 24-year-old sophomore third baseman from Pittsburgh, and the baseball team was touring the Princeton campus on the morning of April 20 before its game that afternoon. As Mason recalled decades later at the dedication of the now-revered Lion Shrine statue: "These two [chaps] escorted us into their beautiful gymnasium, they stopped us in front of a splendid mounted figure of a Bengal tiger. One chap spoke up: 'See our emblem, the Princeton Tiger, the fiercest beast of them all.' An idea came to me, and I replied, 'Well, up at Penn State we have Mount Nittany right on our campus, where rules the Nittany Mountain Lion, who has never been beaten in a fair fight. So, Princeton Tiger, look out.'"

Great response for early 20th-century trash talk, right?

Problem was, as Jackie Esposito and Steve Herb wrote in their book *The Nittany Lion*, the only mountain lion on campus was stuffed and being displayed in a small wildlife museum in Old Main. The last mountain lion seen anywhere in Centre County was in 1893, and that one was killed.

Mountain lions were then on the verge of extinction in Pennsylvania. One of the last known to be close to State College was shot in 1856 by farmer Sam Brush near the tiny, rural community of Brushville, about 175 miles east of Mt. Nittany not far from Binghamton, New York. Sam had the critter stuffed and mounted and in 1893 donated it to Penn State.

The Legend of Princess Nittany

What is a Nittany?

This is the "official" definition as published annually in the Penn State Football Media Guide:

"In regional folklore, Nittany (or Nita-Nee) was a valorous Indian princess in whose honor the Great Spirit caused Mount Nittany to be formed. A later namesake, daughter of chief O-Ko-Cho (sic), who lived near the mouth of Penn's Creek, fell in love with Malachi Boyer, a trader. The tearful maiden and her lost lover became legend and her name was given to the stately mountain."

As the legend goes, Princess Nita-Nee and her Delaware Indian tribe survived wars, disease, and a hostile environment generations ago because of her goodness and grandeur. It all culminated in the Great Spirit causing a mountain to be formed overnight at Princess Nita-Nee's fresh gravesite so that she would protect the valley forever.

The legend may be sentimental and gallant, but it is strictly baloney. It was the invention of a well-to-do New York banker and publisher named Henry Wharton Shoemaker. The first ever mention of a "Princess Nita-nee" was in an article by the 23-year-old Shoemaker in a 1903 newspaper in Centre Hall, a small community at the base of Mount Nittany on the other side of the mountain from Penn State.

Students at Penn State picked up Shoemaker's yarn and wrote their own version for the 1916 school yearbook, *LaVie.* The rest, as they say, is history.

The truth is, Native Americans did call the mountain and the valley Nita-Nee. The word or the phonetic version derives from Algonquin words "nekti" and "attin" that mean "single mountain" or "long mountain," according to native scholars. Another definition means a protective barrier against the elements.

The earliest use of the word "Nittany" to identify the mountain was found in a deed to the Proprietaries (of Pennsylvania) dated September 5, 1768, and the first map that actually shows the Nittany Mountain was published in 1770.

Hogwash. The legend is always more romantic than the truth.

It's doubtful if any of Penn State's 730 students in 1904 looked upon Sam's ugly lion with any pride. The fact was the school didn't have any symbol or mascot comparable to the Princeton Tiger.

However, shortly after Mason's boast, a pair of alabaster African lions 45 inches high sitting on pedestals atop large stone pillars were delivered to Penn State after being on display at the Pennsylvania Mines exhibit at the World's Fair in St. Louis. The pillars were installed at the main college gate at the intersection of College Avenue and Allen Street. From the back, one could see their bushy manes and the tails. Students strolling past the lions daily soon gave them the nicknames of Ma and Pa.

Now, when Joe Mason wasn't in class or playing baseball he was usually writing. Since his freshman year he had been sending stories about Penn State's sports teams to newspapers all over the state—what is known today as "stringing."

Mason also had a great sense of humor. In his senior year of 1906–07 he and a few of his buddies created an independent, unauthorized, and anonymous semimonthly humor magazine to boost the spirits of the students and to tweak the egos and sensibilities of the college administration and faculty. Trying to keep their identities secret, the students called themselves the Ade Family. They listed the family names on the masthead, with the editor being one George (Lemon) Ade, really Joe Mason.

In the St. Patrick's Day issue of March 17, 1907, an editorial signed by editor George Ade urged the adoption of "the Nittany Mountain Lion" as the symbol of the school. "Every college the world over of any consequences has a College Emblem of some kind,—all but the Pennsylvania State College…," the editorial said. "Why not get for State College, Our College, the Best in all the Menagerie of College Pets.—Our College is the Best of all,—Then why not Select for ours, The King of Beasts,—The Lion!!"

The editorial praised the alabaster lions, Ma and Pa, guarding "the entrance to our Campus," and recommended a new statue of "a kingly, all-conquering Lion" be installed at the front of Schwab Auditorium, a few yards from Old Main, with funds from the classes of 1908 and 1909.

A follow-up editorial in the next *Lemon* encouraged everyone to move quickly before another college adopted the lion as its symbol. Before the magazine went out of business after its 13th issue, the class of 1908 chose the lion as the school emblem and the other students agreed. The school yearbook that year had an African lion on the cover. In its dedication, the class wrote: "May we all hail thee with one loud roar. Long live, 'Leo,' King of the living 'Old Nittany.'"

It would be more than 30 years before Joe Mason's ultimate dream came true with the installation of a lion statue on a prominent site as a "permanent guardian" of the college. During that interim, much to Mason's dismay, the lion looked more like the African kind than a mountain lion, starting when the first mascot appeared unexpectedly at the Polo Grounds in New York in 1922.

As for old Ma and Pa, they were removed in 1916 when work began for renovation of the main gate, and they never returned. Years later, everyone learned Ma and Pa had been sent to the rubbish dump.

14 Hail to the Lion

Another Penn State football game is within minutes of kickoff at frenzied Beaver Stadium, and more than 100,000 rollicking fans are hollering. But the home team has yet to appear at the tunnel entrance in the south end zone where it will make its traditional entry onto the field.

Almost all eyes in the crowd are on the Nittany Lions mascot in the middle of the field. He's waving his arms to incite the screaming denizens decked out in their blue-and-white garb to cheer as loud as they can, to let the team that is now streaming out of the locker room toward the tunnel know that the Nittany Nation is with them.

This is a scene that's been repeated at Beaver Stadium every fall for decades. Thank you, Joe Mason and Dick Hoffman. Mason created the Nittany Lion as the iconic symbol of Penn State and Hoffman fathered the Nittany Lion mascot.

And because of what those two started, the 13-ton limestone sculpture of the native Pennsylvania mountain lion—the revered Nittany Lion Shrine—has sat proudly in the center of campus since 1942. It is the most photographic object at Penn State and a must for fans to see, touch, and, yes, be photographed with.

As Jackie Esposito and Steve Herb described in their authoritative book, *The Nittany Lion*, sometime in 1921 Dick Hoffman came up with the idea of wearing a lion costume at a football game. The junior from Harrisburg had worn such a costume the year before in George Bernard Shaw's stage play *Androcles and the Lion*. Hoffman's actual debut is not known. But the first photograph of the mascot was at New York City's Polo Grounds on October 28, 1922, when Penn State played Syracuse for the first time.

Some 25,000 spectators were surprised to see two people in African Lion costumes on their hands and feet, escorting old Andy Lytle onto the field during ceremonies honoring him. Lytle is considered Penn State's most dedicated fan ever because of his near-perfect attendance at home and away games in the early 30-plus years of Penn State football.

Hoffman had persuaded a friend to wear the second costume, but his name has been lost in history. The two lions cavorting on the field on all fours delighted just about everyone but Penn State's cantankerous football coach, Hugo Bezdek. The game ended in a

This is the first known on-field appearance of the Nittany Lion mascot. Actually, there were two mascots at New York's Polo Grounds on October 28, 1922, when Penn State played Syracuse, and they pranced around with loyal fan Andy Lytle.

0–0 tie, and from that day on Bezdek believed the Nittany Lion mascot was bad luck.

The mascot showed up the following Friday at American League Park in Washington, DC in one of the biggest college football games of the year against Navy with Penn State's 30-game undefeated streak on the line. Penn State lost in a 14–0 upset and proceeded to lose two of its last three games of the regular season with the mascot on the field. Bezdek said no more mascots.

After Hoffman's graduation, the costume went into storage in Old Main and everyone forgot about it until someone saw it in 1927. Senior Leon Skinner agreed to wear it at football games, but when Penn State lost all four games, Bezdek banned the mascot for life.

In the fall of 1939, Penn State's 26-year-old gymnastics coach, Gene Wettstone, had an idea to help raise school spirit, particularly for the football team, which had just one winning season in the last nine years. Wettstone had introduced an imitation "three-ring circus" filled with trapeze acts, jugglers, and clowns to promote his gymnastic events, and he figured he could add a lion that would also perform at football games.

Athletic director Carl Schott liked the idea and sent Wettstone to New York to be fitted for a mountain lion costume. When Wettstone returned, Schott told him, "If it fits, wear it." That is how the Nittany Lion mascot reappeared at a Friday night homecoming pep rally and football game against Lehigh on October 14. Penn State won 49–7, eradicating the bad luck demons. The mascot was back forever.

Wettstone had two other students share his mascot duties in 1939, including one of his varsity gymnasts, sophomore George Terwilliger. For the next few years, a Wettstone gymnast would fill the role, but that changed when Wettstone admitted the gymnasts were not funny enough.

Nowadays, there is competition for the honor of being the Nittany Lion mascot.

The mascot even has his own statue, donated by the Back the Lions fan group. The statue is the centerpiece in the lobby of the Penn State All-Sports Museum at Beaver Stadium, perfect for another must-do photograph.

15 Take Photos of Yourself at the Nittany Lion Shrine

If not for periodic student antics that developed into mini-riots and traditional bonfire pep rallies that often turned ugly, Joe Mason's vision of a Nittany Lion statue may never have become a reality.

Just like the occasional student disturbances of today that are centered in the so-called Beaver Canyon apartment and business complex in downtown State College, similar problems in the past often started innocently and transformed into major and minor crises.

On the evening of September 27, 1938, hundreds of male students gathered outside the fraternities and apartment houses in State College and on campus, enthralled by a spectacular lighting display of aurora borealis in the sky. Soon, a throng of pajama-clad students marched down Locust Lane to the Atherton women's residence hall and tried to break in. Failing at that, they proceeded back toward College Avenue.

As the biweekly student newspaper, the *Penn State Collegian*, reported two days later, "They turned down College Avenue, picking reinforcements like a snowball rolling downhill, wrecking and smashing parking meters. And finally with a senseless boyish enthusiasm…they clamored for lumber, for tar, for freshmen… more than 2,000 blockaded the streets, wrecked parking meters and kindled a two-story high bonfire in front of the campus gates at corner of South Allen Street and College Avenue during a three-hour demonstration…."

The bonfire they ignominiously started at the same spot as many others since the late 1890s—particularly when celebrating significant football victories—evoked this bold eight-column headline on the front page of the newspaper: "MOB DAMAGE MAY MOUNT TO $2,000."

In a separate two-column story, Penn State president Ralph Hetzel pleaded with the students to end such "demonstrations… that are harmful to the student body and the College [sic]."

The next Tuesday, the president called a special meeting of the 1939 senior class to help prevent such demonstrations and riots in the future. Shortly after, Hetzel asked a *Collegian* junior associate

Author Lou Prato and his wife, Carole, have visited the Lion Shrine dozens of times since 1956, and this photo shows them there during Lou's 50th class reunion in 2009. (Photo courtesy of Lou Prato)

editor-reporter named Bernie Newman to generate interest for a permanent place on campus to hold bonfires.

Newman or someone else on the *Collegian* editorial staff came up with the ingenious idea of having a lion statue, with the reverent name of the Lion Shrine, built on such a site as a natural drawing card for the celebratory students.

With Newman leading the effort, the *Collegian* started a campaign for the statue in the fall of 1939, and soon the student's All-College Cabinet asked the *Collegian* to poll the student body. Most of the students were apathetic. Of the 6,993 students, just 7 percent voted, but overwhelmingly, 455–45. So much for those historic grand and visionary decisions by passionate students!

Initially, Newman was pressing for an African lion statue, but he and others soon realized it was Joe Mason's mountain lion that was historic to Penn State. Two professors agreed to help Newman find a sculptor. All they needed now was the money to pay for it.

In April 1940 the senior class agreed to fund the statue project as a permanent class gift, but, difficult as it may be to believe now, it was a close vote in favor of the statue over a scholarship fund, 243 to 225.

As described in the book *The Nittany Lion*, Fine Arts instructor Frances Hyslop talked to three prominent sculptors and selected Heinz Warneke, a German native who had moved to the US in 1923 when he was 28 years old.

Once Warneke's design was approved by the student-faculty shrine committee and the board of trustees, Warneke estimated the cost at $6,000 to $8,000, including his commission and the price of the 13-ton limestone block. The senior class had raised just $5,340. Warneke reluctantly agreed to take the offer.

Although the Old Main lawn was the original site picked for the statue, the committee selected a small rise about 20 yards or so in front of the Water Tower, which then served as the football team's dressing room. It was not far from the main gate of New

Guarding the Shrine

Guarding the revered Nittany Lion Shrine "ain't what it used to be."

Almost from the time the shrine was dedicated, it was the occasional target of vandals, typically Penn State's biggest football rivals. The weapons of choice were paints, usually in the school colors of the opposing team.

The first significant painting occurred on Sunday, October 29, 1944, when the lion was smeared with black enamel six days before a home game against Syracuse. Villanova was blamed for a red enamel assault in 1949, and Pitt, Temple, and West Virginia for earlier strikes.

After a white calcimine and blue enamel painting three days before the 1950 season opener against Georgetown, Pi Lamba Phi fraternity sent its pledges for overnight duty Fridays and Saturdays for the rest of that season and for 1951, too. In 1952, the *Daily Collegian* urged the student body to follow Pi Lambda Phi's lead and they did.

Guarding the shrine overnight in the days before big games against the bitterest rivals became a tradition for fraternities, dormitories, and groups like the ROTC and extra-curricular campus clubs. Over the last half of the 20th century, the Shrine was painted many times when the guards were not there.

In 1966, coach Joe Paterno's wife, Sue, and two assistant coaches' wives, Sandra Welsh and Nancy Radakovich, dabbed the Shrine with washable orange paint and orange streamers to boost team morale. Hours later, Syracuse students covered the lion from head to tail and were arrested. No one knew about the wives' sortie until they told their husbands.

The worst damage was on November 16, 1978, when someone smashed the lion's right ear with a hammer or stone and spray-painted the letters "SU" on the body. Syracuse students were suspected but never identified.

The tradition of guarding the Lion Shrine began to fade in the 1990s. Nowadays, the student Lion Ambassadors host a Guard the Lion Shrine event Friday evening before the annual homecoming game, complete with food, drinks, guest speakers, and a disc jockey.

It "ain't what it used to be."

Beaver Field, across the street from Rec Hall, and near the Nittany Lion Inn. That's where it remains today, with only Beaver Field missing, replaced by the Kern Graduate Building and a parking deck, with the site refurbished by landscaping.

Warneke's contract stipulated that the statue be constructed on-site so everyone could see it happen. Warneke and his carver, Joe Garatti, began working on the limestone in June 1942 and the Nittany Lion Shrine emerged just before the first football game on October 3.

At the dedication ceremonies on October 24 before the homecoming game against Colgate, Joe Mason stood on the platform and proclaimed, "We see before us the real Nittany Mountain Lion—alert, resourceful, unafraid, unconquerable, an inspiration to every loyal son and daughter of Old Penn State for generations to come."

Great words, indeed, but shrine or no shrine, the students still go on their occasional rampages. And one more thing you should know: two weeks after the historic 1938 "mob" disturbance, total damage was determined to be a mere $650, not two grand.

Still a small price to pay for the Nittany Lion Shrine.

16 1969: You Can Shove It, Mr. President

President Richard Nixon didn't cost Penn State a national championship in 1969. However, his highly publicized support for the undefeated winner of the Southwest Conference certainly influenced the outcome for No. 1 in the final polls.

The AP and UPI Coaches Polls had determined the mythical national championship for decades and their snub of Penn State in

1969 was a bias against eastern football by college football bigfoots and the media in the Midwest, South, and Southwest. Penn State's 1969 team still might have overcome that bias if Notre Dame had upset Texas in the Cotton Bowl on New Year's Day.

The Nittany Lions could have been in the Cotton Bowl instead of Notre Dame. Why they weren't is partly their own fault, but it is much more complicated. It traces directly to the convoluted way postseason bowl games were arranged in an era before 1992. That was the year the Bowl Coalition was created in the first actual attempt to match the nation's top two teams at the end of the regular season in a bowl game for the national title.

Until the early 1980s, the bowl promoters were permitted to lock in their games in mid-November, two to four weeks before the end of the regular season for all teams. After a surprising undefeated season in 1968 when Penn State won the Orange Bowl and finished No. 2 in the polls, Coach Joe Paterno's 1969 team was on its way toward another unbeaten year when the Cotton, Orange, and Sugar Bowls began talking to Penn State. Saturday, November 15, was bowl selection day. After beating Maryland 48–0 for Penn State's 16th straight game without a loss, the team had to choose between the Cotton and Orange Bowls.

A chance for the national title looked dim. Defending champion Ohio State was cruising along for a repeat and headed to the Rose Bowl. The Cotton Bowl offered the next-best deal, a matchup for the then–No. 4 Lions against either No. 2 Texas or No. 3 Arkansas, both undefeated and seemingly headed for a showdown on December 4.

In his autobiography, *Paterno: By the Book,* Paterno wrote that his five or so African American players, including star running backs Charlie Pittman, Lydell Mitchell, and Franco Harris, didn't want to go to Dallas.

"This was at the peak of the civil rights awareness," Paterno wrote. "They didn't want to go to Dallas, where [President] John F.

Kennedy had been shot [six years earlier]…The revulsion seemed particularly strong among young black people who linked gun-loving Dallas with the lingering racism that had once been taken for granted throughout the South."

Although Paterno preferred to face a higher rated team in the Cotton Bowl, he called a players meeting to discuss it. Dave Joyner, then a sophomore tackle, remembered Paterno starting to talk about the logistics of the Cotton Bowl when Pittman respectfully spoke up. "[Charlie] asked Joe, something like, 'What if we don't want to go to the Cotton Bowl?'" Joyner said. "A discussion ensued about the racial atmosphere in Texas as we perceived it back then, with the team united in their feelings. Joe, to his great credit, allowed the team to decide not to go to the Cotton Bowl."

Why this rationale was never widely reported until years later is still baffling. On Monday, November 17, Penn State announced the players had voted to go back to the Orange Bowl, primarily because there was no chance to play against Ohio State.

Penn State was immediately chastised by the media and many of its own fans for "ducking" the Texas-Arkansas winner. The criticism intensified after the next weekend when underdog Michigan upset Ohio State.

Then, President Nixon, a devout college football fan, got into the act for political reasons to boost his support in the South. Conspiring with ABC, which was nationally televising the Texas-Arkansas game it hyped as the National Championship Game, Nixon went to the game in Fayetteville. After Texas came back in the fourth quarter to win 15–14, Nixon presented his National Championship Presidential Trophy to Texas in the locker room.

The simmering controversy turned into a firestorm. Nixon tried to smooth everything over by announcing he was going to present Paterno and Penn State a plaque for "having the longest winning streak in the country." When the White House telephoned Paterno, a staunch Republican, to tell him, Paterno responded with his most famous words: "You tell the president to take that trophy and shove it."

On New Year's Day, Texas beat Notre Dame 21–17, and Penn State beat Missouri 10–3 to finish No. 2 again.

Almost immediately after they had voted to go to Miami instead of Dallas, several players openly regretted their vote, and their remorse has continued to this day. Even Pittman, Paterno's first All-American, has second thoughts. "But I have no regrets," he told me. "Ohio State was like the team of the century and was just killing everybody. We didn't think we'd have anything to gain by going down there playing Texas on their home field. In hindsight, the better decision would have been to play Texas in the Cotton Bowl. But I learned a great lesson from Joe from this—once you make a decision, you live with it."

Instead of being known for having one of the outstanding defensive teams in the history of college football—as they should be—the Nittany Lions of 1969 are maligned by critics as over-rated bullies who "ducked" a showdown with the nation's No. 1 team. President Nixon was really only part of the reason, but the immortal words of Joe Paterno still reverberate in the Penn State football nation:

"You tell the president to take that trophy and shove it."

17 1994: Undefeated, Untied, and Unappreciated

"Penn State was screwed…they deserved the championship as much as anyone did."

Those words of the famous Las Vegas oddsmaker Danny Sheridan will reverberate throughout the Penn State football nation forever, a perfect epitaph for the frustrating 1994 season when the Nittany Lions were denied a share of the national championship with Nebraska by the pollsters.

None of the voters would admit any bias, but ESPN's Beano Cook came the closest to pointing it out. Cook, who had been one of Penn State's most flamboyant antagonists as the sports information director for State's bitterest rival, Pitt, said, "A lot of coaches voted for [Nebraska's Tom] Osborne and against Paterno."

Meanwhile, the people who then ran the Bowl Coalition that included the four major New Year's Day bowl games outside of the Rose Bowl manipulated behind the scenes to disparage Penn State. The coalition had been created in 1992 to set up a potential national title game after the media and coaches polls had named different champions in 1991 and 1992.

Under the coalition formula, the two teams ranked the highest by the point totals of both polls would play in the championship game. However, the Rose Bowl declined to participate because of its longtime contract with the Big Ten and Pac-8. Since Penn State was in its second season in the Big Ten it was out of the mix no matter what.

Still, it was the bias and empathy for Osborne and Nebraska that was reflected openly in the polls throughout the season that was at the crux of the 1994 team's dilemma. In 1983 Osborne blew his first chance at the championship when he went for a win instead of a title-clinching tie in the last minute against Miami. He missed another shot in 1984 with a defeat in the last game of the regular season, and then lost his only other crack at the crown in 1993 in a showdown with Florida State.

In the 1994 preseason polls, Nebraska was rated No. 4 or No. 5 with Penn State at No. 9. Two weeks into the season the Cornhuskers jumped to No. 1 but then slipped back to No. 2/3 as the Lions moved up.

The partiality of the pollsters was evident after Penn State beat Michigan 31–24 in Ann Arbor in mid-October and jumped to No. 1 in both polls. Ominously, only 19 voters in the AP survey named State No. 1 while 25 still had No. 3 Nebraska at the top of their ballot.

The bias was even more glaring two weeks later when the Lions demolished their biggest Big Ten rival, No. 21 Ohio State, 63–14 but dropped behind Nebraska in the AP voting and held just a two-point margin in the coaches' survey. What galls Penn State fans to this day was the revelation that two of the AP first-place votes for Nebraska came from Ohio State beat writers who covered the Lions' victory. It was downhill for Penn State in the polls from then on.

A week later at Indiana, the Hoosiers scored 15 points in the last two minutes against Penn State reserves. The close 35–29 score caused 12 coaches to switch their first-place votes to Nebraska, which had overwhelmed Kansas 45–17, moving the Cornhuskers up to No. 1 in the USA Today/CNN poll with a 27-point lead over the Lions in total points. In the AP poll Penn State lost eight more first-place votes; only 18 total points separated the teams.

The Nittany Lions came close to ruining their entire season the next week when they had to overcome a 21–0 second-quarter deficit to beat unranked Illinois 35–31 in the nighttime cold and dreary rain of Champaign. In what was one of the greatest series of plays in Penn State football history, Kerry Collins led a thrilling 14-play, 96-yard drive in the last six minutes for the winning touchdown to clinch the Big Ten championship and the Rose Bowl berth.

It all crystalized in the last three weeks of the regular season as Nebraska and Penn State finished as the only undefeated teams. Alabama blew its chance to play Nebraska after a close 24–23 loss to Florida in the SEC title game, and when the final regular-season polls came out, once-beaten Miami was No.3 in Bowl Coalition rankings.

The only chance Penn State had at the championship depended on the Lions beating Oregon convincingly in the Rose Bowl, a Miami upset over Nebraska in the Orange Bowl, and the caprice of the voters who might tab the Hurricanes the champ if they pulled off the upset.

On New Year's Night, Nebraska beat Miami 24–17 in the Orange Bowl and the next day Penn State defeated Oregon 38–20 in the Rose Bowl. Both polls overwhelmingly named Nebraska national champion. Despite playing what the NCAA declared the 17th-toughest schedule compared to Nebraska's 57th, only the *New York Times* and the Sagarin computer ratings made the Lions No. 1.

There has never been a Penn State offense like the one in 1994, one of the most proficient and quick strike offenses in the history of college football. Unlike the four- or five-wide receiver set, no huddle offenses popular today, the Lions' 1994 attack was straight pro-style and featured more passing than any Paterno team before it. Its NCAA record-setting total offense (520.2 yards per game) and scoring (47.8 points a game) was a remarkable achievement in that era before the BCS and the high-scoring style of today.

"What we accomplished was something that very few have done," All-American quarterback and Maxwell Award winner Collins said 20 years later. "My greatest memory of that team is just the quality and character of the guys we had on the team. They were focused [and] had a great work ethic and humility. It was just a special bunch of guys who put together a special year."

Danny Sheridan may have said it best, but the words on a bestselling T-shirt worn for years by Penn State fans still echo throughout the Nittany Nation: "Undefeated. Untied. Unappreciated."

18 Wally Triplett: The Jackie Robinson of Penn State

Wally Triplett met Jackie Robinson in the Brooklyn Dodgers clubhouse at Philadelphia's Shibe Park on June 30, 1947, when the future Baseball Hall of Fame legend was deep into his historic season breaking the major leagues' color line.

At the same time, Triplett was also a racial trailblazer, a 21-year-old Penn State junior who had been the first African American on the football team to be a starter in 1945 and to earn a letter in 1946. They bonded immediately that day, and after the game Triplett invited Robinson to his home in LaMott on the western border of Philadelphia.

"I took him out to my house for Mom's greens and biscuits," Triplett told me. "We played pinochle afterward at my friend's house and then I drove him down to the hotel."

That momentous day for Triplett would not have happened if not for an open-minded, severely wounded combat veteran from World War II named Joe Tepsic, a Penn State teammate in 1945 who befriended Triplett during his trying freshman season. Tepsic left to play for the Dodgers in 1946 and Triplett went to see him a few times when the Dodgers played at Shibe Park. Thus, when Triplett went to try and meet Robinson the next year, the clubhouse attendant remembered him and Tepsic and allowed Triplett into the guarded inner sanctum of a major league locker room.

"I didn't meet Jackie again until a first [African American] sports award dinner at New York's Astor Hotel in January of 1948," Triplett recalled. "He kidded me about being from 'that place Penn State.'"

That was another momentous day for Triplett. He still has the clipping of a photo that appeared in the *New York Amsterdam*

Dave Alston

To understand how important Dave Alston is to Penn State's football history you need to visit the All-Sports Museum located in Beaver Stadium. There are only three statues in the museum— the Nittany Lion mascot in the lobby, a gymnastics figurine in honor of legendary coach Gene Wettstone in the second-floor gymnastics exhibit, and a bronze bust of Dave Alston in the football area on the first level.

Dave and his older brother Harry were Penn State's first African American players in 1941. They were from the industrial town of Midland, near Pittsburgh, where Dave had earned 16 letters in high school—four each in football, basketball, baseball, and track—while also being the president of his senior class and valedictorian. He was a triple-threat tailback in the single-wing formation known for his blazing speed, passing accuracy, and ability to punt a ball 60 yards and drop-kick extra points and field goals.

When the Alstons' father, an ordained minister, told Penn State Dave would not go there without his brother, Coach Bob Higgins took them both. Harry later said Dave could have gone to Cornell but not as a package with Harry.

Dave was a premedical major and quickly became the star of the best freshman team in Penn State history, including future standouts on the undefeated Cotton Bowl team of 1947. The 1941 freshmen rolled over five opponents, scoring 114 points while giving up just 24. Alston scored eight touchdowns, passed for three others (two to his brother Harry), and drop-kicked five extra points.

The word got out quickly. The most famous sportswriter of the era, Grantland Rice, named Alston a preseason All-American and Dave was mentioned in two influential national magazines, the *Saturday Evening Post* and *Colliers*, as well as newspaper and magazine football previews.

Unfortunately, Dave died during a routine tonsillectomy operation on August 15, 1942. His death was later attributed to a blood clot from internal injuries he had previously suffered during a hostile spring scrimmage at Navy. Harry was so devastated he never returned to school.

Despite Dave's death, another well-known *Saturday Evening Post* sportswriter named Francis Wallace named him "sophomore-of-the-

> year in memoriam." Wrote Wallace: "He was one of the finest passers ever and his snake hips made him a running wonder back...He stood head and shoulders above all sophomores."
>
> Visit the Penn State All-Sports Museum and have your photograph taken with the bronze bust of Dave Alston, a true racial pioneer.

showing him posing with Robinson on his left and two other racial sports pioneers to his right, Marion Motley of the Cleveland Browns and Larry Doby of the Cleveland Indians.

When Triplett was in high school, he had met one of the major civil rights leaders in history, Paul Robeson, and that had a big influence on his life.

Triplett was raised in an integrated area that was once part of the so-called Underground Railroad that helped free slaves and then became an army post where the first African American federal troops were stationed. Eventually, African Americans settled there along with Irish immigrants.

He grew up learning to understand prejudice and racism and how to deal with it. That hardened him for more of it while playing for Penn State. Triplett's experience wasn't as overt or as bitter as Robinson's travails, but it was just as spirited and demeaning without the headlines that made Robinson a national hero.

Triplett wasn't Penn State's first African American athlete—that was Cumberland Posey in basketball in 1910—or first African American football player. The Alston brothers were on the freshman team in 1941, and the youngest, Dave, seemed headed for stardom. Dave died unexpectedly in August 1942 during minor surgery and his brother Harry left school.

Coach Bob Higgins recruited Triplett sight unseen, which was standard in those days. In fact, the University of Miami offered Triplett a scholarship until they realized he was African American. Penn State didn't give scholarships but was able to help Triplett obtain a State Senatorial Scholarship. With the assistance of some other African American students, including future Olympic track star Barney Ewell, he got a room in a house where other African American students lived, called Lincoln Hall, and then found a job to help with his expenses.

Triplett didn't play enough as a freshman to earn a letter, but he made history on November 17, 1945, when Higgins started him at left halfback against Michigan State. It wasn't an auspicious debut. He carried the ball 10 times for minus-18 yards as the Lions lost 33–0.

The next season, another African American who had lived in Philadelphia's Overbrook section, not far from Triplett's home, returned to the team after service in World War II. Denny Hoggard had not been on the varsity team before, but now he was a reserve end. He was like an older brother to Triplett.

They banded together, and with the support of their all-white teammates struck a major blow for civil rights, canceling a game at segregated Miami in 1946 and integrating the Cotton Bowl in 1947.

By 1947, Triplett had become a standout wingback. He was an excellent runner, receiver, and defensive back. Twice in his career he rushed for more than 100 yards in an era when few players did, and in 1948 he led the team in scoring with 36 points and in all-purpose yards with 424 rushing, 90 receiving, and 220 on punt returns. He is still second all-time in team career punt returns with an average 16.5 yards on 17 returns for 280 yards and one touchdown.

More meaningful to him was scoring the tying touchdown in the third quarter of that famous Cotton Bowl game on a six-yard pass and making three tackles that saved probable SMU touchdowns.

Even after graduation, Wallace Triplett III was unique. In 1949 he was the first African American to be drafted to actually play in a game in the NFL and then the first NFL player to be drafted into the Korean War. He had a sensational rookie season with Detroit in 1949, starting four games and scoring touchdowns on an 80-yard run and 62-yard punt return. But his four-year career with the Lions and Chicago Cardinals was interrupted by the war, and in 1954 he went into private business. A few years later he became the first African American pari-mutuel clerk in Detroit racing history.

"I'm very proud of being from Penn State," Triplett said. "We changed the course of a lot of other schools in [fighting racism] by what we did. That was the beginning [of the civil rights movement in sports] and we were there." Just like Jackie Robinson.

19 Welcome to the Big Ten

In December 1989 Penn State dropped a bombshell that astonished and bewildered its loyal fans and changed the landscape of college football forever.

The startling revelation that Penn State was giving up 103 years as an independent to join the Big Ten Conference appeared to come out of the blue. Actually, the partnership was the result of 10 years of secret, backroom maneuvering. It did not become official until June 1990 because of the vehement resistance from most of the Big Ten's athletic directors and high-profile football and basketball coaches who were blindsided by the initial announcement.

None of the athletic directors and coaches was more upset than Bo Schembechler, Michigan's celebrated former football coach who was now the athletic director, and Indiana's Bobby Knight, one of the nation's premier basketball coaches.

Schembechler blasted the Big Ten university presidents who made the decisions for not consulting with the athletic directors. "It might be an exciting addition [but] I don't know how they will fit in," Schembechler said. "I, and most of the other athletic directors in our conference, resent the way it was done, and if I offend some presidents, that's too damn bad."

Knight highlighted concern about the logistics and costs of getting to its now-most-rural member—320 miles from the closest conference team, Ohio State, and 975 miles from the most distant one, Minnesota. Only the inimitable Knight could utter the words that would become famous in laconically summing up a large part of the opposition to Penn State's membership.

"I've been to Penn State," Knight told the media, "and *Penn State is a camping trip*. There is nothing for about 100 miles."

Although Joe Paterno is credited with being the instigator of the move for financial reasons when he was athletic director as well as football coach in the early 1980s, the initial contact with the Big Ten was made a few years earlier. President John Oswald and John Coyle, the school's faculty athletic representative, met in Ann Arbor with Michigan president Robben Fleming and athletic director Don Canham.

"[Our athletic administration] had concluded it could not sustain the university's comprehensive athletic program, and its strong emphasis on women's sports, without becoming part of a conference," Coyle told me years later. "The Big Ten seemed like the best fit for us in the quality of our athletics and academics," Coyle recalled, "and Michigan's president and athletic director were receptive."

There was no immediate follow-up, Coyle said, until a strategic plan in the mid-1980s cast doubt on the financial future of Penn State's entire athletic program.

The first inkling of any contact was in an obscure *Sporting News* story on February 21, 1981, about a couple of conversations between Paterno and then–Big Ten commissioner Wayne Duke, including one at the Fiesta Bowl. The information was ignored by the rest of the media.

. It wasn't until early 1989 that things got serious. The key man was Stan Ikenberry, then into his 10th year as president at the University of Illinois, but a high administration official at Penn State from 1971 to 1978. In fact, he was the provost when Penn State had its initial meeting at Michigan about becoming a member.

Ikenberry was serving as the head of Council of Ten (the Big Ten's presidents), which is the actual power broker of the conference. Ikenberry agreed to help Bryce Jordan, Oswald's successor, seek membership for Penn State.

That prompted a series of secret meetings involving several officials, including Big Ten commissioner Jim Delaney, Paterno, Penn State's athletic director Jim Tarman, and chief financial officer Steve Garban, onetime captain of the 1958 football team. Meanwhile, Ikenberry lobbied the Big Ten presidents and eventually had a coalition favoring Penn State's admission as the 11th member of the conference.

On Sunday, December 10, the Council of Ten met in Chicago and voted to invite Penn State, but the decision was kept confidential until more particulars were finalized. Five days later, Ikenberry made the official announcement, saying "We have reached an agreement in principle that Penn State will join the Big Ten. We're proud of their academic standing. We're also pleased with the integrity with which they have conducted their intercollegiate programs."

The vociferous reaction from their athletic directors and coaches gave some of the Big Ten presidents cold feet. When the formal vote was taken in early June, Penn State barely received the two-thirds majority of seven votes required to be admitted. Michigan, Indiana, and Michigan State voted against it.

Some athletic directors and coaches continued to fight against Penn State's admission. Minnesota's athletic director, Rick Bay, a former Michigan wrestler who previously had been the AD at Ohio State, railed, "Penn State wouldn't be a member of the league" if the athletic directors had voted.

Penn State's surprising entry into the Big Ten was a combination earthquake, hurricane, and tsunami for college football. Following the lead of Penn State and the Big Ten, other colleges and conferences scrambled quickly to find new partnerships, and that realignment has continued for 25 years. For better or worse, thanks to Penn State, the college football landscape has changed forever.

20 Saving the Program: Bill O'Brien and the 2012 Team

No one knew what would happen to the Penn State football program when Bill O'Brien became the head coach in early January 2012.

Penn State was in turmoil.

The child abuse scandal that was making Penn State seem like the scourge of the earth was at its height. Legendary coach Joe Paterno had been fired, his saintly image destroyed, and he was literally on his death bed. His onetime respected defensive coordinator, Jerry Sandusky, was in jail awaiting trial. The former school president, athletic director, and financial vice president had also been dismissed and were facing criminal charges.

Yet it would get worse.

On July 12 an in-house investigation commissioned by the board of trustees issued a scathing report asserting a cover-up at the highest levels of the university and blamed it on what it claimed was an out-of-control culture of football.

Eleven days later, in a nationally televised news conference, the NCAA announced unprecedented and extremely severe sanctions that included the loss of 10 scholarships a year for four years, a ban from postseason games for four years, and—the most destructive of all—the right for any current player to transfer to another school before the official opening of preseason practice August 5 and be eligible immediately.

If O'Brien had known about these draconian penalties while he was still the offensive coordinator and quarterbacks coach of the New England Patriots, he might never have accepted the Penn State head coaching job. He could easily have tried to gain his freedom, with legal action if necessary. But that wouldn't have been the Bill O'Brien so widely respected throughout college and professional football.

To the astonishment of much of the public and the NCAA, only eight scholarship players out of a squad of about 105 that included some two dozen walk-ons decided to leave.

Two senior players, in particular, stepped up to help O'Brien save the program. Linebacker Michael Mauti and fullback Michael Zordich were more than ordinary players. They were known as "legacy recruits" because their fathers had played for Paterno. Penn State was in their blood.

Almost from the moment of the NCAA pronouncement, coaches from other teams began making contact with Penn State's players. Illinois was so brazen that its entire staff descended on State College to personally lure any malcontents. After two days of badgering by the outsiders, Mauti and Zordich had enough. They organized a meeting of players who were staying. With 30 of those players behind them during an impromptu news conference without notes Mauti and Zordich spoke out about the loyalty of the players to Penn State and O'Brien. Their words are immortalized in Penn State football history.

"This program was not built by one man, and this program sure to hell is not going to get torn down by one man," Mauti declared. "This program was built on every alumni [sic], every single player that came before us—built on their backs. We're going to take that right now. This is our opportunity to do that."

"We want the nation to know we are proud of who we are," Zordich said. "We're going to stick together through this. We know it's not going to be easy...We know that through this grind that that there's going to be tough times ahead...We have an obligation to Penn State, and we have the ability to fight for not just a team, not just a program, but for an entire university and every man that wore the blue and white on the gridiron before us."

The Penn State fans added their support when a crowd estimated at 3,000–4,000 showed up at the Lasch football building at

Christian Hackenberg

In just two years, Christian Hackenberg is being mentioned in the same stratosphere as Kerry Collins, arguably the best quarterback in Penn State history.

Even though he had to adapt to new coaches and a different offensive system in 2014, Hackenberg entered the 2015 season holding several new Penn State records and is on the verge of breaking many others. One record he now owns is eight games passing for 300 yards or more and he is third in all-time career passing yardage with 5,932 yards and 32 touchdowns on 501 completions in 876 attempts.

Hackenberg climaxed his sophomore year by his selection as the Most Valuable Player of Penn State's first bowl game since the scandal, a 31–30 overtime win over Boston College in the Pinstripe Bowl. (Penn State became eligible to compete for a bowl game in 2014 after the NCAA restored its postseason eligibility.)

Will he be the greatest in school history?

dawn on July 31 for a pep rally initiated by two former players. "It was shocking," said quarterback Matt McGloin.

Despite the determination of the players and O'Brien and his staff, and the support of hundreds of former lettermen and the entire Nittany Nation, the prospect of a successful season was questionable. And when the team lost its first two games, things looked dim.

The team picked itself off the floor and lost just two more games, culminating in the 8–4 2012 season record and earning second place in the Big Ten's Legend Division with an electrifying 24–21 overtime upset over Wisconsin at Beaver Stadium.

Even without Mauti, Zordich, and 29 other seniors who left after 2012, O'Brien and his coaches and the loyal players came through again in 2013, with a 7–5 record and third place in the division, punctuated at the end by a 31–24 upset at 24-point favorite and No. 14 Wisconsin.

The key player for the 2013 success was a talented freshman quarterback who enrolled at Penn State because of O'Brien and despite the scandal. Christian Hackenberg could have gone to Alabama and other elite football schools, but he wanted O'Brien to make him a better quarterback, and O'Brien did.

The NCAA sanctions could have devastated Penn State's football program for a decade or more. O'Brien and the loyal players brought it back from the abyss and earned the respect of some of its most vocal critics.

In December 2013 O'Brien could not resist an offer to return to the NFL as head coach of the Houston Texans. Penn State football moved on, but O'Brien's recruiting of Hackenberg and others in his two years continue to help the Nittany Lions move forward. Bill O'Brien will always be remembered for saving the program during its most horrific and darkest days.

21 See George Deike's Trumpet

George Deike could not have dreamed in 1899 that his bugle from the Spanish-American War would one day spawn a nationally known 315-piece marching band that is one of the jewels of the Penn State football nation.

Deike was a freshman from Pittsburgh studying mining engineering and just back from service with the 14th Pennsylvania Volunteer Infantry. On September 17, 1899, the commandant of Penn State's military training unit spotted Deike's bugle while making his first inspection of the small cadet corps. The next day Deike was appointed the chief musician of the battalion and asked to organize a Cadet Bugle Corps.

Deike recruited three freshman buglers, a senior base drummer, and a junior snare drummer and by October 1, the Cadet Bugle Corps was in business. And that was the birth of Penn State's admired Blue Band, according to the book *The Penn State Blue Band* by Thomas Range II and Sean Patrick Smith.

But Deike and his cohorts wanted more—a full Cadet Band. Twenty-five students signed up, and most of the 364-student body and some faculty joined in to support their cause. Now, all they needed was money to pay for instruments and other necessary expenses.

When the board of trustees refused to allocate any funds, board president General James Beaver and school president George Atherton donated $50 each and trustee H. V. White gave $100. Beaver, the onetime governor and Penn State's most consequential benefactor, asked trustee Andrew Carnegie, the wealthy steel industrialist, for another $100. Carnegie responded with a cashier's check for $800, prompting this gracious response from the board's executive committee:

"No single act in many years has awakened so warm an enthusiasm among the entire body of students, and the friends of the College regard this gift as one of the most stimulating and healthful towards the growth of vigorous and manly College spirit."

The words are as true today as they were then.

President Atherton officially authorized the Cadet Band on October 23, 1901, but there are indications it had begun making public appearances earlier, including at football games. However, *The Penn State Blue Band* book cites the *Times* newspaper of State

The Cadet Bugle Corps organized in 1899 by George Deike transformed into Penn State's famous marching Blue Band. Deike is in the front row holding his bugle from the Spanish-American War that started it all.

College as being the first known mention of the band at a football game in Williamsport against Lehigh on November 16, 1901. Penn State won 38–0, which may be why some fans believe the Blue Band is a good-luck charm for the team.

In 1911, *Cadet* was eliminated from the name and the group became the College Band. By 1923 the band had grown to 125 members and the name was officially changed to the Blue Band. The name came about because the best 50 musicians were wearing dark blue uniforms instead of the band's standard drab brown or khaki uniforms. Those elite 50 also were the only ones to travel because of expenses. They made the first official appearance of the Blue Band at a football game on October 26, 1923, at New York's Yankee Stadium against West Virginia. (It ended in a 13–13 tie, so no luck there.)

Until 1914 students were in charge of the band. Since then there have been just six directors—Wilfred "Tommy" Thompson; Hummel Fishburn; James Dunlop; Ned Deihl; Richard Bundy; and, starting in 2015, Gregory Drane.

A drum major was added in the 1930s, and in 1971 drum major Jeff Robertson created the now-traditional, fan-pleasing "flip" before the entrance of the Blue Band from Beaver Stadium's south end zone. First, the drum major runs 50 yards to midfield and does a complete somersault. Then, as the band marches downfield, the drum major runs back through the band and repeats the flip near the goal posts. Fans believe if the drum major makes the flip without fail, the Nittany Lions will win the game that day. Okay, it's not true, but it's the school spirit that counts.

Another pregame tradition created for the 1965 Pitt game is the Floating Lion. The full band marches down the entire field and back in a formation spelling "L-I-O-N" while playing the traditional tune, "The Nittany Lion" (better known to fans informally as "Hail to the Lion"). The song was written in 1919 by Penn State graduate Jimmy Lyden, then a prolific New York songwriter. As a sophomore Lyden also wrote his first traditional song, "Victory," and graduate Joe Saunders wrote another in 1915, "Fight on State." They're all part of the school's fight song repertoire that all true Penn State fans must sing along with the Blue Band at Beaver Stadium.

Although women have been part of the Blue Band's concert unit since 1930, the Blue Band was an all-male bastion until 1972, not coincidentally the same year of the landmark Title IX that legislated equality for women in athletics. That fall 12 majorettes made their debut at Beaver Stadium, and a year later four coeds were playing instruments and another was carrying a flag. Today, 40 to 45 percent of the Blue Band is composed of women and competition to be in the band is strong with a failure rate of about 33 percent.

George Deike would be proud of today's Blue Band, and his pioneering bugle is on display in the lobby of the Richard Bundy Blue Band Building not far from Beaver Stadium—another must-see for Penn State fans.

22. 1972: Redemption in the Cotton Bowl

As I wrote in *The Penn State Football Encyclopedia* in 1998, "If there is one game in the Paterno era that any of his 31 teams 'had' to win it was the 1972 Cotton Bowl." That still holds true today after Joe Paterno's 46-year career ended with 409 victories in 548 games.

Three years earlier, in his fourth season, Paterno and Penn State were heavily criticized by the college football world for supposedly ducking a chance to play Texas for the national championship in the 1970 Cotton Bowl. It was an era when bowl matchups were arranged before the end of the regular season, and the 1969 situation that led Penn State to play Missouri instead in the Orange Bowl was complicated. That controversy didn't matter when the No. 10, once-beaten Nittany Lions faced off against the No. 12, twice-beaten Longhorns as a six-point underdog.

What made everything worse for Penn State was an embarrassing, mistake-prone 31–11 loss to twice-beaten Tennessee in the last game of the regular season, after the bowl pairings had been set. The defeat had ruined Penn State's third undefeated record in four years.

Even before that loss in Knoxville, many in the media were mocking the Lions for their supposedly "soft" schedule, with one Chattanooga newspaper labeling them "imposters." It was a typical refrain that would follow Paterno's teams for decades.

The alleged weak schedule included nine wins by 25 points or more, against such intersectional opponents as Iowa, TCU, and North Carolina State, with just one close win over Air Force 16–14.

"If an Eastern team beats a club from another section of the country, it's regarded as a fluke because your opponent didn't take you seriously," Paterno once complained. "If we lose, it's because we're lousy."

Texas coach Darrell Royal and his team didn't believe the 1971 Nittany Lions were lousy. But there definitely was a lack of respect for Penn State's talent and the caliber of Penn State opponents in recent years when compared to the Southwest Conference.

Royal's Longhorns had stormed to prominence in 1968 with a potent wishbone offense and had only lost four games and tied one since then. Two of those defeats had occurred midway through the 1971 season in tough back-to-back losses to Sugar Bowl–bound Oklahoma and Arkansas.

Both Penn State and Texas could score, went the pregame analysis, but since the Nittany Lions had never played against a wishbone team, their defense would wear out and the Longhorns would dominate with ball control.

The fans and media also bought into the myth that Paterno and his players intentionally avoided Texas in 1969 because they knew Texas was the better team.

"We weren't very popular when we went down there [in '72]," Paterno recalled years later, "but that was a psychological carryover from the ratings of 1969...."

The critics appeared to be right in the first quarter when, in a steady rain, Texas went on long drives to the Penn State 30- and 1-yard lines but only scored a 29-yard field goal. The Longhorns continued the attack in the second quarter, but Penn State tied the game with a 21-yard field goal after forcing a fumble. Then, with 30 seconds left in the half a Texas interception at midfield led the Nittany Lions to a then–Cotton Bowl record 40-yard field goal on the last play.

Although the score was close, Texas' wishbone was dominating the game and a second-half rout appeared imminent. As the Lions trotted into the dressing room, co-captain Dave Joyner, an All-American offensive tackle, told his concerned coach not to worry, saying, "We got 'em where we want 'em."

Three plays into the second half, Penn State recovered a Texas fumble, and within moments the Lions took the lead and never looked back. It turned into a rout, all right. Penn State's withering defense shut down the wishbone, which couldn't score a touchdown for the first time in 80 games, while its offense controlled the ball for almost 13 minutes of the fourth quarter en route to a stunning 30–6 victory.

"I don't think we've ever had a game that we had to win more than this one," Paterno said in the locker room and repeated over the years. "There was so much that had been done that was ready to go down the drain if Texas had beaten us."

23 Don't Go Pro, Joe: 1972 Sugar Bowl

The buttons, signs, and bumper stickers began popping up nearly two weeks before the 1972 Sugar Bowl, after reports surfaced that the New England Patriots were seriously pursuing Joe Paterno to be their next football coach.

"Don't Go Pro, Joe," the message implored, and it was directed at one man, Penn State's popular head football coach.

Some 20,000 Christmas cards with that succinct and direct phrase and Paterno's photo on the front were distributed free in State College on December 22. That was timed for the day after his 47th birthday, so that the football team's most avid fans could send him a personal plea. The innovative campaign blitz was launched by a local advertising agency and publishing company run by a prominent community leader and Penn State booster-alumnus, Mimi Barash Coppersmith, and her husband, Sy.

"I couldn't help but feel good about the cards and flashing labels…," Paterno wrote in his 1989 autobiography, *Paterno: by The Book.*

When the fans gathered in New Orleans for the New Year's Eve game against Oklahoma, they added a "Don't Go Pro, Joe" chant to the buttons they wore and the blue-and-white signs they carried. They shouted the mantra whenever Paterno appeared in public and even during the Sugar Bowl night game at Tulane Stadium.

Paterno had been contacted several times about coaching elsewhere since becoming Penn State's head coach seven years earlier, including by Michigan and the Pittsburgh Steelers. He had resisted all the other concrete offers for a variety of personal and professional reasons, but this one was enticing.

St. Joe

Joe Paterno's very public rejection of the Boston Patriots' lucrative offer thrust him into a new level of class and respect. Here was a big-city guy stuck in the middle of nowhere Pennsylvania being so loyal to his players and dedicated to their well-being off the football field that he turned down the buckets of money and lifetime security that college and professional football coaches at that time could only dream about.

Paterno began talking more and more about his Grand Experiment and making sure his players graduated. He campaigned openly against teams and peers who violated NCAA rules or cheated in other ways.

Invited by the Penn State board of trustees to speak after his team won its first national championship in 1982, Paterno challenged them bluntly to make the school one of the greatest public universities in the world, saying, "I am ready to help where I can to make 'Number One' mean more than when we stick that finger up." And he put his money where his mouth was, eventually giving more than $4 million to help fund myriad projects, including a new wing on the school library.

Paterno's words and action brought down the wrath of many fellow coaches who gave him the sarcastic nickname St. Joe. He made national headlines in 1980 when a Pittsburgh sportswriter wrote about Paterno's flippant criticism of fellow coaches Barry Switzer of Oklahoma and Jackie Sherrill of Pitt in what Paterno thought was an off-the-record conversation at a private party. Asked if he would retire from coaching and go into politics, Paterno snapped, "I'm not going to give up college football to the Jackie Sherrills and Barry Switzers of the world."

Paterno apologized to Switzer a couple years later, and finally in 2004 he made up with Sherrill, who spent a football weekend at the Paterno home with his wife.

The 2011 scandal has damaged Paterno's once-pristine image, and whether it will ever be restored is unknown. He never liked being called St. Joe anyway.

When Patriots owner Billy Sullivan telephoned him in late November before Penn State's annual end-of-season rivalry game against Pitt, Paterno was surprised by Sullivan's proposal for part ownership in the team and the title of coach and general manager with complete control of all team decisions. Paterno agreed to talk to Sullivan after the Pitt game. When they met in New York a few days later, Sullivan proffered a financial package Paterno could hardly believe: a four-year contract worth $1.4 million and 5 percent worth of stock in the Patriots.

Paterno, who was then making $35,000 a year with no perks, later wrote about his instant reaction. "I looked at the salary part, then the stock part, and said to myself, 'Holy Smoke.'"

Paterno told Sullivan he didn't want to talk any further until after the Sugar Bowl, but that wasn't good enough for the aggressive Patriots owner. Sullivan flew to New Orleans and showed up at a private dinner for both teams and the media at one of New Orleans' classic restaurants, Antoine's. "He threw me a big wave and a significant smile that made me want to shrink," Paterno recalled.

Sullivan also joked with Paterno and the crowd about the Patriots job. The room buzzed all night over Sullivan's presence, and the media reports of the event added to the intrigue of the Penn State coaching situation.

The Sugar Bowl had its own unique circumstances. This was the first game played on New Year's Eve instead of New Year's Day and for first time in its 39-year history, there was no team from the Southeastern Conference in the game.

No. 2 Oklahoma entered as a 13-point favorite and beat Penn State 14–0. "Lions Offer No Excuses," read the headline in the *New Orleans State-Item*. However, with their star running back John Cappelletti, missing the game because of a virus infection and his backup, Walt Addie, nursing a bruise, the Lions' passing game could not overcome Oklahoma's harassing defense and the four lost fumbles. (Weeks after the game, the NCAA made Oklahoma forfeit all its games that season because two of its freshman players had been ineligible. However, Penn State does not recognize the forfeit in its official records.)

Paterno went back to State College to ponder over the Patriots job. "I knew there was no way I could turn down Sullivan's deal," he wrote later. "It gave me everything I ever dreamed of...."

Paterno discussed everything with his wife, Sue, and called Sullivan. They agreed to meet the next morning in New York. Paterno knew his wife was not "crazy" about the new job, but they celebrated that night with Louise and Jim Tarman, Penn State's sports information director who would be going with him to Boston.

"At bedtime, I said to Sue, 'Okay, kid. Tonight you get to sleep with a millionaire,'" Paterno recalled often over the years.

Paterno had a sleepless night wondering if he was making the right decision. When Sue woke up the next morning, Paterno uttered one of his more famous quotes: "You went to bed with a millionaire, but you woke up with me. I'm not going."

"I now knew clearly, exactly," he later wrote, "just what college football means to me—and what professional football never could."

If you've never seen one of those "Don't Go Pro, Joe" buttons, you need to visit the Penn State All-Sports Museum. It's on display in the Paterno display case.

24 Play Days: Women Pioneers before Title IX

Eight years before the groundbreaking Title IX legislation forced colleges to have varsity sports programs for women, Penn State started one at the University Park main campus, but hardly anyone on or off campus knew it.

President Eric Walker and athletic director Ernie McCoy had approved the 1964 plan for nine varsity sports proposed by the athletic department's two women administrators with one caveat.

"He said, 'Please, do me a favor and do not call it varsity or intercollegiate,'" remembered Marty Adams, chairperson of the Women's Physical Education Department. "'Call it extramural because too many of the staff might be opposed to competition for women but they won't know what extramural is.'"

So Della Durant, who had been the advisor to the student-run Women's Recreation Association (WRA), was given the bizarre title of Director of Extramural Sports for Women. In came extramural sports and out went Play Days.

Before 1964 women had competed in intramurals with club teams advised by a faculty member under the auspices of the WRA.

"In those [WRA] years we had what we called Play Days" Durant told me a few years before her death. "We would have intramural competition on campus and then we would take our teams to Wilson College or other colleges and there would be other schools there. But we wouldn't compete against each other as a Penn State team against another school. We would take two girls from Penn State and two from other schools and form teams that would have informal competition. It was more social than anything."

Soon Play Days transformed into Sports Days, where they actually competed as a Penn State team against other college teams. But the women wanted more. The student funds office balked at paying for more competition between schools. So the women faculty in the athletic department boldly went to McCoy, who was also dean of the College of Health and Physical Education. He was enthusiastic and so was President Walker.

The faculty volunteered to coach the teams.

"We had nine teams ready to compete in 1964, but we couldn't find enough teams to play us," Durant remembered. "In that first year, our golf team competed once against Bucknell and twice against the women in the Centre Hills Country Club because some of the other schools didn't have teams available."

On October 13, 1964, the field hockey team made history by beating Susquehanna 2–0 at home in the first official women's varsity game. In May 1965 the golf team made its historic debut by defeating Bucknell 4–0 at the Centre Hills Country Club.

The following season, in 1965–66, Penn State had women varsity teams in basketball, fencing, gymnastics, lacrosse, rifle, softball, and tennis. Bowling was added in 1968 and swimming and diving in 1970.

"At first, the women's faculty set the rules and some were a bit bizarre," Adams recalled. "We could have no more than two contests in one week, and then if you had two contests you could not have any the next week," said Adams. "It was strange...Is it a little wonder with this name [extramural] why it took us so long to be known?"

Extramural be damned, Adams, Durant, and another faculty member, Lucille "Lu" Magnusson, also wanted to overcome the bias by the chauvinistic NCAA. In 1967 the NCAA formed a feasibility committee to study "the development and supervision of women intercollegiate athletics."

The women in collegiate athletics knew that meant years of stalling. They set up their own organization in 1967 to oversee varsity sports, the Commission of Intercollegiate Athletics for Women (CIAW). That group evolved into the Association for Intercollegiate Athletics for Women (AIAW) in 1971 with 275 institutions. For the next decade while the NCAA dawdled, Penn State would win 12 AIAW national team championships and five Nittany Lions women would be honored as Player of the Year in their sports.

Prodded by Title IX and the success of the AIAW, the NCAA adopted another resolution in 1975 "calling for the orderly development of women's intercollegiate athletics." That was enough for the women and the federal government. The hammer came down the next year with Title IX.

Still, it would take another eight years before the foot-dragging NCAA would fully accept women's athletics as equals. In the fall of 1980, the NCAA proposed competition for women in Divisions II and III with the stipulation that the AIAW dissolve. There was intense opposition from both sides. The AIAW leadership, including Adams and Durant, believed the women were still being treated like second-class members.

"They weren't treating us like equals, particularly in leadership roles," Durant said, "We also didn't like the NCAA's positions on recruitment, financial aid, the transfer rule, and other things."

The Penn State women continued to get help from the school's new president, John Oswald; Robert "Bob" Scannell, who succeeded McCoy as dean of the redesignated Penn State's College of Health, Physical Education and Recreation in 1970; and the new athletics director, Ed Czekaj. They and other male supporters pushed for equality inside the byzantine NCAA power structure, and in 1983 the NCAA formally absorbed women's varsity sports as the AIAW dissolved.

Play Days were finally over for the NCAA.

25 Tailgate on Game Day

Tailgating at the Beav is a must-do for any Penn State fan and especially if it is a "whiteout" night game.

The experience is unique, with its own style, traditions, and food. The location itself is like none other either.

Beaver Stadium is on the eastern edge of the Penn State property in a onetime cow pasture, partially moved and reconstructed there at the end of the 1959 season. Original seating capacity: 46,000. Seating capacity since 2011: 106,572, down 650 seats since the last major expansion in 2001 to ADA standards.

Once the third-largest Pennsylvania city when filled on game day, Beaver Stadium is now fourth after Philadelphia, Pittsburgh,

A Traffic Jam Created Tailgating

When the Penn State administration drew up plans to move the football field to its new location and rename it Beaver Stadium, some prescient officials envisioned tailgating, but they didn't call it that. A planning document hoped "that pre-game picnic lunch will be increasingly a Penn State tradition, such as it is now at the Ivy League schools, permitting the station wagon set to arrive an hour or two before kick-off [sic] and enjoy fried chicken, sandwiches, etc. under the cool shade of sturdy oak trees." A preliminary design included a special area with picnic tables adjacent to the west side of the stadium.

By the time the first game was played on September 17, 1960, the "special area" had been eliminated. Because students had not returned for the fall semester the crowd that day was far less than capacity. When 33,613 turned out for the homecoming game against Missouri two weeks later, traffic was literally a mess. A front-page story in the Monday *Centre Daily Times* recounted the nightmare: "The traffic pileup before and after the game had police swearing, drivers cursing and pedestrians jumping for their lives. The blockage seemed concentrated on the campus before the game and in town after the game...There were some reports of traffic using lawns and private driveways to get around the jams." An accompanying front-page editorial signed by editor Jerry Weinstein suggested fans avoid the traffic jams by bringing "picnic lunches to be eaten before the opening kickoffs" and "a picnic supper" for after the game.

Weinstein's idea began to pick up some adherents and—voila— Penn State's tailgating was born. Even Weinstein could not have envisioned the tailgating fanaticism of today.

and Allentown. With a population of some 42,000 in the borough of State College that doubles when students are there and a rural Centre County populace of 155,400, it takes loyal Penn State fans from all over the East and elsewhere to make the Beav the second-largest stadium in the nation after Big Ten rival Michigan's 109,901.

It's a picturesque setting in a rustic atmosphere. Visitors are always impressed in the fall when the leaves are changing on the small mountain ranges north and south of the stadium, with a grand view of the fabled Mt. Nittany from every tailgate lot and most of the stadium seats. For years in the 1970s and 1980s, a wide shot of Mt. Nittany and the south end of Beaver Stadium became the standard opening for the network television cameras as the sportscasters extolled the charm and warmth of Happy Valley.

The parking lots around Beaver Stadium are jammed from early morning to late at night with enthusiastic Penn State fans tailgating before and after home games in the fall.

The scene inside the stadium is even more exhilarating at night. That all started in 1982 when portable lights were trucked in for a 3:45 kickoff against Nebraska in what turned out to be a come-from-behind last-second 27–24 victory in one of the classic games in Penn State history. Two years later permanent lights were installed. In recent years, Penn State has hosted at least one game before November with a late start and the whiteouts—where all the fans dress in white—have made the atmosphere second to none, including LSU's legendary Death Valley.

The RVs start cruising into town four days before the game. Parking in the special RV grass lots catty-corner to Beaver Stadium is not permitted until noon Friday, but the two Walmarts and one Sam's Club located about three to four miles from the stadium allow RVs to park overnight until then. Other RV drivers wait until game day to pull into their reserved spaces closer to the stadium.

Three large paved lots reserved for the Penn State regulars encircle three-fourths of the Beav. Other spacious grass lots are available for game day parkers who have to walk farther to reach the stadium gates, although special buses are provided for ADA patrons.

And when all those lots open at 7:00 AM for noon kickoffs and 8:00 AM for all other games, there already is a line of assorted vehicles ready to move in and start the party. The fans pour their Bloody Marys and mimosas, nibble at the salsa and chips, and fire up their gas grills and camping stoves for the steaks, hamburgers, barbecue ribs, pastas, and lobster bisque. And no tailgate at the Beav is complete without Pennsylvania's own Yuengling beer.

In 1988 the Penn State Alumni Association published a hardcover cookbook of some of the school's best tailgating recipes titled *Cookin' with the Lion* that included such food as Fiesta Bowl Albondigas, Crush 'Em Lion Salad, and Lion's Paw Ribs.

Three hours before kickoff, a large crowd of tailgaters gathers outside the south end of the stadium to greet the traditional

Blue Buses that transports the players from the team hotel to the stadium. For 35 years, the players embarked in front of the team entrance at the middle of the south façade. James Franklin modified that tradition in his first year as head coach in 2014 by having the buses stop at the southeast corner so that the players can walk through a small roped-off path in the crowd to the entrance. It was an instant hit.

The earlier bus stop also has been a boon for the devoted students who camp out for days in tents at that southeast corner to get the best seats when the nearby student gate opens an hour and a half before kickoff. The camp out is a relatively new tradition the students started in 2005 before the midseason clash with Ohio State that was the biggest game in a stretch of four losing seasons since 2000. Initially named Paternoville by the students, they now call it Nittanyville. And rain, shine, or snow, the students are there.

In recent years, dozens of media outlets have produced lists of the best college football tailgate experiences. As one might expect, the accounts are usually written with a bias for or against certain schools. Every fan believes their school has the best tailgating, and why not? Penn State has received its share of recognition.

A few years ago *Newsweek* magazine cited tailgating at the Beav as "the biggest pregame party in the United States." Joe Cahn, the self-proclaimed commissioner of tailgating who runs a tailgating website and has written about his tailgating around the nation, claims Penn State's only rival as the best is his favorite team: LSU.

Penn State touts its game day experience—from tailgating to whiteouts—as "the Greatest Show in College Football," a phrase first uttered by a former Ohio State quarterback–turned–ESPN sportscaster, Kirk Herbstreit. So true, Brother Herbstreit, so true.

26 1947: The Cotton Bowl Team

No Penn State team in any sport accomplished what the 1947 football team did on and off the field. It stands alone atop Penn State's Mount Everest.

The term "great" is frequently overused. Not this time. The 1947 team not only went undefeated and set NCAA defensive records that remained in place for years, but what the nearly all-white players did for civil rights in an era before the 1960s marches in Alabama and Mississippi and the riots in Detroit and Newark is their crowning achievement.

It all started the year before with the 1946 team, and almost all of those players were back in 1947.

There were two African American players on those basically 45-man squads of '46 and '47. Denny Hoggard had been an ineligible freshman in 1942 and returned in 1946 after service in World War II. Wally Triplett became the first African American to start and earn a letter in 1945 and was on the verge of becoming a star wingback.

Hoggard and Triplett reflected Penn State's African American student enrollment of 25 to 35. Triplett and Hoggard encountered racism, particularly from opposing teams, and even from some teammates. But the bulk of the players, many of them veterans of the war who had played on integrated high schools in Pennsylvania, treated them well.

"We did take a few punches sometimes under the pile during a game and in scrimmages," Triplett told me.

A few months before the 1946 season, Penn State scheduled a game at Miami after the traditional season-ending game against Pitt. Whoever set up the game may not have realized that the city of Miami was segregated and so was the college's football team. In late October, the University of Miami told Penn State to leave the African American players home or the game would be canceled.

Head coach Bob Higgins called a team meeting. It was tense but short, as a couple players described it to me. After a couple players said they wanted to play at Miami, several team leaders took charge and demanded an immediate vote to cancel the game. Hands went up slowly, and there was a definite majority.

"That's when someone said, 'Let's make it unanimous,'" Triplett remembered, "and the guys said, 'Yeah, let's get it over with and get on out of here.' You could have bowled me over."

That was the moment the 1947 squad became a great team.

The 1946 team lost its final game of the season against Pitt 14–7, but it would be the last Penn State defeat until Pitt did it again in 1948 7–0.

Penn State's undefeated team of 1947 integrated the 1948 Cotton Bowl with two African American players in a 13–13 tie against SMU. Starting wingback Wally Triplett is in the third row and reserve end Denny Hoggard is in the second row.

In 1947 Penn State was loaded with a mix of tough 25-year-old (or so) war veterans and younger, experienced talent at every position. Higgins' dilemma was getting them all on the field, especially in a period when everyone in college football had to play offense and defense.

Utilizing the power of Higgins' single-wing offense with clutch passing and a modified 5-3-2-1 blitzing defense, Penn State rolled over nine opponents with only two victories by margins less than 13 points and won its first Lambert Trophy as the best team in the East. When the final AP poll was released on December 8, the Nittany Lions were ranked No. 4, behind No. 1 Notre Dame, Michigan, and an equally surprising SMU team.

By winning the Southwest Conference, SMU was the host team in the Cotton Bowl, and SMU Coach Matty Bell said he wanted to play the highest-ranked team. That meant Penn State because Notre Dame didn't go to bowls then and Michigan was in the Rose Bowl. But there was a major obstacle. Dallas was segregated.

Bell conferred with Cotton Bowl officials and then met with his team, led by junior halfback Doak Walker, who would win the Heisman Trophy the next season. He asked if anybody objected to playing against African American players. "Nobody did," Walker's backup Frank Payne told the *Dallas Morning News* 63 years later.

Penn State still had to obey Dallas' segregation laws, which is why the team spent 11 days living at a Naval Air Station 14 miles from town. That caused so much dissension that many players hopped the fence and went into the city, bringing down the ire of some sportswriters for "partying" and not taking the game seriously.

The writers were wrong. The game was an exciting one, highlighted by missed extra points by Walker and the Lions' Ed Czekaj (a future Penn State athletic director) and came down to the last play of the game in a 13–13 tie.

The outcome of the game was inconsequential in comparison to the fact that Triplett and Hoggard made history as the first

African American players in the Cotton Bowl game. First Miami and then the Cotton Bowl. A nearly all-white Penn State team hit a grand slam for civil rights.

"They didn't understand the significance of what they did [and] I didn't either," Triplett recalled decades later. "For years, none of them thought they had done anything."

On October 12, 2010, the 1946 and 1947 teams received the Heroes Amongst Us Award, from the National Consortium for Academics and Sports at its annual awards dinner in Orlando. At the same dinner the group inducted South Africa's Nelson Mandela and 1968 Olympians Tommie Smith and John Carlos into its Hall of Fame.

The consortium, an organization that focuses on using sports for social change, honored the 1946–47 teams "for the bond and togetherness among teammates during a time of tension and prejudices." They are still the only sports team to win the award since its creation in 2007.

What those teams accomplished is noted at Beaver Stadium with a historical marker near the entrance to the All-Sports Museum. It's a must-see for every Penn State sports fan.

27 Lenny Moore

The greatest player in Penn State football history is not and never will be in the College Football Hall of Fame.

Of course, that definitive claim about halfback Leonard Edward Moore is guaranteed to start an argument. After all, a few thousand men have played for Penn State since 1887, and 23 of them are enshrined in the pantheon of college football, two as head coaches.

One, tailback John Cappelletti, is the only Penn State player to win the Heisman Trophy. He also won the Maxwell Award as "the most outstanding player in college football." Three other Hall of Famers have also have won the Maxwell Award as well as two Nittany Lions All-Americans runners-up who were in the Heisman.

Don't take my word for placing Lenny Moore at the top of Mt. Nittany.

"Lenny Moore is the best all-around player I ever coached," the late Joe Paterno said frequently. Paterno was an offensive backfield assistant to head coach Rip Engle during Moore's Nittany Lion career from 1953 to 1955.

"[Lenny is] the greatest back I ever coached and the best two-way halfback in the game today," Engle told *Pittsburgh Press* writer Carl Hughes as Moore was getting ready to end his collegiate career against Pitt in 1955.

Hughes also asked Engle's predecessor, Bob Higgins, to evaluate Moore. Higgins, a two-time All-American end at Penn State in 1915 and 1919 and the head coach from 1930 until 1949, spent three of his retirement years watching Moore at Beaver Field. "Moore is the best I've ever seen," Higgins replied.

"I am truly humbled," Moore said when he learned of Joe Paterno's supreme compliment. "When I'm told things like that I wonder how can that be because there have been so many great players at Penn State for over 100 years."

Moore wound up at Penn State because of his high school coaches at Reading, Pennsylvania. "I wasn't even sure I wanted to go to college," Moore said. Head coach Andy Staple convinced his parents about that, and line coach Bob Perugini, a Lions letterman in 1941–42, pointed him toward Penn State. Assistant Penn State coach Tor Toretti recruited him.

Although Penn State had been an integrated team since the 1940s, there were still few African Americans on campus, let alone playing football, and an undercurrent of racism was part of the

Lenny vs. Jim Brown

No one in the standing-room sellout crowd of 30,321 at Beaver Field, including me, knew they were watching what would become one of the classic games in Penn State's football history.

It was November 5, 1955, and neither team was having a good year. Penn State was 3–3 and would finish 5–4 while 3–2 Syracuse would wind up 5–3. What the fans really wanted to see were the star running backs of each team, Lenny Moore and Syracuse junior Jimmy Brown. They weren't disappointed.

Moore and Brown were sensational on both offense and defense. Brown was almost a one-man team, scoring all of slightly favored Syracuse's 20 points. Twice Penn State had to rally from 13-point deficits in the first and second halves. With the Lions trailing 13–7 at halftime, the crowd came alive on the second-half kickoff when Moore's ankle tackle on Brown saved a touchdown, only to see Brown score his third touchdown a few plays later.

In the end, the difference in the final 21–20 score was starting sophomore Jack Farls' block of Brown's extra-point kick attempt after Brown's second touchdown midway in the second quarter. Penn State's junior quarterback Milt Plum kicked all three of his extra-point attempts, and with his passing on offense and tackling and interceptions on defense Plum was the near-equal that day of the two future Pro Football Hall of Famers.

Jim Brown ran for 159 yards and two touchdowns on 20 carries; caught two passes, one for a six-yard TD; returned three kickoffs for 95 yards; and intercepted one pass. Moore rushed for 146 yards and a touchdown and was all over the field on defense, making tackles and defending passes.

"Lenny never in his life was greater," Coach Rip Engle said after the game.

"Jimmy and I talked about the game later in the pros," Moore told me years later. "He said, 'You had a very good game, man.' And I said, 'So did you.'"

Classic understatements from the players who made it a classic game.

atmosphere in the State College community. Engle and his coaches wanted to change that.

Moore was the linchpin in Engle's early 1950 recruiting of African American players that included Rosey Grier, Jesse Arnelle, and Charlie Blockson—each of whom would become famous in their own right.

"I loved Tor," Moore said years later. "I loved Rip Engle, too, because not only was he my coach but a great human being, and I admired him. All the coaches made me feel like a big part of the Penn State family despite some of the little negative things that were going on there."

What made Moore stand out above all others was his consummate skill and versatility. He did everything except pass and kick, and he would have done that if asked to by Engle.

Nicknamed the Reading Rambler after his hometown, his high-stepping running style was a trademark that carried over into an illustrious pro career with the Baltimore Colts during their heyday. Moore is still one of the school's career all-purpose offensive leaders (No. 14) with his running, receiving, and kickoff and punt returns.

He also was the first Lions player ever to gain over 1,000 yards in a season, in his junior year, when he was the second-leading ground gainer in the nation with 1,082 yards on 136 carries for a phenomenal 8.0 yards per carry. His 11 touchdowns, including two 80-yard runs, set a team single-season record that stood for 14 years. He is fourth in career punt-return average (15.8 yards on 24 returns for 378 yards and a touchdown) and 10th on career kickoff-return average (24.3 yards on 23 returns for 560 yards).

The aging generation that saw Moore play also remembers him as an outstanding defensive back. He remains tied with four players for sixth in career pass interceptions with 10 (for 136 yards and a touchdown), leading the team in interceptions as a junior (three for 40 yards) and senior (six for 96 yards and a touchdown).

Selecting Moore as the greatest may strike some as unreasonable when comparing a glamorous halfback to a grunt lineman. It also may seem unfair to put more emphasis on the players who played both offense and defense that were the foundation of college football until unrestricted substitution starting in 1966 made way for the modern-day specialists. So be it.

There are a few linemen who would be contenders as the Nittany Lions' all-time best player, as well as several backs. At the top of the lineman list are Glenn Ressler and Mike Reid, who both won the Maxwell Award. Harry "Light-Horse" Wilson, an All-American at both Penn State (1923) and Army (1926), ranks right behind Moore. All three are in the College Football Hall of Fame.

Moore never will be because the No. 1 criteria for eligibility is being a first-team All-American. Unlike today, there were few qualified All-American teams back in the 1950s, and Moore was only a second-team choice in 1954 and 1955, primarily because the Penn State teams of that era were vastly underrated.

However, Moore is just one of six Penn State players in the Pro Football Hall of Fame, and the second one inducted (1975) after an All-Pro career as a running back and receiver with the Baltimore Colts from 1956 to 1967. He is still 13th in the NFL records with 113 career touchdowns.

The next time Penn State retires a jersey number it should be No. 42, worn by one of the greatest players in college football history.

28 Mike Reid

Mike Reid is Penn State football's Renaissance man.

No player has been as distinguished off the field as well as on it as the outstanding defensive tackle and co-captain of the great undefeated 1968–69 teams. He is one of just three Penn State athletes to receive the NCAA's prestigious Silver Anniversary Award for his exceptional postcollegiate career achievements.

"Of all the great players I've had here," Joe Paterno once told *Sports Illustrated,* "Mike Reid remains near the top."

Reid's athletic accomplishments at Penn State culminated in his senior year of 1969 when he won the Maxwell Award as the country's best football player, finished fifth in the Heisman Trophy voting, and became the only Penn State player to receive the Outland Trophy as the nation's most outstanding interior lineman. In his sophomore year, Reid won the Eastern Intercollegiate Wrestling Association heavyweight championship and almost made it to the finals of the NCAA tournament before losing to the eventual champion. The first time he picked up a shot put for the track team with no prior experience, he set a school record and then broke it twice.

Off the field, Reid's five years on campus were marked by classical piano recitals, the lead role in the musical comedy *Guys and Dolls,* and playing the organ in church. All the while he was earning plaudits in the classroom after switching his major from business to music before his junior year.

Historian Ridge Riley summed up Reid's diversity perfectly in his book, *Road to Number One,* after Reid had scored the only touchdown of his career with a 26-yard interception against Maryland in 1969. "Fond of ham on likely occasions, Mike held the ball high in the air as he crossed the [goal] line," Riley wrote. "That night he played Liszt for Heywood Hale Broun on [the] CBS [Evening News] in the course of a chat about the compatibility of football and music."

Reid's sense of humor is inherent to who he is. After listening to all the acceptance speeches of other award winners thanking parents and teammates at the 1969 Maxwell Awared banquet, a smiling Reid told the audience, "Gentlemen, I did it myself, and to hell with you."

As to his ability at the piano, he once joked with author Frank Bilovsky, "I know I look a lot like [more] a piano mover than a piano player."

The piano would lead to his enshrinement in the Nashville Songwriters Hall of Fame in 2005 as a Grammy-winning writer or co-writer of more than 20 country music hits, including 12 songs that became No. 1 on the charts for Ronnie Milsap.

However, it wasn't for his wizardry at the piano that he was inducted into the College Football Hall of Fame in 1987 or named to *Sports Illustrated*'s 75-man All-Century team in 1999.

Reid also might be in the Pro Football Hall of Fame today if he hadn't quit after his five-year All-Pro stint with the Cincinnati Bengals. In their third year of existence in 1970, the Bengals made him their first draft choice and the seventh overall NFL selection behind No. 1 Terry Bradshaw. Reid, an aggressive pass-rusher, was in the Pro Bowl twice, a first-team AP All-NFL selection once (1974), and was either a first-team All-Conference and/or second-team All-NFL selection in his last four years.

"Whenever I produced, they tore up my contract and gave me a new one without asking," he recalled. "My rookie year was a lot of fun...but I don't remember a particular enjoyable season after that...it was the same everything...I might have had it left physically, but mentally I was burned out."

So he walked away and has never regretted it. At first he formed a band that played various music and then went on his own for a while. After sending a demo to Nashville, he was hired to write songs.

"I was absolutely the greatest songwriter the NFL ever produced," Reid once quipped in an interview with the *Los Angeles Times*.

Reid has branched out from country music and in recent years has worked on two disparate musical productions, a play based on the middle life of the 18th-century lover Casanova and a smaller four-character chamber musical that revolves around a couple in their late twenties whose automobile crashes in a Pennsylvania snowbank. "This is absolutely the best work I can do," Reid told me a few years ago.

Reid almost became a linebacker-fullback at Penn State, and that's where he played on the freshman team. Paterno moved him to middle guard, and he became a star from Paterno's first game in 1966 when he was credited with a school-record three safeties. A wrestling injury sidelined him in 1967, but when he returned he was elected co-captain and became the consummate leader of the 1968–69 teams.

More than 30 years ago, Reid looked back at his life at age 34 and told Bilovsky, "I'm real lucky. I'm one of the most fortunate people in the world to have done one thing, to have experienced the power of being in the athletic environment, and then turn around here [in Nashville]…to become involved in something with more passion than ever before."

One of his closest friends, Dr. Dave Joyner, who received the NCAA's Silver Anniversary Award two years after Reid did in 1995, said nothing has changed for his onetime teammate.

"Mike was the greatest football player and athlete in Penn State history," Joyner said. "More important, he was and is an outstanding person and artist."

29 Rip Engle: The Mule Driver from Elk Lick

They were an odd pair, the soft-spoken, prematurely grey-haired man who once drove mules for a coal mine in the backwoods of Pennsylvania as a 20-year-old and the mouthy, wise-cracking Italian, 20 years younger, who grew up playing football on the streets of Brooklyn.

Neither Charles "Rip" Engle nor Joe Paterno knew it in 1946 when Engle gave a football scholarship to Paterno and his younger brother George, but Engle would became the biggest influence on Paterno's professional life. As Paterno wrote later in his autobiography, Engle "was a perfect father figure."

From the time Paterno became a defensive back for Engle at Brown University in his freshman year until the end of his legendary career, the coaching traits and philosophy of Engle were inherent in what Paterno did or didn't do throughout his 62 years of coaching at Penn State.

"In the old days [as the head coach] I used to wear good dress shoes to games [because] Rip Engle did...." Paterno once admitted.

It's a familiar story of how Paterno, Engle's star quarterback in 1948–49, delayed law school to help Engle for a year when Engle became the new head coach at Penn State in the spring of 1950. He simply needed the money to pay for Boston University's law school.

The year turned into 16 before Paterno succeeded his mentor. What's not so familiar is how Engle's amiable and collegial approach to the job, stressing loyalty and family, filtered into Paterno's mindset and became the heart of Penn State football for 70 years.

Engle may not have been as street smart as a youth like Paterno, but he knew what hard work, determination, and a smile could get you. He lived in the tiny mining town of Elk Lick (now Salisbury), about 30 miles from Somerset, now famous as the site of one of the 9/11 terrorist planes that crashed nearby.

Engle's high school didn't have a football team and he worked in a coal mine until he was 19. He saw his first football game when he played in one for little Blue Ridge College (it no longer exists). After transferring to Western Maryland (now McDaniel), he became an All-Maryland end for Coach Dick Harlow, and it was Harlow, a onetime Penn State player and head coach, who steered Engle into coaching.

"I never expected to be a coach," Engle told Ken Rappoport in his book *The Nittany Lions*. "I got out of school right after the Depression and that was the only job I could get. Coach Harlow had two jobs for me coaching, and I couldn't find another job to save me. Otherwise, I would never have been a coach."

After 11 years of success at Waynesboro High School, Engle went to Brown as an assistant in 1942. He became the head coach in 1944, and with Paterno as his clutch quarterback he turned a struggling program into a winner. That led to a job offer after the 1949 season from Penn State's biggest rival, Pitt, which he rejected. He then accepted the one from Penn State.

The Penn State position came with the unusual requirement that Engle keep the previous staff, including the man he was succeeding, erstwhile longtime assistant Joe Bedenk. The staff was edgy and concerned about their futures. They were single-wing coaches and didn't know much about the new man except he helped innovate a new offense called the Wing-T formation.

Engle's warm personality and attitude about family made it work, right from the beginning and all the way to his retirement at the end of the 1965 season. Four of those six 1950 holdover coaches were still with him: Jim O'Hora, Frank Patrick, Earl Bruce, and Tor Torretti (who moved into recruiting in 1963). Those assistants also stayed with Paterno until their retirements. So did four other assistants Engle had hired: J. T. White (1954),

Dan Radakovich (1960), Joe McMullen (1963), and George Welsh (1963). Eventually, Radakovich, McMullen, and Welsh left on good terms.

That, my friends, is loyalty.

Engle ran an open, freewheeling staff, where everyone could give their opinion on team matters, but the give-and-take never spiraled out of hand. There were occasional personality clashes, with Paterno sometimes in the middle of it, but they got along like a family and they socialized like one, too, after hours and with their wives. Paterno even wound up living with the O'Hora family for an amazing 10 years before his marriage.

Engle revitalized the Penn State football program. He beefed up recruiting, made it a point to go after African American athletes, and gradually attracted national attention with turning point upsets over Big Ten powers Illinois, Purdue, and Ohio State that transformed the Nittany Lions into an Eastern power and winner of bowl games.

Paterno was Engle's heir apparent almost from the start. When Engle retired after the 1965 season, Paterno stepped up. Engle eventually succumbed to Alzheimer's, and two months before he died his star pupil won Penn State's first national championship at the Sugar Bowl.

30 1968: Chuck Burkhart and the 12th Man

Joe Paterno's first great team would not have finished undefeated and No. 2 in the nation after a thrilling last-second victory in the Orange Bowl without a bespectacled, slow-footed junior quarterback, a quick-thinking tight end, and an absentminded linebacker.

Only two of them played for Penn State. At the end, it was the linebacker who enabled the quarterback to help Paterno win his first Coach of the Year Award from his peers.

As the 1968 season began, Penn State was riding an eight-game undefeated streak, including a surprising 17–17 tie with favored Florida State in the Gator Bowl. He had a young but semi-experienced team loaded with juniors. Two of them, defensive tackles Mike Reid and Steve Smear, were elected co-captains, the first underclassmen so chosen since center Bas Gray in 1924.

Paterno knew he had a potentially outstanding defense, but his offense was a mix of veterans and newcomers. He felt everything would depend on the cohesiveness of the offense and the quarterbacking of junior Chuck Burkhart, who had not lettered in 1967. Burkhart had been a high school teammate in McKees Rocks of returning All-American tight end Ted Kwalick and Burkhart had never lost a game. Still, there were questions about his talent.

Burkhart wasn't especially fast and lacked a quick release when passing. Sportswriters claimed he was erratic, and the contact lenses he wore didn't help mince the criticism. However, he rarely made a mistake and always was his best under pressure in the clutch.

Despite some misgivings about the 1968 team, it was rated No. 10 in the AP preseason poll with three foes in the top 20: UCLA (16), Syracuse (19), and Miami (20). With the confident Burkhart getting better each game, the Nittany Lions steamed past their first five opponents. They almost blew it all against Army on Homecoming Day until Kwalick made the play of the game.

Army had rallied to come within six points with two and a half minutes left and then went for an onside kick. In the scramble for the ball it disappeared under a pile of players. Suddenly, the ball squirted out. Kwalick, standing alone a few feet away, swooped down, picked it up, and ran 53 yards for the game-clinching touchdown that saved the season.

The 31-Game Undefeated Record 1967–70

1967 [Won 8, Lost 2, Tied 1] Captains: Bill Lenkaitis, Jim Litterelle

				Attend.
Oct. 7	L	UCLA [3]	15–17	46,007
Oct. 14	W	at Boston College	50–28	15,500
Oct. 21	W	West Virginia (Homecoming)	21–14	44,460
Oct. 28	W	at Syracuse	29–20	41,750
Nov. 4	W	at Maryland	38–3	34,700
Nov. 11	W	North Carolina State	13–8	46,497
Nov. 18	W	Ohio U.	35–14	29,556
Nov. 25	W	Pittsburgh	42–6	36,008
Dec. 30	T	Florida State (Gator Bowl)	17–17	68,019

1968 [Won 11, Lost 0] Captains: John Kulka, Mike Reid, Steve Smear

				Attend.
Sept. 21	W	[10] Navy	31–6	49,273
Sept. 28	W	[4] Kansas State	25–9	45,024
Oct. 5	W	[3] at West Virginia	31–20	34,500
Oct. 12	W	[3] at UCLA	21–6	35,772
Oct. 26	W	[4] at Boston College	29–0	25,272
Nov. 2	W	[4] Army (Homecoming)	28–24	49,653
Nov. 9	W	[4] Miami (Fla.)	22–7	50,132
Nov. 16	W	[3] at Maryland	57–13	30,000
Nov. 23	W	[3] at Pittsburgh	65–9	31,224
Dec. 7	W	[3] Syracuse	30–12	41,393
Jan. 1	W	[3] Kansas [6] (Orange Bowl)	15–14	77,719

1969 [Won 11, Lost 0] Captains: Tom Jackson, Mike Reid, Steve Smear

				Attend.
Sept. 20	W	[2] at Navy	45–22	28,796
Sept. 27	W	[2] Colorado	27–3	51,402
Oct. 4	W	[2] at Kansas State [20]	17–14	37,000
Oct. 11	W	[5] West Virginia [17] (Homecoming)	20–0	52,713
Oct. 18	W	[5] at Syracuse	15–14	42,291
Oct. 25	W	[8] Ohio U.	42–3	49,069
Nov. 1	W	[5] Boston College	38–16	46,652
Nov. 15	W	[5] Maryland	48–0	46,106
Nov. 22	W	[5] at Pittsburgh	27–7	39,517
Nov. 29	W	[3] at North Carolina State	33–8	24,150
Jan. 1	W	[2] Missouri [6] (Orange Bowl)	10–3	77,282

1970 [Won 7, Lost 3] Captains: Jack Ham, Warren Koegel

				Attend.
Sept. 19	W	Navy	55–7	48,566
Sept. 26	L	[4] at Colorado [18]	13–41	42,850

Penn State went on to win the rest of its games without being seriously challenged again. With No. 1 undefeated Ohio State meeting No. 2 once-tied USC in the Rose Bowl, No. 3 Penn State was matched with No. 6 Kansas on New Year's Night.

Although defense was the strength of both teams, nearly everyone figured the game would be a shootout between Penn State's run-oriented offense that averaged 34 points a game and the pass-happy attack that had made Kansas the nation's highest-scoring team, averaging 38 points per game.

The game turned into a defensive struggle with fumbles, interceptions, and goal-line stands. With two minutes remaining, Kansas led 14–7 with the ball at its own 38-yard line and could clinch the game with a first down. But the Lions forced a punt that was partially blocked and Penn State had the ball at the 50 with 1:16 left.

Boom! Burkhart threw a bomb to halfback Bobby Campbell that wound up at the 3-yard line. On third down with 20 seconds remaining, Burkhart suddenly realized the play he called in the huddle with halfback Charlie Pittman running around right end wouldn't work. He surprised all his teammates by faking to Pittman, keeping the ball himself, and bootlegging around left end for the touchdown, the first of his collegiate career.

"I said I'd save my first touchdown for a time when it counted," Burkhart said after the game.

There was no overtime then, and Penn State went for the win. Kansas batted down Burkhart's pass into the end zone and the Jayhawks began celebrating. Wait. Umpire Foster Grose waved the yellow flag. Kansas had one too many linebackers on the field. Junior Rick Abernethy accepted the blame, saying, "Nobody tapped me to come out."

Days later, the game film would reveal that Kansas also had 12 men on the field for three previous plays, too.

With a second chance, Campbell took a pitchout and with a mass of blockers ran around left end for the winning two points.

It was an incredible finish that had repercussions for decades. As Paterno often said, "This Orange Bowl game put us on the map."

The thrilling 15–14 victory is now a featured display in the Penn State All-Sports Museum and a must-see for all Penn State fans.

The next season, Penn State went undefeated again behind the quarterbacking of Burkhart. The Nittany Lions did not lose until setting a school record 31-game unbeaten streak, thanks in part to a slow-footed quarterback, a quick-thinking tight end, and an absentminded linebacker.

31 Visit the All-Sports Museum and Tour Beaver Stadium

As the first director of the Penn State All-Sports Museum who was instrumental in its development and construction, I could easily have ranked a visit to the facility in Beaver Stadium the first thing Penn State fans need to know (about) and do before they die.

Other than Coach Joe Paterno, the museum is mentioned the most times in this book. And why not? All the memorabilia, photographs, and miscellaneous information displayed there are inherent to the heritage and achievements of Penn State athletes and coaches—John Cappelletti's Heisman Trophy, Horace Ashenfelter's Olympic gold medal, the four straight NCAA championship trophies won by Coach Cael Sanderson's wrestling team, and much more.

Some 250,000 visitors have passed through since the doors opened on February 17, 2002. Most are surprised the space devoted to the school's premier sport, football, is so small, even though it is the largest area in the 12,000 square feet of exhibit space that covers two floors. Since the addition of men's and women's ice hockey as a varsity sport in 2012–13, the museum now features exhibits on 33 sports, including three no longer active, like boxing, which was Penn State's dominant winter sport from the 1930s until the post–World War 1940s.

It's impossible in this chapter to describe everything visitors can see. Interactive displays and video presentations are spread throughout the museum, giving visitors the opportunity to punch a heavy boxing bag or lift a 100-pound wrestling dummy or see football game film from the 1930s and 1940s. An area on the second floor enables the museum to present timely temporary exhibits, such as the one in 2014 on the 50th anniversary of Penn State's vanguard women's varsity sports program.

"We update each active sports exhibit annually so that the achievements of our current athletes are recognized as well as the stars of the past," said my successor as director, Ken Hickman. "We also sponsor special lectures and panels on various subjects and host special events for children such as a Halloween night and birthday parties."

The lobby atrium features a statute of the Nittany Lion mascot, an academic All-American wall, and a floor-to-ceiling trophy case that contains 66 of the school's 75 national championship trophies through 2014–15. Several cannot be found, including the first one from 1921 in wrestling, seven years before the start of the NCAA tournament. A timeline just inside the entrance to the exhibits traces the birth and development of each sport and a distinctive medallion marks the year of every national championship.

A large football trophy case contains nearly every major trophy won by a Penn State player. Cappelletti's Heisman stands alone several feet away so that visitors can take photographs with it. One of the most unusual items in the case is a 1920s nose guard worn by All-American Joe Bedenk. The oldest memorabilia is there, too: an 1894 football Penn State won by beating Lafayette 72–0.

Visitors certainly have been impressed.

"Another glorious and spectacular facility for Penn Staters and the rest of the world to see. We are Penn State 'Proud,'" wrote Paul Malin of Hackensack, New Jersey, in a comment card.

"Excellent," wrote Steve Duncan of Harrison Township, Michigan. "Really fills every PSU fan's heart with pride for such a great university."

At one time in the early 1990s, the athletic department had envisioned a separate building for the museum across the street from the stadium. "We began raising funds for that building," said Tim Curley, then the athletic director. "When we decided to expand the stadium, we realized this would be a perfect place for the museum."

The only drawback is the museum is closed on many game days when visiting the museum would be a natural thing to do. Opening hours depend on a late kickoff because the entrance also is used as a gate for the Mount Nittany Club and seating area on the fourth level and the football recruiting lounge on the second floor. "If the kickoff is at 3:30 PM or later we are open from 9:00 AM until three and a half hours before that kickoff," said Hickman. However, hours are expanded on Fridays and Saturdays of football weekends to accommodate out-of-town visitors.

It's best to check the museum's website (http://www.gopsusports.com/museum) for opening hours because they vary during the winter months and holidays. A donation is suggested.

You can get a brief look inside Beaver Stadium on your visit or arrange to take one of the special guided group tours of the stadium that are scheduled about eight times a year. The special tour includes the Penn State locker room, the media room, the field, the football lettermen's lounge, and the private Mt. Nittany Club.

Naturally, I'm proud of the Penn State All-Sports Museum. It's No. 1 in my book. Okay, in this book it's No. 31.

32 See the Olympic Medals of Horace and Barney

Long-distance runner Horace Ashenfelter is the only Penn State athlete to win an Olympic gold medal in individual competition, while just two others earned gold medals in relays and team events: sprinter Barney Ewell and basketball player Suzie McConnell-Serio.

If you didn't know their names, you do now.

Ashenfelter's upset of Russian Vladimir Kazantsev in the 1952 3,000-meter steeplechase shocked the world. It was at the height of the Cold War and made the 29-year-old FBI agent from New Jersey a national hero. Months later, he was honored with the prestigious Sullivan Award as the nation's Amateur Athlete of the Year.

"Of all the gaudy accomplishments of the Americans in this strenuous pageant," wrote the great sportswriter Red Smith at the time, "this may have been the most extraordinary."

Four years earlier, Ewell won his gold as an unscheduled substitute in the 4x100-meter relay race that ended with Ewell involved in a controversial passing zone exchange that initially disqualified the US team. Before that race, Ewell won silver medals in the 100- and 200-meter dashes, with the 100 so close the Olympics' first official photo finish was needed to determine the winner.

Ashenfelter's gold medal and Ewell's 100-meter silver are on display in the track-and-field exhibit at the Penn State All-Sports Museum. Ashenfelter's Sullivan Award and his shorts, shoes, shirt, warm-up suit, and the number he wore are also in a special trophy case, along with a photo of the key moment in his upset. The historic photo finish of Ewell's heartbreaking loss to Harrison Dillard in the 100-meter is on a nearby wall with his silver medal.

This is the moment of truth as Horace Ashenfelter upsets Russian Vladimir Kazantsev in the 1952 Olympic 3000-meter Steeplechase. Kazantsev stumbles at the last water jump and Ashenfelter (No. 998) moves ahead and sprints to the finish line.

You'll also find a large color photograph in the museum's basketball area of McConnell-Serio with the gold medal around her neck.

Nearly 160 athletes, coaches, and administrators with Penn State ties have been involved in the Olympics from 1904 through the winter Olympics in Japan in 2014. So the gold medal accomplishments by Ashenfelter, Ewell, and McConnell-Serio are in rarified air in Penn State athletics and shared only by John Cappelletti and his Heisman Trophy.

Ewell is one of just five Nittany Lions to win silver medals. Mike Shine also won his in an individual event, 400 hurdles in 1976, while the others were in relay or team competition: Harold Barron (4x400 relay, 1920), Arthur Studenroth (team cross country, 1924), and Susan Rojcewicz (basketball, 1976). Nine others won bronze medals, including McConnell-Serio (basketball, 1992), Mary Ellen Clark (two in diving, 1992 and 1996), and Char Morett (field hockey, 1984).

Morett has been Penn State's field hockey head coach since 1987. Clark's 1992 bronze medal, her colorful outfit from the opening ceremony, and her Olympic diving flag autographed by fellow Olympians can be seen in the museum's diving exhibit.

Ewell was already a household name in track-and-field when he became teammates with Ashenfelter in 1946 under Coach Chick Warner. As a freshman from Norristown in 1940, Ewell won the NCAA and IC4A championships in 100- and 200-meters and long-jump titles and repeated the feat in 1941 and 1942. Known then as "the fastest man alive," he would have been a cinch for the 1940 Summer Olympics but the games were canceled because of the war. Ewell was in the army when the 1944 Olympics also were cancelled.

By the 1948 Olympics in London, Barney Ewell was 30 years old, an "old man" by standards for sprinters but not for the steeple-chase, which is more a test of endurance and tactics, and age is less of a factor. USC's Mel Patton, 23, was then "the World's Fastest Human" and favored in the 100-meters. Ewell beat Patton but 25-year-old Harrison Dillard won in a record time of 10.2 seconds. Patton was favored again in the 200-meter. Ewell was in the lead briefly when Patton passed him.

Ewell was devastated, but when a US teammate in the 400-meter relay became ill, Barney replaced him as the leadoff man. The US team won but was disqualified because of Barney's handoff. Days later, news film showed Barney had not violated any rule and Barney and his teammates received their gold medals.

Ashenfelter's gold medal four years later was equally dramatic. US runners rarely scored in the nearly two-mile steeplechase, which required jumping over little fences and running through a wading pool. Ashenfelter studied the European runners and noticed a flaw in their technique at the wading pool. Although the Russian Kazantsev owned most of the world steeplechase records, Ashenfelter thought he could beat the entire field on the flat track and win the race at the wading pool. That's exactly what happened.

With Chick Warner watching as one of the US coaches, Ashenfelter faltered at the start, but by the third lap, he and Kazantsev were battling for the lead ahead of the pack. In the backstretch of the final lap, the Russian was in front, but at the last water jump he stumbled and almost fell. Ashenfelter went over the barrier in stride, landed with one foot in the shallow end of the pool, and sprinted to the finish line, leaving the Russian almost 50 yards behind. The scoreboard showed the record winning time of 8:45.4.

"What Horace did was a great accomplishment," said the late Olympic historian John Lucas, the official lecturer for the International Olympic Committee and a onetime Penn State track coach. "But Barney Ewell is without a doubt the best Penn State Olympian ever."

33 Jack Ham

Don't be shocked. Jack Ham may be the greatest linebacker in Penn State history but he was not the best linebacker on the outstanding back-to-back defensive teams of 1968–69.

Yes, Ham was good enough to be inducted into the College Football Hall of Fame in 1990. But it wasn't until his senior season of 1970 that he blossomed into a consensus first-team All-American.

Ham was asophomore and junior on those shutdown defensive units that were the foundation of the undefeated seasons and Orange Bowl victories that boosted Penn State to No. 2 in the nation. Although he was starter at outside linebacker from his first varsity practice in the spring of 1968, he was overshadowed in 1968 and 1969 by two-time All-American Dennis Onkotz, and Ham was no better than an honorable mention.

By the 1970 season, Onkotz and two other starting linebackers had graduated and their replacements were relatively inexperienced. Ham, the defensive captain, had to take charge while his teammates developed. After losing three of its first five games, the 1970 team won five straight and finished 18th and 19th in the final rankings. Even though he is still 16th in career tackles for the Lions with 251, including 151 solos, Ham didn't lead the team in tackles that season. Junior linebacker Gary Gray did.

Ham admitted he didn't play as well as he should have in his senior year because the coach who taught him everything about linebacking, Dan Radakovich, had left after the 1969 season. Radakovich's replacement was a former offensive line coach whom Radakovich had just taught how to coach linebackers.

"Rad made me be better every year I played at Penn State, but he wasn't around my senior year when he would have made me even better," Ham told me a few years ago. "Rad did more for me than anyone at Penn State except Joe Paterno. He was a great coach."

Ham says Radakovich continued to help him when Radakovich became the Pittsburgh Steelers' defensive line coach for one year in Ham's rookie season of 1971 and then came back in 1974 to coach the offensive line. "He wasn't my [position] coach but he was a friend and he'd point out things to me," Ham said.

Ham was the No. 2 choice of the Steelers, the 34th overall pick, in an NFL draft loaded with future star players, including four now in the Pro Football Hall of Fame—first-rounders John Riggins and Jack Youngblood and second-round picks Dan Dierdorf and Ham. Ham was inducted into the Pro Football Hall of Fame in 1988 after a brilliant 12-year career that included eight Pro Bowls and six selections to the All-Pro first team. Ham played on four Super Bowl championship teams (1974, 1975, 1978, 1979), and, according to the Elias Sports Bureau, still holds the NFL record for most career forced turnovers by a non-defensive back with 53.

Ham and Dave Robinson, an All-American end at Penn State but an All-Pro linebacker in Green Bay in the 1960s, are the only Nittany Lions in both the College and Pro Football Halls of Fame.

The NFL tacked on another honor in 1994 by selecting Ham as one of seven linebackers on the league's 50-member all-time team in conjunction with the NFL's 75th anniversary.

It's the combination of his outstanding careers with Penn State and the Steelers that has made Ham Penn State's all-time best linebacker in poll after poll and in the opinions of historians and most of the media. Ham welcomes the accolade but can cite other Lion linebackers who were his equals if not better. He also has a germane reason for his success.

"There was a parallel between my playing days with the Steelers and at Penn State," he wrote in the book *What It Means to be a Nittany Lion.* "I had a dominant defensive line in front of me with guys like Steve Smear and Mike Reid [at Penn State] just like I later had with [Steelers] players like Joe Greene and L. C. Greenwood."

The story of how Ham found himself at Penn State is familiar to most Penn State fans. He was a scrawny 180-pound guard on the second team in his senior year at Bishop McCort High School in Johnstown. After graduation he went to a military prep school with the intention of enrolling at VMI. One of his Johnstown pals and teammates was Steve Smear, whom Penn State recruited to play tight end.

After Smear's year on the freshman team, Paterno asked him to switch to defensive end. Smear was ready to quit. Assistant coaches, including Radakovich and George Welsh, talked Smear into staying, and he mentioned Ham. The coaches looked at game film of Ham. "He couldn't block anybody," Radakovich recalled, "but he was impressive on defense as he ran in pursuit across the field." Radakovich and Welsh convinced Paterno to offer Ham the last scholarship available.

Ham's fortes were his speed, quickness, and instincts. He could roam the field in almost an instant, sacking the quarterback on one play, defending on a potential receiver the next, and fighting off would-be blockers to tackle the runner on the third. His times in

10-yard sprint drills were almost always the fastest at Penn State and for the Steelers.

You won't find Ham's name too often in the Penn State record book, but he and linebacker Andre Collins still share the records for most blocked punts during a season (three in 1968 for Ham) and a career (four).

Ham set a new Penn State football record in 2012 that nobody realized until three years later. In 2000 Ham became part of the broadcast team for the radio network's football games and in 2012 he surpassed George Paterno with the most successive years as the network analyst.

That's Jack Ham, Penn State's greatest linebacking radio analyst.

34 Penn State Royalty

Before the Paternos, the royal family of Penn State was the Higgins-Suhey family.

The patriarch was Bob Higgins, who had stepped on campus as a highly sought-after football recruit from a New Jersey prep school by way of Corning, New York, in 1914. He became the Nittany Lions' first two-time first-team All-American at end in 1915 and 1919, and retired before the 1949 season as the then-longest-tenured head coach in Nittany Lion history with a 97–57–11 record after 19 years.

The oldest of Higgins' three daughters, Ginger, married his feisty but kind-hearted guard from Cazenovia, New York, Steve Suhey, who became a first-team All-American in 1947 as captain of Higgins' greatest team. His youngest daughter, Nancy, married another of Dad's players, Jim Dooley, who was a second team All-American center in 1952.

Steve and Ginger produced three grandsons for Higgins and they would play football for Joe Paterno. Larry may have had the most talent, but he also had the worst luck with injuries. Paul, a linebacker, would be a co-captain on the first Penn State team to become No. 1 in 1978. Matt, the junior starting fullback on that team that almost won the national championship, went on to help the Chicago Bears win the Super Bowl in 1986. In turn, the Suhey brothers sent two of Higgins' great-grandsons, Kevin and Joe, to also play for Paterno.

Higgins could have attended an Ivy League school, but Penn State's young assistant coach Dick Harlow convinced him to enroll at Penn State. Both would one day be inducted into the College Football Hall of Fame. When Harlow became the team's head coach in 1915, his prized recruit was his best player as an offensive and defensive end. The team finished with a 7–2 record and the International News Service named Higgins to its All-America first team, making him the second Penn State player so honored, following Mother Dunn in 1906.

After missing the 1917–18 seasons because of World War I, where he was in the thick of heavy combat, Higgins led the 1919 team to a 7–1 record as its captain and was again selected as a first-team All-American, this time by Walter Camp.

However, it was as a coach that Higgins became a Penn State legend and earned the endearing nickname of the Hig from his players. His low-key style and personality made him a players' coach.

As Ridge Riley, historian and Higgins' longtime friend, described Higgins in his book *Road to Number One,* Higgins was "easy going, patient, tempering criticism with humor" but he "could be severe at times."

After two years as an assistant under Hugo Bezdek, Higgins was promoted in 1930 just as Penn State was deemphasizing all intercollegiate athletics by eliminating scholarships and scouting and severely reducing the spending on varsity sports teams, particularly football.

Higgins had four straight losing seasons before some of his friends skirted the rules and arranged for some players to get room, board, tuition, and books through jobs and other aboveboard means. By 1940 Higgins had one of the best teams in the country and seemed headed to the Rose Bowl until a 20–7 upset at Pittsburgh caused the team to finish 6–1–1.

After that season, Higgins' onetime teammate and the mastermind behind the financial aid strategy, Casey Jones, helped recruit the players who would be the foundation of his greatest team—the undefeated 1947 squad that finished No. 4 in the country and tied No. 3 SMU in the Cotton Bowl. Included among them was Steve Suhey, who was invited to live in the Higgins home during his freshman year.

"Higgins typically put two top athletes on the top floor [of his three-story house]," wrote his biographer Rich Donnell in his 1994 book, *The Hig*. "The players would perform various chores around the house." Now we know how Steve and Ginger fell in love.

With a sensitivity for the plight of African American players, Higgins and Jones also recruited Penn State's first-ever African American players, Dave and Harry Alston. Dave was the star quarterback for the best freshman team in school history, but he died unexpectedly from tonsillectomy surgery in April 1942 and his brother left school and never returned.

It was this same empathy for African American players that Higgins showed as he supported his players when they declined to play at segregated Miami in 1946 and helped break the color line at the Cotton Bowl in 1947.

With many of those same players from the Cotton Bowl team back in 1949, like backs Wally Triplett, Woody Petchel, Fran Rogel, and linebacker Chuck Drazenovich, Higgins' 1948 squad almost went unbeaten again. They seemed headed back to the Cotton Bowl until another upset to bitter rival Pitt 7–0.

Higgins retired after that 1948 season, just as the athletic department was restoring scholarships and increasing funding for football. He lived another 20 years, and one of his joys in retirement was spending some Saturday afternoons in the fall with his three grandsons watching Penn State football games at Beaver Field.

Steve Suhey and Joe Paterno became friends, and for more than a year in the early 1950s Paterno lived with Steve, Ginger, and their firstborn, Larry. Paterno also spent a lot of time around Higgins, and later wrote the foreword for *The Hig* biography:

"These are special people who established a special relationship with a great University—a committed family who joined together for three generations and influenced for good thousands of individuals who would be bounded together by being Penn Staters... [They] synergized those intangible qualities inspire people; that make people want to be with them; and whose common sense and commitment to their traditional values and their families carried over into their loyalty to friends and institutions."

That, readers, is royalty.

35 Discuss the Best Coach in Penn State History

When Joe Paterno was alive he often called women's volleyball coach Russ Rose the best coach ever at Penn State.

It takes one to know one. Paterno is considered one of the greatest coaches in college football and Rose is similarly recognized in college volleyball.

Are either of them the best coach in Penn State history?

Perhaps?

Two old-timers, Gene Wettstone in gymnastics and Bill Jeffrey in soccer, along with Penn State's current wrestling coach, Cael Sanderson, would certainly challenge Paterno and Rose.

The history of Penn State head coaches stretches back to 1892, to the school's first head football coach, George Hoskins. Hoskins' duties were truly more than a century different from what coaches do today. He really was in charge of physical training for the entire 287-member student body and simply advised the football team. Well, he actually did more later by playing in some games, but that's another story.

W. B. Burns in baseball was Penn State's second head coach in 1900. That was 64 years before Pat Seni in field hockey and Mimi Ryan in golf became the first head coaches of a women's team at the start of Penn State's groundbreaking varsity sports program for women.

There has been an Airbus load of head coaches since Hoskins, and at least a dozen would be the equals of Paterno and Rose in their own sports.

Paterno stands out in a class by himself for at least one reason. He had a lot more assistants than the others. No Penn State team has ever had more official assistant coaches than football, and that goes back to Hugo Bezdek, the Hall of Fame head coach from 1918 to 1929. In Paterno's last season (2011), he had nine assistants. Rose has had two for several years. Wettstone and Jeffrey didn't have any for a long time before adding one. Of course, football has the most players to coach, too.

Coaches with fewer players usually do more personal one-on-one coaching than football head coaches. Even in his seventies and early eighties, Paterno loved to demonstrate blocking, tackling, and pass defending to errant players.

Paterno's NCAA record of 409 victories in his 46 years pales in comparison to Rose's record of 1,161 victories in his 34 seasons from 1981 through 2014, but volleyball plays more than three times as many games a season than football. Maybe that's a tie.

Rose is in the American Volleyball Coaches Association (AVCA) Hall of Fame and Paterno was inducted into the College Football Hall of Fame before the child abuse scandal. Both have been honored as Coach of the Year by their coaching peers. And both have a Hall of Fame ice cream named after them at Penn State's popular Creamery. Three more ties.

The tiebreaker may be national championships. Rose won his NCAA-record seventh national championship in 2014, with four straight from 2007 to 2010 during an unprecedented stretch of 109 straight wins, including back-to-back 38–0 seasons in 2008 and 2009. Paterno won just two national titles in 1982 and 1986, but his undefeated teams in 1968 and 1969 that helped set a school record unbeaten streak of 31 games, as well as his 1973 and 1994 undefeated teams, were snubbed by the pollsters.

Wettstone's credentials may top all others. In his 38 years (1939–76), Wettstone won an NCAA-record eight national championships with 35 of his gymnasts winning individual national championships, including 11 titles in the premier all-around competition. He also coached the US gymnastics team in the 1948 and 1956 Olympics and served as an official at the 1952 Olympics while 11 of his athletes also competed in the games from 1948 to 1976.

One also needs to give Wettstone a bonus for his showmanship that packed Rec Hall for three decades and another for being the third person to be Penn State's Nittany Lion mascot. In the early 1940s, Wettstone used his gymnasts to produce crowd-pleasing circuses, complete with trapeze acts, rope climbing, flying rings, clowns, a circus band, and an effervescent ringmaster played by Penn State's extroverted boxing coach Leo Houck.

Wettstone made Rec Hall an international showcase with exhibition meets against teams from such countries as Japan, Sweden, the Soviet Union, China, and Bulgaria while also attracting large crowds with dual meets against regional and national rivals as well as with Olympic trials and NCAA championship tournaments. For years, gymnastics was the most popular winter sport on campus.

Soccer reached the pinnacle of success under Bill Jeffrey. In his 37-year Penn State tenure (1926–52), Jeffrey's teams won an impressive 74 percent of their games, winning 153, losing 24, and tying 29. And in the decades before the NCAA tournament, Jeffrey's teams won nine national championships as recognized by the Intercollegiate Soccer Football Association of America (ISFA),

Even more amazing is Jeffrey's 65-game undefeated record between 1932 and 1941 where his teams outscored opponents 689 to 184. His 1950 team became world news in the winter of 1951, during a controversial three-week, four-game goodwill tour of Iran sponsored by the US State Department. Today, Jeffrey's name is still a presence at Penn State's soccer stadium named in his honor.

If the 36-year-old Sanderson coaches at Penn State as long as Wettstone and Jeffery, he might equal if not surpass their accomplishments. Since becoming the head wrestling coach in 2009 to 2010, Sanderson's team has captured four straight NCAA championships from 2011 to 2014, with 10 of his Lion wrestlers winning individual national titles. That's a remarkable achievement for a coach in any sports era.

The best coach in Penn State history? You decide.

36 Jesse Arnelle

If not for football coach Joe Paterno, Penn State's only first-team All-American basketball player, Jesse Arnelle, would have gone to an Ivy League college or another school renowned for its academics.

Arnelle was an outstanding high school football and basketball player with good academic credentials in New Rochelle, New York, just north of New York City. In the early winter of 1949–50, Brown University's head coach, Rip Engle, was recruiting Arnelle to play football at the school in Providence, Rhode Island.

After Engle accepted an offer to take over the faltering Penn State football program in April, he sent his new young assistant and former Browns quarterback, Joe Paterno, to New Rochelle to convince Arnelle to enroll at Penn State.

That's how in May 1950, the 6'5", 200-pound Arnelle and his working-class African American parents were sitting in their living room listening to the slightly built Italian with a Brooklyn accent telling them about the state school in the middle of rural Pennsylvania, then a drive of several hours over dangerous two-lane roads from New Rochelle.

"I was trying to find the ideal setting that I felt I wanted," Arnelle told me years later, adding that he had been most interested in Brown, Columbia, Penn, and Colgate. "I was all set to go to Brown until Joe's visit.

"He started talking about the value of a college education, and what that could mean, depending on what I wanted to do with my life, what were my dreams and ambitions…and if I could create the best scenario for the next five, six years from the standpoint of doing things that I enjoy doing in sports and getting a college education, what kind of setting [and] what kind of experience would

I want to have…it was all wrapped in the total college experience. I hadn't thought a lot about it that way. It had nothing to do with just playing football. He didn't talk much about that."

Paterno persuaded Arnelle to visit Penn State and see it for himself before making the first major decision of his life. "Had it come from anybody else but Joe, I would not have considered it," Arnelle said. Once on the relatively small, tree-filled, picturesque campus and mingling with some of the 11,000 or so students, he was sold. "It was one of those moments in your life when you just know this is the right place…an epiphany."

Arnelle also wanted to play basketball. Basketball coach Elmer Gross was delighted. Penn State's basketball program had limited funds, with only a couple players getting financial aid of some type. Half of its roster was composed of football players, and Engle had just given him another one. The biggest football prize of all time.

Arnelle played a lot of football in his freshman year, starting most of the season at defensive end. Over the next three years as a two-way end he was good enough to be an honorable-mention All-American and be drafted in the 10th round by the Los Angeles Rams.

As a power forward he was an instant star on the basketball court, leading Penn State to its first NCAA tournament in 10 years (and second in history) and was selected a third-team All-American. Two years later, he was a first-team All-American as the underrated Nittany Lions shocked college basketball with a third-place finish in their only appearance in the NCAA Final Four. The next season Penn State was in the NCAA tournament again and Arnelle was a third-team All-American.

Arnelle also was a star in the classroom and with his mostly white collegiate peers. In his senior year, he became the first African American student elected president of the student body. That took the sting off some of the racism he encountered on and off the court and field.

Despite playing in a slowed-down basketball era with the jump ball and no shot clock or three-point scoring, Arnelle's statistics are overwhelming. He held the Penn State career scoring record of 2,138 points for 56 years until Talor Battle broke it with 2,213 points. He still holds dozens of other scoring and rebound records and here are just a few:

- First in points for one season (731), single-season scoring average (26.1 in 1955), most 30-point games in career (15) and season (11 in 1954), field goals scored in career (738) and season (260 in 1955), free-throw points in career (662) and season (243 in 1955), free-throw attempts in a career (992) and season (346 in 1955), and rebounds in career (1,238), season (428 in 1955), and game (27 in 1955).

- Second through sixth in most points in one game (spanning 44 to 38) behind Gene Harris' 46 points, scoring 44 in a 94–45 win over Bucknell in 1955.

As Arnelle was graduating with a degree in political science, the Fort Wayne Pistons drafted him in the second round as the 13th overall pick. Red Auerbach, the legendary basketball coach of the NBA's Boston Celtics, summed up Arnelle's talent for *Sport* magazine: "He is a rare athletic specimen, big and strong and extremely graceful. He has a handsome build and the classic moves of an athlete. He could probably play any sport."

Ultimately, Arnelle played a short time with the Harlem Globetrotters and one season with the Pistons before obtaining his law degree from Dickinson and embarking on a distinguished legal career. He also served more than four decades on the Penn State board of trustees, including 1996–97 as president.

That's a long way from that living room in New Rochelle.

37 Dave Robinson and the Play of the Century

Junior end Dave Robinson leaped over two blockers, grabbed the surprised Georgia Tech quarterback around the neck, and slammed him to the ground, forcing a fumble that Robinson quickly recovered at the Tech 35-yard line.

Philadelphia Daily News sportswriter Larry Merchant, who was covering that 1961 Gator Bowl, called it "possibly the play of the century." With a national television audience still marveling at what they had just seen midway through the third quarter, Penn State's touchdown pass on the next play virtually clinched what would be a 30–15 upset victory.

"One of their guards tried to take my legs out," Robinson later remembered. "He was coming so low I just went over him. I was still airborne when I struck the quarterback and he fumbled the ball. I would have scored but in those days you couldn't advance the ball."

The Robinson play typified the ferocious style that would help him become one of only two Penn State players in both the College and Pro Football Halls of Fame.

Robinson also was a racial pioneer. He was the first African American to play in the Gator Bowl in 1961, 16 years after the postseason game began.

On that December 30 afternoon in Jacksonville, Robinson's dramatic play put an exclamation mark on the racism he had confronted for years, and particularly earlier in Gator Bowl week. Because Jacksonville was still segregated, the Penn State team was forced to stay in the nearby resort town of St. Augustine, which was dreary and barren at that time of the year, with most of its hotels and restaurants closed until New Year's Day.

Robinson stayed away from the all-white businesses, but one day a teammate coaxed him into going to a drugstore where some of the Penn State players hung out. A waitress refused to serve him coffee. He also received threatening letters, including one written by a man claiming to be an army sharpshooter.

"I didn't start the game and found out afterward…it was because he was going to shoot me on the 50-yard line on national TV," Robinson said. He also remembered hearing racial slurs from the crowd but not the opposing Tech players.

When Penn State returned to the Gator Bowl the next year to play Florida, Robinson was not only a first-team All-American end, but the first African American Penn State player to be selected a first-team All-American. This time, the major racial incident occurred when the team's chartered plane had to divert to Orlando for a few hours because of the weather. The airport restaurant manager would not serve Robinson, and the entire team and coaches walked out.

Except for the Florida helmets having stickers of the Confederate flag, nothing racially happened in the game. Robinson was at his best again and was selected the Most Valuable Player despite a 17–7 loss to Florida.

Although it was his defensive prowess that made him an All-American, Robinson was also praised for his blocking and pass-catching on offense. Penn State was not much of a passing team back then, but if it had been keeping track of tackling and sacks at the time, Robinson would have been among the team leaders of his era.

"[Robinson is] the greatest lineman and the greatest natural athlete I've ever coached," head coach Rip Engle said.

Yet Robinson achieved his greatest fame after Penn State. The Green Bay Packers drafted him in the first round, 14th overall, in

1963 and Robinson became a star on one of the most dominant sports franchises in history. The Packers switched him to left linebacker, where he teamed with Ray Nitschke and Lee Roy Caffey as the best starting linebacker corps in the NFL from 1964 to 1969. The Packers won three straight NFL titles from 1965 to 1967 and the first Super Bowls in '66 and '67.

The Pro Football Hall of Fame website describes Robinson as a "big-play performer on Packers dynasty," adding, "Robinson maintained a consistently high level of play but competed for national notoriety with many great defensive stars including numerous future Hall of Famers on the Packers roster." Robinson is among 11 Packers from a span of 1961 through 1972 enshrined in Canton.

Robinson left the Packers after 1972 and started for the Washington Redskins in 1973 and 1974 before retiring. He was selected on the NFL's All-Decade Team of the 1960s and to the Pro Football Hall of Fame in 2013, 16 years after his induction into the College Football Hall of Fame.

And what did Robinson think of "possibly the play of the century"?

"That big play of mine was a bad one, really," he told the *Daily Collegian* after the game "I should have gone for the blocker, but I decided to jump and before you knew it I had the ball in my hands and we were on the way."

38 View Game Film of McCloskey's Controversial Catch

Although the younger generation of Penn State fans may not know it, the 1982 Nebraska game is considered by the Nittany Nation as the greatest ever in the history of Beaver Stadium.

"No doubt about it," said Fran Fisher, Penn State's broadcasting icon, who did the play-by-play for the radio network that day. "In fact a lot of people consider that the National Championship Game in many respects."

It wasn't simply because the Nittany Lions won on a thrilling, 10-play, 65-yard drive led by quarterback Todd Blackledge in the last 1:14 of the game.

It wasn't only because Penn State would not have won its first national title that year without the 27–24 victory over a versatile team with at least four future first-team All-Americans, including junior I-back Mike Rozier, the 1983 Heisman Trophy winner.

And it wasn't just because of the pregame hype and the electrifying atmosphere created partly because of artificial lights needed to televise the game nationally for what was then the latest start of any home game in history—3:45 PM.

It was all three of those elements mixed in with a dramatic fourth one—a controversial pass reception by tight end Mike McCloskey in the last 10 seconds that was ruled in bounds but wasn't.

The controversy over McCloskey's catch at the 2-yard line on the left sideline of the south end zone near the Penn State student section continues to this day. It is the linchpin that turned a then-friendly nine-game intersectional rivalry since 1920 into a resentful one that has intensified with Nebraska's entry into the Big Ten in 2010.

No. 2 Nebraska, which had scored 110 points and given up just seven in its first two games at Lincoln, was a slight favorite over a No. 8 Penn State team that had averaged nearly 40 points in three games while giving up at least two touchdowns per game.

Penn State coach Joe Paterno told the media the Lions needed a high-scoring game to win, and asked the fans "to bring a light to St. Jude," the patron saint of lost causes.

Instant Replay

When Joe Paterno chased Big Ten referee Dick Honig and yanked his shirt after a controversial officiating decision had just cost Penn State a 42–35 overtime loss to Iowa at Beaver Stadium on September 28, 2002, he made national news. That was the defining moment that eventually led to instant replay in college football in 2005.

Paterno and other coaches had been complaining for years about inconsistent officiating. Paterno was the most prominent of the coaches advocating for instant replay, particularly because the NFL had been using instant replay since 1986, except for a seven-year period of restudy from 1992 to 1998.

Many media outlets criticized Paterno for his "assault" on Honig, and the Big Ten warned him not to cross a line "imputing bad intentions." Paterno told reporters, "I thought they made a couple of lousy calls on the other side of the field." He was particularly irate about a pass incompletion for Iowa in overtime that set up the winning touchdown. Television replays indicated Paterno was correct.

Paterno and Penn State had their share of officiating going their way. The controversial late pass reception by Mike McCloskey in the 1982 Nebraska game was one. When another pass reception call favored Penn State the next season against Alabama in the same south end zone of Beaver Stadium, *Sports Illustrated* published a humorous drawing credited to ABC-TV's Beano Cook, a longtime Penn State adversary. The diagram showed part of the end zone extended where McCloskey made his catch and another nearby part of the end zone cut out where the controversial Alabama pass was ruled incomplete. Game film proved the officials made the right decision on the pass but blew an Alabama motion penalty and two offsetting offside infractions.

Two years after Paterno pursued Honig, the Big Ten used instant replay on a one-year test basis approved by the NCAA. The next season the NCAA formally adopted the use of instant replay in college football.

As of the 2015 season, Honig is working as an instant replay supervisor for Big Ten games and still being booed by Penn State fans.

Paterno may have been concerned after a scoreless first quarter, but within six minutes of the second period, the Lions had a surprising 14–0 lead on long drives of 83 and 71 yards. In the last minute of the first half, Nebraska exploded, going 80 yards on seven quick passes, and the Lions led 14–7 at the half.

Another long march of 83 yards in the first 5:14 of the second half increased Penn State's lead to 21–7. However, Nebraska stunned the record crowd of 85,304 and dominated the rest of the game—or almost—with a touchdown in the third quarter, a field goal early in the fourth, and an 80-yard, 13-play drive in the last six minutes of the game to take the lead 24–21 with 1:18 left.

A personal foul penalty by Nebraska on the kickoff that went into the end zone put the ball on the Lions' 35-yard line, but Penn State had no timeouts. "There was no panic," Blackledge said later. "Everybody was calm…I didn't know if we could take it all the way for a touchdown. But I felt pretty confident we could get in range for at least a field goal to tie it."

Two quick 16-yard passes reached the Nebraska 33-yard line as the crowd screamed. Moments later it was fourth-and-11 at the 34 with 32 seconds left, and Paterno thought of going for a field goal. Instead, Blackledge scrambled and passed to Kenny Jackson for a first down at the 23 and then scrambled out of bounds at the 17 for another six yards with 13 seconds remaining.

On second-and-4, Blackledge found McCloskey tiptoeing down the sideline. McCloskey caught the ball as he stepped out of bounds at the 2. The official signaled it was good. Across the field, everyone on the Nebraska sideline protested.

This was before instant replay, or Penn State's 1982 season might have ended right there. Game film would later show McCloskey was out of bounds, but he never came close to admitting it until 16 years later when he was the guest speaker at a Boys Town event in Omaha.

"The ref said I was in," McCloskey said after the game, "and that's the only fact that mattered. I played the ball like I was in... the referee's the boss."

McCloskey still is unsure. "Quite honestly, it's hard for me to know," he told me a few years ago. "It was pretty much bang-bang, and we had to hurry and get back in the huddle for the next play." Blackledge wanted to throw to McCloskey again, but he was covered. So he passed to an ex-tackle–turned–tight end with the nickname Stonehands for obvious reasons. Blackledge's pass to Kirk Bowman was low near the back end zone line, but Bowman dove for the ball and rolled to the turf for a touchdown. Nebraska protested again to no avail. This time game film would prove it was the correct call.

The fans were delirious, tearing down the goal post and celebrating into the night.

A disheartening defeat at Alabama two weeks later seemed to end Penn State's national title hopes. But things happened as they usually do in college football, and the Nittany Lions were crowned champions after beating Georgia 24–21 in the Sugar Bowl on New Year's Night.

If you want to see what the controversy is all about, view the game film at the sports archives in the Penn State Paterno-Patee library.

Nebraska has never forgotten the controversy, either. It is No. 73 in *100 Things Nebraska Fans Should Know & Do Before They Die.*

39 1967: The Legend Begins

Joe Paterno knew he had been a flop in his first year as Penn State's head football coach in 1966. It had been a year of confusion with questionable decisions about everything from his handling of the players to the offensive and defensive formations he was using. The only thing that saved him from a losing 4–6 record was a 48–24 win at the end over a lousy Pitt team that only won one game.

And when Paterno's 1967 team looked erratic and shaky on defense in losing the season opener at Navy 23–22—blowing a five-point lead in the last minute—Paterno knew he was in trouble. "After the game I felt, for the first time, concerned about my future as a coach," he later wrote in his autobiography, *Paterno: By the Book.* "I knew I needed a drastic change…."

On the team's depressing bus ride back from Annapolis, Paterno had a "crazy thought…of dumping almost the whole [veteran defensive] crew and starting from scratch with fresh kids." He had discussed it with his staff after spring practice, but they were reluctant to make such a radical move that could backfire if the inexperienced kids didn't live up to expectations. Now he was ready.

Paterno didn't tell the players what he was going to do during the following Friday night game at 11-point favorite Miami. Before that, he made a defensive alignment change in practice, dumping the 5-2-4 for an attacking 4-4-3 that he and linebackers coach Dan Radakovich had designed.

Paterno made one position change before the game, moving sophomore Steve Smear in at defensive tackle because of an injury. As steady drizzle fell in the Miami heat and humidity, Paterno began inserting a new sophomore defender every play or so. By the end of the first quarter, the defense was loaded with the "kids" who would become the foundation of Penn State's great defenses in 1968 and 1969, including future All-Americans Dennis Onkotz and Neil Smith.

The first half was mostly a punting duel until junior Bobby Campbell's zigzag 50-yard punt return late in the second quarter set up a 15-yard touchdown pass from Tommy Sherman to tight end Ted Kwalick. The Lions missed the extra point but made a two-point conversion after a third-quarter seven-yard touchdown pass to Don Abbey. Abbey's 24-yard field goal increased the lead to 17–0 before Miami took advantage of a botched punt return in the last 30 seconds to make the final score 17–8.

The next week at Beaver Stadium Penn State almost beat No. 3 UCLA and its eventual 1967 Heisman Trophy winner, quarterback Gary Beban, losing 17–15. "I don't think I've faced a tougher pass rush," Beban said. Paterno and his Nittany Lions would not lose another game until 1970.

Penn State slowly began attracting attention as it beat traditional opponents on the road—Boston College, Syracuse, and Maryland—and West Virginia on homecoming. But it was a 13–8 win over No. 3 North Carolina State on November 11 that thrust Paterno and Penn State into national prominence.

NC State, coached by Penn State alumnus Earle Edwards, had not given up a first-quarter score all season, and the Lions shocked them. Kwalick made a sensational reception for an 18-yard touchdown less than four minutes into the game, and three minutes later Onkotz intercepted a pass and ran 67 yards for another touchdown, giving the Lions a 13–0 lead and helping Onkotz earn AP Lineman of the Week honors. "That was the big play of the game," Paterno said. "It's what gave us momentum to win."

The second big play came with 40 seconds left in the game after NC State had kicked two field goals to narrow the score to 13–6 and then drove 67 yards in the last nearly five minutes for a

Earle Edwards and His Penn State Coaches

If not for some backdoor political maneuvering in the Penn State athletic department, Earle Edwards would have become the Nittany Lions' head coach instead of Rip Engle and his protégé Joe Paterno.

Edwards had been a starting end for Penn State from 1928 to 1930, and in 1936 he returned to be an assistant coach under Bob Higgins. Joe Bedenk, a Nittany Lions All-American guard in 1923, had been an assistant since 1929 and Al Michaels, quarterback of the 1933–34 teams, was hired the same year as Edwards. Those Penn State coaches brought Penn State back to national prominence in the 1940s, and when Higgins decided to retire after the 1948 season, Edwards was his handpicked successor.

Bedenk didn't want to apply for the job, but friends in the athletic department and some ex-teammates manipulated behind the scenes and Bedenk was named head coach instead of Edwards. After spring practice, the disappointed Edwards left to be an assistant at Michigan State. Early in the 1949 season, Bedenk made it privately known he wanted to be an assistant again and concentrate on his baseball coaching responsibilities. He resigned in March 1950 and Engle became the head coach, bringing Paterno, his Brown quarterback, with him.

In 1953, Michaels reunited with Edwards at Michigan State, and when Edwards left to be head coach at North Carolina State the next season, Michaels went with him. Edwards also hired another former Penn State player, Bill Smaltz, who was one of the best quarterbacks in the country from 1939 to 1941.

With his Penn State alumni assistant coaches, Edwards carved out his own legend at North Carolina State. His 77 victories are the most by any of the other 33 NC State head coaches, and no one is close.

Before Edwards retired after the 1970 season, he and his two assistants coached three games against their alma mater in 1956, 1967, and 1969 and lost all of them. Must have been the curse of Joe Bedenk.

fourth-and-goal at the 1. The Lions defense stopped tailback Tony Barchuk's blast up the middle, gave up a safety, and won 13–8.

It was the Gator Bowl on December 30 that made Paterno a household name in college football. Leading favored Florida State 17–0 with 5:30 left in the third quarter after a goal-line stand and with a fourth-and-inches at his own 15-yard line, Paterno decided to go for it. Watching up in the press box, athletic director Ernie McCoy exclaimed, "My god, he's going for it!"

Sherman and center Bill Lenkaitis were certain the quarterback sneak was successful. "I looked down and the ball was more than a foot past the line," Sherman said. The officials disagreed.

Two plays later Florida State scored, and when the Lions fumbled the ensuing kickoff at the 23-yard line, the Seminoles quickly made it 17–14. Yet there was no more scoring until the final 10 seconds of the game, when Penn State's defense halted Florida State's 52-yard drive, and with a fourth-and-goal at the 9, a 26-yard field goal tied it.

Paterno was heavily criticized for what appeared to be a foolish gamble. He admitted he blew it but later told Sandy Padwee of the *Philadelphia Inquirer* if he hadn't made the call, "I wouldn't have the courage to be the football coach I want to be."

Reflecting on the play later, Paterno said, "In the long run that fourth-down call may be the best thing I ever did for Penn State football."

40 See the Final Four Trophy

Penn State's 1954 basketball team may not be the best in school history, but it is the only one to reach the fabled NCAA Final Four.

"I think it was amazing what happened to us in '54," Jack Sherry, the team captain, said decades later. "It was like an act of God."

Prior to the 1953–54 season, Penn State had been to the NCAA tournament twice since it started in 1939, first in 1942 and again in 1952. What makes the accomplishment in 1954 even more astounding is just five other Nittany Lions teams have reached the NCAA playoffs in the last 61 years with only one, 2000–01, getting as far as the Sweet Sixteen.

In fact, the 1954 team's NCAA appearance was bracketed around two others coached by Elmer Gross and led by power forward Jesse Arnelle in 1952 and 1955. The '52 team may have been better than '54 and was the first to win 20 games since Penn State basketball began in 1897.

That 1951–52 team was 17–1 at one juncture, played 15 games away from Rec Hall, and lost three close road games in a row near the end of the regular season—one by three points and two in overtime. The victories included two historic upset wins over top-ten-ranked West Virginia, 61–60 at Morgantown and 84–65 at home.

Unfortunately, in the first round of the tournament, the Lions were matched up against defending champion No. 1 Kentucky and lost 82–54.

"I've always felt the 1952 team never got the recognition it deserved," said Sherry, then a sophomore starter along with freshman Arnelle. Substitutes Ed Haag, Ron Weidenhammer, and Jim Blocker joined Arnelle and Sherry as starters in 1954.

A few months after the 1952 loss to Kentucky, the defeat took on a different meaning when Kentucky was caught up in the infamous point-shaving scandal that led to the arrest of 32 players at seven colleges. Up to that point, the National Invitational Tournament, which started a year before the NCAA playoffs, had more prestige, and teams often participated in both events.

Still, it was a major accomplishment when Penn State was invited to play a first-round NCAA game in 1954 against Toledo

Penn State's 1954 basketball team is the only men's team to reach the NCAA Final Four. Coach Elmer Gross is in the second row (far left). The starting five are in the front row, including star Jesse Arnelle (far left) and captain Jack Sherry (holding the basketball).

at Fort Wayne after a 14–5 regular season. The Lions surprised favored Toledo 62–50 on Tuesday, March 9, and moved on by train to Iowa City for a Friday matchup with SEC champion and No. 8 LSU.

Using a full-court defense as part of their patented sliding zone, the Nittany Lions shocked LSU and the basketball world with a 78–70 win. The next night they repeated the scenario in a more startling upset, by snapping Notre Dame's 18-game winning streak 71–63.

The team received a shock of its own when they returned to State College and some 4,000 fans welcomed them home in front of the Corner Room Hotel at 2:00 AM. "What we didn't know was everyone on campus was listening to the games being broadcast on radio by Mickey Bergstein, who wasn't even there," Sherry said.

Bergstein, the manager at WMAJ, had recreated the action with audio-taped crowd noise by having Penn State's sports publicity director Jim Coogan feed information in a terse code via Western Union. However, contractual arrangements prevented the station from broadcasting the Final Four in Kansas City.

Unfortunately, the Nittany Lions picked the wrong day to play one of their worst games of the season. Cross-state rival LaSalle, featuring All-American Tom Gola and favored to win the tournament after Notre Dame had eliminated Indiana, beat the Lions 69–54. But in that era, the semifinal losers met for third place. The next day Penn State beat pre-tournament No. 11 USC 70–61 and another large, but less subdued, crowd greeted the team at Rec Hall.

"Gross did an outstanding coaching job," wrote *Kansas City Star* sportswriter Bob Busby in the 10-page summary of the tournament published in the official *NCAA Guide*. "Furthermore, Jesse Arnelle, the Penn State center, was one of the most underrated individual performers of the past season."

Two significant facts stand out in the makeup of the 1954 12-man roster. Financial aid for basketball players was usually limited to tuition and other fees, and not everyone received that perk. At least three players were walk-ons while Sherry and Arnelle were on football scholarships. Three of the teams at the Final Four did not have an African American. Penn State had four: Arnelle, Jim Blocker, Earl Fields, and Jim Brewer.

Today, the third-place trophy from the 1954 Final Four is prominently displayed in the Penn State All-Sports Museum.

"Playing in the Final Four was really no big deal back then like it is today with all the hype and television coverage," Sherry recalled over the years. "Nobody believes Penn State went to the Final Four."

41 1973: The Heisman Team the Media Scorned

None of Joe Paterno's greatest teams were more maligned than the undefeated, untied squad of 1973 that helped John Cappelletti become Penn State's only Heisman Trophy winner.

From the time Paterno produced his first unbeaten team in 1968, a large segment of the media—based mostly in the South and Southwest—denigrated his accomplishments and his teams. They not only mocked Penn State's Eastern-based schedule but also questioned the talent of the players.

The condemnation heated up when Paterno's 1969 squad was accused of ducking Texas and a chance at the national championship at the Cotton Bowl. It intensified when Tennessee ruined another unbeaten season in the last game of 1971 31–11, and then beat the Lions again in the opening game of 1972 28–21, with both games before hostile crowds in Nashville.

Even the 1971 team's stunning upset of Texas in the 1972 Cotton Bowl didn't mollify many critics. Nor were they impressed or influenced when, after the 1972 season, Paterno rejected a lucrative salary and ownership offer from the New England Patriots to be the head coach with complete control over all team decisions on and off the field.

Paterno's life-changing decision came a few days after his 1972 team had lost 14–0 to Oklahoma in the Sugar Bowl without star running back Cappelletti, who had a viral infection.

No one was more critical of Penn State than Dan Jenkins of *Sports Illustrated*, a Texas native who had covered Southwest Conference football for 15 years before joining *SI* in 1963. His belittling of Penn State was best epitomized after the Sugar Bowl loss when he wrote: "For some reason, Penn State has the knack of bringing out the worst in good teams. Maybe that's because the Nittany Lions do not command enough respect, being from the East and all...."

Then, in the preseason analysis of the 1973 team a few months later, *Sports Illustrated* again ridiculed Penn State, and one can be sure Jenkins was involved: "Given its schedule—oh so easy with the Maryland's and Navy's—10–1 is the worst it can be."

Still, *Sports Illustrated* picked Penn State to finish No. 3 behind Texas and USC while the Associated Press placed State at No. 7 and the United Press International coaches at No. 10. As the regular season progressed, State made it as far as No. 5, but no further.

Yet the media was impressed by Cappelletti. After the Lions beat Air Force 19–9 in the televised fourth game of the season which they were expected to lose because of the high altitude in Colorado Springs, on October 6, Cappelletti began getting mention as a Heisman Trophy candidate. His stock went way up three weeks later when he scored four touchdowns in a 62–14 thrashing of West Virginia. But the team's stock went down as the skeptical pollsters dropped the Lions to No. 6 and leapfrogged previously No. 8 Notre Dame into fifth place.

Cappelletti may have all but clinched the Heisman Trophy on November 10 at Beaver Stadium when Penn State beat the North Carolina State team coached by Lou Holtz 35–29. Cappelletti had his best running day ever, gaining 231 yards with three touchdowns on an all-time school record of 41 carries that still stands.

Shortly after Penn State beat Ohio University 49–10, the Orange Bowl announced a matchup between the Lions and unde-feated No. 7 Louisiana State. Penn State would beat Pittsburgh 25–13 in the regular-season finale, but LSU lost its final two games to Alabama and Tulane, taking the luster off the Orange Bowl despite the Heisman Trophy winner.

Penn State defeated LSU 16–9 before the smallest Orange Bowl crowd (60,477) since 1949 in a defensive battle with all but two points by LSU scored in the first half. It was a solid win for the Lions but not with the media.

"The match was so lackluster that I had hoped that some of the Penn Staters would be honest enough to say 'we don't deserve to be No. 1.' That didn't happen though," wrote John Crittenden, Sports Editor of the *Miami News*.

"Had the Lions beaten LSU more convincingly, they might have been able to make a better argument for the national championship," another Miami reporter wrote. "In truth, however, Penn State just didn't play like the nation's best collegiate football team."

When the votes were counted in the AP and UPI polls, Notre Dame was No. 1 and Penn State was No. 5, despite being the only two undefeated teams left.

"We felt we could have played with anybody," quarterback Tom Shuman said years later.

Mark Markovich, the offensive co-captain who was selected a second-team All-American guard, recalled that his talented senior class lost only three games in their entire career: "Of the original 22 guys, 17 were still on that '73 team and 13 of our class were in the NFL the next year."

In the locker room after the game, Paterno told the media his team deserved to be No. 1 as well as any other, and he reiterated his six-year campaign for a playoff. "This was the best team I've ever coached," he said. "We have as much right to claim the top place as anyone else." Then he uttered one of his most famous off-the-cuff quotes that, in the end, is the real legacy of the 1973 team: "I have my own poll—the Paterno poll. The vote was unanimous—Penn State is No. 1."

42 Paul Bunyan and His Ox

Glenn Ressler is the preeminent two-way interior lineman who ever played for Penn State, at least in the modern era since the demise of the single-wing offense starting in 1950.

In his senior year of 1964, Ressler became the second Nittany Lion to win the Maxwell Award as the nation's most outstanding player, following quarterback Richie Lucas in 1959. He also was a consensus All-American at guard that season, the last time only 11 players were so honored in the consensus selections compiled annually by the NCAA since 1889. Even though Ressler only played middle guard on defense but center on offense, the center on the consensus squad that year was a guy named Dick Butkus from Illinois.

Rip Engle called Ressler "the best interior lineman I ever coached."

However, Ressler was the second-team center most of his career. But in the way that Engle utilized two different 11-man teams during that now-passé period of limited substitution, Ressler was on the field enough for him to earn the quirky nickname Paul Bunyan for his outstanding blocking.

Ressler was a linebacker and offensive guard on his freshman team; he didn't become a center and defensive middle guard until his junior year. That season of 1963 was a breakthrough year for the onetime backwoods farm boy not far from Selinsgrove.

"I can remember when we first got electricity [in our house]," he told Frank Bilovsky for the 1982 book *Lion Country*. "We never did have indoor plumbing."

Although Ressler played every offensive line position, linebacker, and defensive tackle at Mahanoy Joint High School (with

88 students in his senior class), he was still a raw talent when Penn State surprised him with a scholarship offer. Army and Wichita State had shown interest, but assistant coach Jim O'Hora drove to the Ressler farm with the offer, and that impressed Glenn.

"I doubt I would have gone to college without the scholarship," said Ressler, who eventually graduated with a degree in Agriculture Engineering.

Since 1959, Engle's team's had been one of the best in the East with four straight postseason bowl games. Nineteen sixty-three looked like a rebuilding year, especially at running back and both offensive and defensive lines. However, behind the quarterbacking of Pete Liske and the power running of junior Tom Urbanik, who had not lettered before, the Nittany Lions won five of thier first seven games.

It was in the eighth game against Ohio State in Columbus where Ressler would become a star and he and Urbanik would become folk heroes. Penn State was such an underdog that the *Columbus Citizen-Journal* called it "non-league nonsense." In what was a blistering defensive struggle, the Lions won 10–7, with Ressler leading the way on defense with 14 tackles and four assists. Three times on fourth-and-short situations, he was the stone wall in front of linebackers Ralph Baker and Joe Sabol in stopping Ohio State. His crushing blocks also helped keep the offense moving.

The 1963 team split its last two games to finish with an unexpected 7–3 record. Ridge Riley, the longtime writer of the popular *Alumni Newsletter*, was impressed with Ressler's crunching blocking and tackling and Urbanik's bull-like running. Before the 1964 season Riley gave the duo the nickname of Paul Bunyan and His Ox, referring to the gargantuan lumberjack and his blue ox, Babe, of Minnesota folklore. With the help of Penn State's sports information director, Jim Tarman, the rest of the media picked it up.

The 1964 Nittany Lions may have had Paul Bunyan and His Ox but they weren't enough to prevent Penn State from losing the first three games of the season for the first time ever. It started to turn around with a 6–2 win over Army, but everything was pointing to a disastrous losing season for the first time since 1938 when the 3–4 Lions went back to Columbus as 14-point underdogs to No. 2 Ohio State.

In what the Associated Press later selected as College Football's Upset of the Year, Penn State stunned Ohio State 27–0, holding the potent Buckeyes to 30 yards rushing and 30 yards passing. Ressler, alias Paul Bunyan, dominated the line of scrimmage on both sides of the ball and was given the game ball by his teammates. A few days later the AP and *Sports Illustrated* named him the Lineman of the Week.

"That game probably made my career," Ressler has said repeatedly since.

Years later, Paterno revealed in the book *Football My Way* that he and assistant Frank Patrick, who scouted the Buckeyes, had noticed on game films that the position of the hands and feet of OSU's backs and linemen gave away the play. They changed the defense and moved Ressler over the center. "We always knew where the play was going before the ball was snapped," Paterno stated.

Penn State went on to beat Houston 24–7 and Pitt 28–0 and win the Lambert Trophy, with Urbanik the leading rusher for the season with 625 yards and eight touchdowns on 134 carries. The players rejected a firm invitation from the Gator Bowl, telling the media the team had done enough.

A few months later, Ressler was drafted third by the Baltimore Colts (as well as the AFL's Denver Broncos) and played 10 years, starting at offensive guard on two Super Bowl teams and winning it all in 1970.

In 2001 Ressler became the third Penn State lineman after Steve Suhey and Mike Reid to be inducted into the College Football Hall of Fame.

No one has called him Paul Bunyan for decades.

43 Ted Kwalick

"Ted Kwalick is what God had in mind when he made a football player," Joe Paterno often said.

That's the epitaph for Penn State's indestructible 6'3", 240-pound two-time All-American tight end who finished fourth in the 1968 Heisman Trophy vote behind O. J. Simpson.

Twenty-one years later Kwalick would be inducted into the College Football Hall of Fame, and in 1999 *Sports Illustrated* selected Kwalick and his defensive tackle teammate Mike Reid to its 75-man All-Century team.

Kwalick was one of the original prototypes of the modern-day tight end who must be able to block and catch passes over the middle and downfield.

Passing always was secondary to the running phase of Paterno's offense. Only two receivers or ends who played before 1970 are still in Penn State's career records: Kwalick and split end Jack Curry, a senior teammate on Paterno's first team in 1966 when Kwalick was a freshman.

As of the start of the 2015 season, Kwalick's 86 receptions, including a team-leading 31 in 1968, were 18th all-time, and the 1,343 yards he gained were 16th. More significantly, until broken in 2014 by Jesse James he held the school mark for most career touchdowns by a tight end with 11.

Kwalick's most famous and memorable touchdown did not count in those receiving stats because it was scored on an onside kick against Army in 1968, saving an undefeated season for a team that went on to win the Orange Bowl and rank second in the nation. It was the sixth game of the year on Homecoming Day at Beaver Stadium, and Army had come back late in the fourth quarter to narrow Penn State's lead to six points. Army's onside kick wound up under a pile of Nittany Lions and Cadets and suddenly squirted out.

"Dave Bradley jumped on it, and one of the cadets punched it out of his leg and it popped into my hands," Kwalick recalled in Ken Rappoport's 2005 book *Penn State Nittany Lions: Where Have You Gone?* "I was lucky to run down the sideline to score. That put the game out of reach."

Kwalick is reminded of that 53-yard touchdown whenever he meets Nittany Lions fans.

"I went back in 1989 for my induction in the College Football Hall of Fame…and everybody that came up to me said, 'Oh, I remember you, you're the guy that ran back that onside kick against Army,'" he said.

Kwalick is also remembered for his block that helped beat Kansas at the 1969 Orange Bowl in what was his last college game. Penn State had rallied in the last minute to score a touchdown to trail by one point. A pass for two points into the end zone to a well-covered Kwalick that would have won the game sailed over his head. However, Kansas was penalized for having 12 men on the field, giving the Lions another shot.

"We called a running play," Kwalick recalled, "and I was blocking John Zook [Kansas' All-American defensive end]. Bobby Campbell got the ball and I was lucky to get a good block on John, and Bobby got into the end zone." The 15–14 victory is one of the most celebrated in Penn State history and a must-see featured exhibit in the Penn State All-Sports Museum.

Kwalick came from a humble family in suburban Pittsburgh and was the first of his mother's and father's 15 siblings and all of his cousins to go to college. He is most proud of the fact that his mother and father never missed a game of his in high school or college.

Ted Kwalick was the prototype for the modern-day tight end. He was a Penn State All-American in 1967–68 and inducted into the College Football Hall of Fame in 1989.

In Kwalick's sophomore year at Penn State, Paterno hired his head coach at Montour High School, Bob Phillips, to be the Lions' receivers coach. With his high school quarterback, Chuck Burkhart, also there, it felt like home to Kwalick, except when he was in the doghouse for one reason or another.

"When you got in some little scrapes or minor problems… they'd call you into the coaches' office," Kwalick remembered in a 1986 interview with Gerry Dulac of the *Pittsburgh Press.* "They would sit you in a chair in the center of a ring and the coaches would sit in a ring around you. They would start asking you questions and before you could answer one, one on the other side would ask you and they would get you turned around. They would get you turning so fast the chair would start smoking. I think I was in there six times. Paterno said no one has come to that record."

Kwalick was the first junior at Penn State to be selected a first-team All-American in 1967. When he was a consensus All-American the next year, he became just the second two-time All-American, following the Lions' legendary coach and end Bob Higgins in 1915 and 1919.

The San Francisco 49ers drafted Kwalick in the first round (seventh overall). He was in three Pro Bowls and made first-team All-NFL in 1972 before joining the Oakland Raiders and playing on the Raiders' 1976 Super Bowl champion team.

After leaving the NFL soon after the Super Bowl, he went into business, and in 1996 started a company in Santa Clara that manufactures large surge-protection equipment for both home and industrial use. He is still president of ProTech Voltage Systems, but full-time retirement is in his future.

Thank you, God, for creating a football player named Ted Kwalick.

44 2005: Saving Paterno's Career

Joe Paterno knew he was fighting to keep his job.

He had another meeting coming up with his bosses, this time at his home, to talk about his future as head coach, and they were nudging him toward retirement.

Paterno's 2004 team had just lost its sixth straight game and the seventh of the season. Their only victories had been over the weakest teams in the second-tier Mid-American Conference, Akron and Central Florida. He knew this could be worse than 2003, when his team won only three games: one against one-win Temple, one against Mid-American Kent State, and the last against perennial loser Indiana.

With just two more losses in 2004 at Indiana and against Michigan State a week later, this could be a low point in his 39-year career. That would please a lot of fans and many in the media who urged or demanded that he retire or be fired.

One irate fan made his case to Neil Rudel of the *Altoona Mirror*, then Penn State's senior beat writer: "Sorry to say, JoePa must go. Right now he is destroying his legacy and destroying the PSU program by hanging on too long."

Nothing had gone right for Paterno since the upset loss to Minnesota in 1999. That miracle last-second Hail Mary pass and field goal had knocked his second-ranked Nittany Lions out of the BCS national championship "millennium" game in the Sugar Bowl January 4.

The next season was his first losing one in 12 years and only the second in Penn State history since 1938. But it got worse. There was another losing year in 2001 before Paterno and his assistant coaches stopped the bleeding in 2002 with a 9–3 record that earned them a New Year's Day game in the Capital One Bowl against Auburn. But the team did not play well against Auburn, and the 13–9 defeat was deflating.

Since the win in 1999 over Illinois before the Minnesota disaster to the latest 2004 loss against Northwestern, Paterno's Nittany Lions had lost 36 games and won 25. A defeat at Indiana could mean the firing squad, or at least forced retirement.

Some critics were citing his age or claiming the game had passed him by. But at nearly 78 years old, Paterno believed he and his loyal assistants could coach Penn State to another national championship. Just give him a little time. He knew he had some good young players on the 2004 team and he was recruiting some blue-chip talent.

That's what Paterno told university president Graham Spanier and athletic director Tim Curley when he secretly met with them a few days before the Indiana game. He repeated it in another meeting that also included two members of the board of trustees a day after the end-of-the-season game against Michigan State. At least it's what Paterno said a year later when the public first learned about the post–Michigan State meeting from an exclusive story by *Pittsburgh Post-Gazette*'s beat reporter Chico Harlan. Only Spanier has talked publicly about the meetings in recent years, and his version is different.

Penn State had beaten Indiana 22–18 in 2004 in a tight game that came down to a four-down goal-line stand starting at the Lions' 1-yard line with 2:18 left. The next week, the Lions smashed three-point favorite Michigan State 37–13 in an offensive blitz not seen earlier in the year.

Paterno recalled the Sunday meeting after Michigan State as cordial but confrontational.

"The direction they wanted to take," Paterno told Harlan, "was, 'maybe it's time to go, Joe. You ought to think about getting out of it.' I had not intended to discuss that with them, because I felt I would know when to get out of it...That's all I said to them. They didn't quite understand where I was coming from or what it took to get a football program going....I said, 'Relax. Get off my backside.'"

Spanier privately challenged Paterno's account almost from the day the *Post-Gazette* published the story on December 25, 2005, as Penn State's once-beaten 2005 team was preparing for its Orange Bowl game against Florida State. But Spanier never said anything publicly until an interview with columnist Dave Jones of the *Harrisburg Patriot-News* a couple weeks after both he and Paterno were fired in 2011 in the repercussions from the child abuse scandal.

Spanier asserted that Paterno was not asked to quit. "There was a point in time in our program where Joe was thinking about getting the program in good shape for a successor, and we met at his invitation," Spanier said. "But there wasn't just a meeting. There were a series of discussions, at Joe's initiation," including the two meetings at Paterno's home. "I think these were good, open, back-and-forth discussions. And what came out of those discussions was a mutual interest in continuing to work toward the future."

Regardless of what actually occurred, Paterno proved to be right about his Penn State football team. With a squad of determined veteran players led by quarterback Michael Robinson and linebacker Paul Posluszny and a half dozen or so highly rated recruits like receiver Derrick Williams and defensive back Justin King, the 2005 team surprised the college football world. They won the Big Ten Championship Game and the Orange Bowl in triple overtime and finished third in the national rankings, missing an undefeated season by a whisker in a last-play defeat at Michigan.

In the last six years of his Hall of Fame career, Paterno would not have another losing season and each of his teams would play in a major bowl game, including the 2009 Rose Bowl. On January 10, 2006—one year, one month, and sixteen days after the last meeting at his home with his bosses—Joe Paterno was selected National Coach of the Year by his peers in the American Football Coaches Association for an unprecedented fifth time.

45 1959: Close, but No Cigar

Rip Engle's 1959 team led by Heisman Trophy runner-up quarterback Richie Lucas came close to playing for the national championship, and if they had they might have won it.

A missed extra point early in a game at Beaver Field on November 7 against Syracuse, hyped as the Battle of Unbeatens, eventually created the circumstances that led to the 20–18 loss, when a pair of two-point conversions failed later on.

Syracuse finished the regular season No. 1 in the polls and then beat Texas 23–14 for its first and only national title.

A deflated Penn State team, already knowing it had to play in the first Liberty Bowl at Philadelphia because of Pennsylvania politics, was then upset by its traditional nemesis Pitt 22–7 in the last game of the regular season.

"There was some disgruntlement on the team playing in the Liberty Bowl [which had been set up before Pitt]," Lucas recalled. "Sometimes we didn't play as well as we could have [at Pitt] because some people were not happy with the situation."

The players redeemed themselves a few weeks later in a 7–0 win over Alabama in the frigid bowl game, but it didn't help them in the final polls released December 7 before the bowl game. The Lions finished 10th in the United Press International coaches' rankings and 12th in the Associated Press media vote.

Sam Stellatella, the player who missed the extra-point kick that changed everything in the Syracuse game, has tried to make it up to the players ever since by organizing reunions every five years at Penn State and having the team recognized as "the only Penn State team to beat Bear Bryant."

A record crowd of 34,000 had jammed New Beaver Field, despite 30-degree temperatures, expecting to see a classic, and they did. At 7–0 and rated No. 4, Syracuse was a six-point favorite over the No. 7 Nittany Lions, unbeaten in six games. Not surprisingly, the game was not on TV in an era when televised games of every NCAA school were severely restricted, but it was broadcast by a national radio network.

Penn State took command immediately. The Lions forced a Syracuse punt after the kickoff and just missed a 45-yard touchdown pass that was dropped. Shortly after, they recovered a fumble at the Orange 45-yard line that set up a touchdown by sophomore Roger Kochman on a fourth-down, 17-yard run up the middle.

Stellatella, a guard on the red team who took over the place-kicking earlier in the year, had hit on 15 of 16 attempts, but this kick was wide right.

"With better luck the Lions would have come out of that first period with a two-touchdown lead…and that would have put an entirely different complexion on the game," Gordon White of the *New York Times* wrote the next day.

The miss revitalized Syracuse. An end zone interception by Penn State thwarted one Syracuse drive of 66 yards but a short punt led to a 45-yard drive for a touchdown and extra point in the second quarter and another touchdown in the third. With 11:20 left in the fourth quarter the Orange scored again on a short, 41-yard drive, but this time the Syracuse kicker missed his extra-point attempt.

What happened in the next few minutes were two of the outstanding plays in Penn State history, and they nearly cost Syracuse its national championship.

Integrating Alabama in the 1959 Liberty Bowl

Penn State's 1959 team did not realize it would be making college football history when it played in the first Liberty Bowl. It was years later before the players realized the significance of being the first integrated team to play against Alabama.

Coach Bear Bryant, who was more prescient than most of the prejudiced fans of Southern college football teams, was in his second year at his alma mater. When the Liberty Bowl invited Alabama to play Penn State with African American Charlie Janerette as a starting tackle, Bryant made it happen despite vociferous complaints from racists in his state.

Actually, the fact that Alabama was playing against an integrated team for the first time hardly made news outside of the South. It was mentioned briefly in the last paragraph of an AP dispatch announcing the game and not at all in the lengthy postgame story in the *New York Times.*

Despite the racial history, the focus of the matchup was on the two coaches: Penn State's Rip Engle and Bryant. This was Engle's best team and his first to play in a bowl. Alabama's last bowl game had been in 1953 when Bryant was at Kentucky, where he had produced three bowl teams.

The two teams designed their game plans around the probability of bad weather on December 19 in Philadelphia, but the 30 mph winds made the wind chill far below freezing, and passing was almost impossible. The game turned into a classic defensive struggle, with both teams losing four fumbles and Alabama never getting past the Lions' 27-yard line.

As the first half was winding down, a short Alabama punt into the wind gave Penn State the ball at the Tide 22-yard line with no timeouts. With 18 seconds left, Penn State scored on an 18-yard pass to Roger Kochman off a fake field goal, and that was all the Lions needed to win 7–0.

"We're the only Penn State team to beat the great Bear Bryant," said Sam Stellatella who earlier missed the extra point against Syracuse.

Yes, and the first integrated team to play against Alabama.

Kochman took the kickoff on the goal line and ran 100 yards for a touchdown that sent the crowd into a frenzy, but it was short-lived as the Syracuse defense forced Lucas' pass attempt for two points to fall short. After trading punts, the Orange punted again. Tackle Andy Stynchula crashed through the line, slammed into the three-man protection, leaped with his knee planted in the back of a blocker, and hit the ball with his right forearm. End Bob Mitinger recovered at the 1-yard line, and on the next play sophomore fullback Sam Sobczak had the touchdown.

Lucas called the same play for two points that gave Penn State its first touchdown, faking a rollout to the left and giving the ball to Kochman. Syracuse was ready and stopped it. The clock showed 4:15 to play, and that was too much time left for an onside kick.

Penn State still had a chance when Syracuse's sensational sophomore Ernie Davis took the Lions kickoff near the sideline and absentmindedly stepped out of bounds at the Orange 7-yard line. "But here the Orange proved its greatness, its gameness and its poise," Ridge Riley reported in his detailed weekly newsletter to alumni. "Under extreme pressure from Penn State and certainly somewhat shaken by the sudden change in the character of the game, Syracuse slowly and methodically pushed up field for four consecutive first downs to run out the clock."

When the teams left the field, the Penn State crowd gave them both standing ovations. In the locker room, Syracuse coach Ben Schwartzwalder told reporters this Penn State squad "was the greatest team I've ever come up against."

In the end, Syracuse deserved to win. Yet, as always in tight games where a few plays make the difference, one can only speculate what would have happened if Stellatella had made that extra point. Stellatella, an extrovert from New Jersey whose high school sweetheart at one time was a teenager who would become world famous named Martha Stewart, has his own view:

"Everybody blamed me, and said I lost the national championship because if I would have kicked all three points we would have won the game," Stellatella said. "No one felt worse after that game than me. When you make the kicks you take the glory and when you miss you take the blame."

46 Dennis Onkotz: The First Great Graduate of Linebacker U

Dennis Onkotz was a better linebacker at Penn State than Jack Ham.

That may seem an outlandish statement to the younger generation of Nittany Lions fans. Ham is regarded by fans and the media as the school's best-ever linebacker. But much of that opinion is based on Ham's superlative career with the Pittsburgh Steelers that landed him in the Pro Football Hall of Fame.

Ham didn't become an All-American until his senior year, 1970, when he was a consensus first-team choice. Onkotz was second-team All-American as a sophomore in 1967 and then a first-team consensus All-American the next two seasons. Onkotz's name is all over the Penn State record books, while Ham's is almost extinct.

They're both enshrined in the College Football Hall of Fame. Yet, despite Onkotz' superior three years on the field, Ham was inducted first, in 1990, and Onkotz had to wait another five years. Dan Radakovich, the man who coached them both, believes Ham's pro career probably gives Ham the edge. Radakovich was their linebackers coach at Penn State, helped coach Ham on the Steelers, and tried to save Onkotz's pro career after a devastating leg injury.

"Dennis was as good at Penn State as Jack—maybe even better," Radakovich wrote in his 2012 autobiography, *Bad Rad: Football Nomad*. "But he never had a chance to prove it in the pros."

Radakovich believes Onkotz "was the linchpin" for Penn State's now-famous nickname of Linebacker U. "Denny was not only a great linebacker but his exceptional talent as a punt returner was unusual for a linebacker," Radakovich wrote. "Add that to the focus off the field on his colorful and scholarly academic endeavors—that also were highly-unusual [sic] for a football player at the time—and all that brought attention to Penn State as Linebacker U—an assembly line, if you will, for producing linebackers."

Onkotz earned a national reputation for going to class on Saturday mornings before home football games. It's not like it was basket weaving. His major was Biophysics and he eventually graduated with a 3.5 GPA. "I remember one time when the team stayed Friday night at a hunting camp in the woods at least a half hour away from the stadium," Radakovich told me. "Onkotz was very upset that he'd miss his class, but we had someone drive him there long before the team left in buses."

In what may have been Onkotz's best-ever game, he was at his 8:00 AM German class before the 1:30 PM kickoff against No. 3 North Carolina State in 1967. In the first quarter, Onkotz returned an interception 67 yards for a touchdown that put the Lions ahead 13–0. Coach Joe Paterno called it "the play of the game." Still, it took another big play from Onkotz with 40 seconds left on fourth-and-goal at the Penn State 1-yard line to get the win. The score was 13–6 when Onkotz, linebacker Jim Kates, and tackle Mike McBath stopped NC State tailback Tony Barchuk short of the goal line. The Lions then took a safety for the 13–8 victory, and the Associated Press named Onkotz Lineman of the Week.

To this day, Onkotz doesn't believe he was doing anything unusual on Saturday mornings because going to class "was the norm," as he wrote in *What It Means to Be a Nittany Lion*. "We went to class. We graduated. We did all those things you're supposed to do. We were the symbols of what Joe [Paterno] was pushing, the scholar-athlete."

Onkotz was in Paterno's first recruiting class when he became the head coach in 1966. He was from a large working-class family near Allentown, and became a starter in the second game of 1967 at Miami when Paterno replaced a bunch of seniors with sophomores early in the first quarter. Penn State stunned Miami 17–8, and after a loss the next week to UCLA, Onkotz and his sophomore teammates never lost another game. The 1968–69 teams finished No. 2 in the nation and won two Orange Bowls behind two of the greatest defensive squads in Penn State history.

The three touchdowns on interceptions that the 6'2", 215-pound Onkotz scored in his career still comprise the team record, although Darren Perry tied it in 1991. Onkotz remains tied with Don Eyer at fifth in career interceptions (11) and is tied with nine others for most interceptions in single-season (six in 1967). He also is sixth in career tackles (287), ninth in one season tackles (118 with 74 solos in 1967), and—get this—eighth in career punt returns with an average of 13.2 yards, and third in most returns (47).

The New York Jets drafted Onkotz in the third round and he was eager to prove himself in the NFL. In his ninth game as a backup and punt returner, be broke his leg so severely that he missed the next season. Radakovich talked the Steelers into trading for Onkotz before the 1972 season. "After he limped around practice with us…[we] knew that Dennis was not healed enough to play—and sorry to say, he never did," Radakovich said.

Onkotz moved to State College, and for decades he has been a financial consultant with an office close to Beaver Stadium.

So is Dennis Onkotz or Jack Ham Penn State's best-ever linebacker?

47 Lydell and Curt

Neither Lydell Mitchell nor Curt Warner expected to play football for Penn State. It's fortunate that they did. One can only speculate how their absence would have changed the outcomes for the Nittany Lions teams they played on: Mitchell from 1969 to 1971, including the back-to-back undefeated teams that finished No. 2 in 1968 and 1969, and Warner from 1979 to 1982, including the 1982 team that played for the national championships and the 1986 team that won it.

Their exceptional abilities on the field landed them both in the College Football Hall of Fame just five years apart, Mitchell in 2004 and Warner in 2009. Only five other Penn State running backs—Pete Mauthe, Glenn Killinger, Shorty Miller, Harry Wilson, and John Cappelletti—were enshrined before them.

"If Joe Paterno had not made me mad when he was recruiting me, I would have gone to Ohio State," Mitchell wrote in *What It Means to Be a Nittany Lion*. When Mitchell, who was from Baltimore, told Paterno on the telephone he had chosen Ohio State, Paterno told him, "Well, you're afraid to come to Penn State because Charlie Pittman is there and you can't play."

Warner might have played for Nebraska or Notre Dame. "[Nebraska] was too far away, and being kind of a mama's boy, I really didn't want to be that far away from home," Warner wrote in the same book. So the kid from rural West Virginia picked Penn State.

Pittman would become Paterno's first first-team All-American running back in 1969. Mitchell was next in 1971, followed by Cappelletti in 1973 and Warner in 1982. There have been only six others since: D. J. Dozier (1986), Blair Thomas (1989), Ki-Jana Carter (1994), Curtis Enis (1997), and Larry Johnson (2002). Mitchell and Warner set Penn State records that still remain.

Mitchell is still the leader in rushing touchdowns for one season, 26 in 1971, when he led the nation in scoring with 174 points (with three other touchdowns on receiving and kick/punt returns). At the time, his points, 29 touchdowns, and rushing touchdowns were three NCAA records. Mitchell held the team's single-season rushing record for 31 years with 1,567 yards until Johnson broke it in 2002 (2,087 yards) and the career rushing record for 17 years with 2,934 yards before Warner passed him (3,398 yards).

Warner's rushing mark lasted longer, 29 years, before it was snapped by Evan Royster's 3,932 yards in 2010, but he still is the leader for most 100-yard rushing games (18), one more than Carter, Enis, and Thomas. He might have more such games, and more total yardage, if Paterno had not thrown the ball more in the first five games of 1982. That all changed after Alabama beat the then–No. 3 Nittany Lions 42–21 to seemingly knock them out of the national championship race.

"After that game, we started emphasizing the run more," Warner recalled, "and that made us a more balanced offense." With Warner running for more than 100 yards in six of the last seven games, Penn State won its first national championship with a 27–23 win over Georgia.

In that last 100-yard game against Georgia, Warner outdueled the Heisman Trophy winner Herschel Walker. As the Lions defense held the prolific Walker to 103 yards and one touchdown on 28 attempts, Warner was following his blockers for 117 yards and two touchdowns on 18 carries.

Winning that game and the national title was the highlight of Warner's career, and he credits his teammates.

"It's a great feeling to know you're undisputed national champion," Warner wrote. "I'm most proud of the fact that we had a bunch of guys who were in it together, played together, and had an opportunity to win it all and did it."

As one would expect, Mitchell also credits his teammates for his success, especially Franco Harris. They were New Jersey high schoolers being recruited by Penn State when they met on their first

In this historic photograph from the 1970 season, Lenny Moore, arguably Penn State's greatest player, stops by the Nittany Lions bench to talk to All-American running backs Lydell Mitchell and Charlie Pittman.

visit to Penn State. They have been fast friends ever since and later in life went into business together.

But it was Joe Paterno who motivated Mitchell, even at times he didn't realize it. And it started with that phone call telling Mitchell he was afraid of Pittman.

"That ticked me off," Mitchell wrote, "and within 10 seconds I replied, 'I'm coming to Penn State and I'm going to break all the

Charlie, D. J., Blair, and L. J.

Although they were All-American running backs, Charlie Pittman, D. J. Dozier, Blair Thomas, and Larry Johnson have never reached the historical stature of Mitchell and Warner. When they played they were Penn State's best running backs.

Pittman was the consummate leader on and off the field and a major influence with his African American teammates. Dozier was the offensive star of the 1986 national championship team, but he shared the spotlight with Thomas, then a sophomore.

In his autobiography, Coach Joe Paterno wrote that Thomas "is the best all-around back I have ever coached in thirty-eight years. Lydell Mitchell might compare, but Blair is quicker."

Paterno's loyalty to his seniors kept Johnson as a reserve until his own senior season when he had a record-setting season in winning the Maxwell and Walter Camp Awards as Player of the Year and the Doak Walker Award as the most outstanding running back. He led the nation in rushing with 2,087 yards (and 20 touchdowns) on 271 carries when he also broke the school single-game rushing record held by Warner, not once but four times. His 327 yards (and four touchdowns) on 28 carries against Indiana was still the team record in 2015.

Johnson finished third in the Heisman Trophy voting, while Dozier was eighth and Thomas 10th. Pittman never made the top 10 but his teammate at defensive tackle, Mike Reid, did, finishing fifth. Johnson may have the best credentials to follow Mitchell and Warner into the College Football Hall of Fame but his well-publicized bickering with Paterno and subsequent off-field problems after graduation could be a major deterrent.

records there.' That's exactly what I said to him, and with a lot of help from my teammates, I was fortunate enough to fulfill my promise."

Mitchell believes his last game was his best, when Penn State upset Texas 30–6 in the 1972 Cotton Bowl. It was Paterno's watershed game, in which Penn State silenced many of its critics and proved it was a football power and not a weakling from the East.

"People didn't take us seriously," Mitchell said. "They didn't think we played good football up north. We were the laughingstock everywhere we went. It was very gratifying not only to play against a great Texas team...but to go out there and just completely dominate them."

Mitchell was the Offensive Player of the Game after rushing for 146 yards and a touchdown on 27 carries.

Warner probably summed up both of their Penn State careers at a news conference in New York preceding his induction into the College Football Hall of Fame.

"When I look back over my career," he said, "it's a humbling time to reflect upon family, friends, teammates, coaches...and I'm just privileged and proud to be a part of the Penn State family...I'm deeply humbled, and deeply honored and proud."

48 Ki-Jana and Kerry

Ki-Jana and Kerry. You don't have to say the last names for true blue-and-white Penn State football fans. They know automatically.

Ki-Jana Carter and Kerry Collins should be enshrined in the College Football Hall of Fame one day. They've been eligible since 2004, 10 years after they led the 1994 team to an undefeated Rose

Bowl championship season, but they had never been on the ballot until Collins made it for the voting for the 2016 classes. The Hall of Fame selection process is filled with as much politics and bias as anything else in life. So who knows if they'll ever be inducted?

Politics and bias is nothing new for Carter and Collins and the 1994 football team. It was outright bias by the voters in the media and coaches polls that cost Penn State at least a share of the national championship (see Ranking No. 17). And it was also that same media bias in the Heisman Trophy voting that denigrated Carter and Collins and made Colorado halfback Rashaan Salaam the winner that year when all three were consensus All-Americans.

Carter was the Heisman runner-up with 901 votes to Salaam's 1,743 votes. Collins was fourth (639) behind quarterback Steve McNair (655). Even the total of voting for the Penn State duo did not top Salaam's numbers. Salaam isn't in the Hall of Fame either, although he ran for more than 2,055 yards that year. Obviously, those numbers stood out at Colorado.

Yet Carter and Collins were the stars of one of the greatest and most proficient offenses in college football history. The quick-strike 1994 offense set several school records, plus two NCAA marks for average points (47.8) and total offense (520.2 yards) per game (47.8). If the Lion offense had not scored touchdowns so quickly, the individual statistics of Carter and Collins would have been even more impressive.

Carter ran for 1,539 yards and 23 touchdowns on 198 carries. Those 23 touchdowns are second in school history only to Lydell Mitchell's 26 in 1971, and Carter still holds the record for most 100-yard rushing games in a season (10) and most career touchdown runs for 80 yards or more (three). His 83-yard touchdown on Penn State's first offensive play in the 1995 Rose Bowl is one of the most memorable plays of all time and prompted his induction into the Rose Bowl Hall of Fame in 2014.

Brady, Engram, and Hartings

The bias against Penn State in 1994 also was exposed when tight end Kyle Brady, wide receiver Bobby Engram, and guard Jeff Hartings were chosen on bona fide All-America teams but not enough of them to be consensus All-Americans.

Brady may have been overshadowed by his teammates on the Lions explosive offense, but his clutch receiving and exceptional blocking was continually praised throughout the season by the media, particularly TV game commentators. That was most evident in Penn State's historic come-from-behind, 14-play, 91-yard touchdown drive late in the fourth quarter that beat Illinois to clinch the Big Ten Championship Game when Brady caught two key passes and didn't miss a block.

The blocking of Hartings was also crucial in that drive against Illinois and he was the man who led fullback Brian Milne through the off-tackle hole for the three-yard winning touchdown. Hartings was an Associated Press and Walter Camp All-American that season as a junior. The next year, Walter Camp, the United Press International, and other groups helped Hartings become a consensus All-American, making him one of just 11 two-time All-Americans of Penn State's 84 first-team selections.

What's inexplicable is why Engram, chosen a Walter Camp All-American in 1994, was not a consensus All-American that season after winning the first Biletnikoff Award as the "outstanding college pass receiver." Engram was equally as valuable as a senior on a less talented Nittany Lions team, and was only a second-team All-American choice that year.

Engram was the first Penn State receiver to gain more than 1,000 yards in a season, and he did it twice, in 1994 and1995. Only Alan Robinson in 2013 has more yards, but Engram still holds the school record for career yardage (3,026), career touchdowns (31), single-season receiving touchdowns (13 in 1993 and 11 in 1995), and most games with 100 yards or more (16).

Brady and Hartings were No. 1 NFL draft choices and Engram was a No. 2 selection. Brady played for 13 years, Hartings for 11 years, and Engram for 14 years. Not one of college football's 1994 consensus All-American wide receivers, tight ends, or guards lasted longer than eight years. No bias, huh?

"Carter's been a phenomenal football player," Coach Joe Paterno said soon after Carter left Penn State. "Every time he's had to do something, he's made big, big plays."

During the Rose Bowl Hall of Fame ceremonies in Pasadena, Carter thanked Paterno and then read the names of Penn State's offensive team that started the 1995 game against Oregon, beginning with the five offensive linemen from tackle to tackle. "I wouldn't be here without my teammates," he told the crowd.

Collins' credentials for the College Football Hall of Fame may even surpass Carter's. He won the Maxwell Award as the nation's most outstanding player, the Davey O'Brien Trophy as the best quarterback, and ABC-TV's award as Player of the Year. His 172.86 percent passing efficiency that once led the nation remains the Penn State record. Collins set several school records in 1994 but most have been surpassed since the Lions started upgrading their passing attack in the mid-2000s. Among the records he still holds for a single season are completion percentage (66.7 percent) and yards per attempt (10.15 yards) while his passing yardage (2,679) is now fourth after being surpassed in 2009.

Paterno had high praise for Collins' leadership. "The elements of leadership and poise make the difference between a guy who's a really good quarterback and a great one," Paterno told the *Philadelphia Inquirer*. "Kerry has them."

Collins also singled out his teammates in an interview with this writer. "My greatest memory of that team is just the quality and character of the guys we had on the team," he recalled. "They were focused [and] had a great work ethic and humility. It was just a special bunch of guys who put together a special year."

Carter and Collins were both No. 1 draft choices in 1995, but here is where their paths went in different directions. Carter was the first overall selection in the draft when picked by Cincinnati, but injuries severely curtailed his seven-year career.

Collins was chosen four places later as the franchise quarterback and first-ever draft choice by the then-new Carolina Panthers team. He went on to play 17 years in the NFL—tied with kicker Matt Bahr's record for Penn State players in pro football—with six different teams and took the New York Giants to the Super Bowl in 2000.

A coin flip determined the title of this chapter, but it could have been named "Kerry and Ki-Jana." And they both belong in the College Football Hall of Fame.

49 The Legacy Recruits

Earl Hewitt Jr. was the first legacy recruit in 1927, and Kevin Reihner and Sterling Jenkins were the latest in 2015.

There have been some 60 legacy recruits in the past, and there could be more in the future. But there won't be any who play for Hugo Bezdek, Bob Higgins, Joe Bedenk, Rip Engle, and Joe Paterno, Penn State's head coaches from 1918 through 2011.

The term legacy recruit is usually defined as a son or grandson who followed their fathers and/or their grandfathers to play football at Penn State, but it can also include brothers, cousins, and nephews. The original legacy recruit was a walk-on reserve right halfback named Earl Hewitt Jr. who lettered in 1927, and the son of Earl Hewitt Sr., a star running back from 1898 to 1901. That was long before the descriptive term became common.

No one knows who coined the phrase legacy recruit. It didn't become popular until the early 2000s after many years of Penn State football progeny playing for Coach Joe Paterno.

Some of the legacy recruits have become stars, equaling or surpassing the achievements of their kin. Others could not match their elders on the field. Leo Wisniewski was a very good defensive lineman and co-captain of the 1981 team, but his younger brother Steve became a two-time All-American guard in 1985 and 1986 and his son Stefen an All-American guard in 2010.

Jim Garrity led Penn State in pass receiving in 1953 and 1954. His son Gregg did it in 1981. A year later Gregg caught one of the most famous passes in school history for a touchdown in the Sugar Bowl that helped give the Lions their first national championship in 1982. Gregg's son, Gregg Jr., is a junior wide receiver on the 2015 team.

John Bruno was a reserve halfback in 1956. His son, John Bruno Jr., walked on in 1982 and became one of the outstanding punters in school history and a crucial player in the Fiesta Bowl upset of Miami for the 1986 national championship.

Another father-son combination is one of the least known legacy recruit families. Father Dave Truitt backed up All-American end Bob Mitinger in 1960. Son Greg is the best long-snapper in school history. His Penn State résumé includes two teams that played for national championships in 1985 and 1986 as well as the 1988 squad. What's also significant is Greg's five years as the long snapper for the Cincinnati Bengals (1992–96). No other Nittany Lion long snapper has even come close to his NFL tenure.

No family can match the enduring lineage of Higgins, a two-time All-American end in 1915 and 1919. His All-American guard Steve Suhey married one of his daughters, and three grandsons and two great-grandsons played for Paterno.

The Hostetler-Stupar clan includes brothers Ron, Doug, and Jeff and their brother-in-law Steve Stupar (from 1979–80) and his son Nate (2008–11). John Gilmore (1999–2001) is a nephew of Bruce Gilmore (1956, 1958).

Then there are the five Collins brothers of Cinnaminson, New Jersey. Andre was first (1986–89) and became a first-team All-American linebacker in his senior year. Gerry was next (1989–91), then Phillip (1993–94), and finally Aaron (1994–97), who started 36 consecutive games at linebacker. The capstone of the legacy recruit history was in 2012. Four years earlier Paterno recruited Michael Mauti and Michael Zordich. Mauti followed his father, Rich (1975–76), and brother Patrick, a walk-on in 2005 who lettered in 2009. Zordich's father of the same first name had been an All-American and co-captain on the 1985 team that played for the national title in the Orange Bowl. The two Michaels were crucial in helping Penn State overcome the severe NCAA sanctions in 2012, and Mauti became a first-team All-American linebacker.

Mauti's successor as starting linebacker in 2013 was Mike Hull, whose father, Tom, also was a linebacker (1971–73). In 2014, Hull was honored as the Big Ten's Butkus-Fitzgerald Linebacker of the Year.

As a four-time Academic All-Big 10, Hull also fit the Paterno mold of a scholar-athlete, with talent on the field and in the classroom. Lance Hamilton, Tony Pittman, Arron Collins, and Stephan Wisniewski are the high priests of the legacy recruits academic temple. All followed a family member to Penn State: Lance (1984–85) after his brother Harry (1980–83); Tony (1992–94) after his father Charlie (1967–69); Arron (1994–97), the last of five brothers to follow his brother Andre (1986–89); and Stephan, after his father and uncle. The Hamiltons, Pittmans, and Stephan were all CoSIDA Academic All-Americans. More significantly, Lance, Tony, Arron, and Stephan are among just 17 Penn State players since 1971 to receive $18,000 postgraduate fellowships from the National Football Foundation as Hall of Fame Scholars.

Hull, Mauti, Wisniewski, and Gilmore were in the NFL as of the 2015 season. The latest legacy recruits are offensive linemen. Tackle Kevin Reihner transferred in 2015 as a fifth-year graduate student from Stanford to follow his offensive lineman father,

George (1974–77) and his uncle John (1972–75). Sterling Jenkins' grandma is the sister of running back Chappie Hill (1956).

Who's next in the pipeline?

50 Franco and Munchak

Franco and Munchak.

If those names are not familiar to a Penn State fan, then they should be.

Franco Harris and Mike Munchak are two of just six Penn State players in the Pro Football Hall of Fame. They were both superb players on outstanding Penn State teams, but they were overshadowed by their All-American teammates.

In Franco's three years at fullback from 1969 to 1971, All-American tailbacks Charlie Pittman and Lydell Mitchell were the headliners while Harris hardly made honorable mention.

Munchak was good enough to be selected a second-team All-American guard in 1981, but on the other side of the center Sean Farrell was a consensus first-team All-American. Munchak might have made it to the first team the following year, but with one year of eligibility left he departed for the pros. Farrell repeated as a first-teamer in helping Penn State win its first national championship in 1982, while Munchak was earning plaudits as the No. 1 draft choice (eighth overall) of the Houston Oilers.

By his second full season, the Scranton native was in the Pro Bowl, the first of nine in his 12-year career. He was also a first-team All-Pro selection by the pro football writers in 1987 and 1991. When he retired at the end of 1993 he was still a starter.

Even before Munchak was drafted, Franco was helping the Pittsburgh Steelers win Super Bowls. Pittsburgh had chosen him in the first round (13th overall) of the 1972 draft and he was an instant star, earning the first of nine successive Pro Bowl honors. During the span of his 13-year career, he was the primary running back that helped the Steelers win four Super Bowls from 1975 to 1980. When he retired, he was second in all-time rushing to Jimmy Brown, and as of the end of the 2014 season, Harris was still 13th in career NFL rushing with 12,120 yards on 2,949 carries and 91 touchdowns.

Harris, whose mother was Italian, was so popular with the fans that in his rookie year they created Franco's Italian Army to vocally support him. Later that season singer Frank Sinatra, who was a New Jersey native like Harris, personally joined the army when the Steelers were in San Diego near Sinatra's home.

For all his statistics, Franco is more famous for the miracle pass reception—forever known as the Immaculate Reception—that he made as a rookie for the winning touchdown in the last seconds against Oakland in the AFC playoffs. The 25-yard pass from Terry Bradshaw toward Frenchy Fuqua bounced off Raiders back Jack Tatum and bounced into the air. Harris scooped it up at Oakland's 42-yard line and ran untouched into the end zone. To this day, Harris credits Paterno.

"Joe would always [tell us] certain things about, 'going to the ball,'" Harris told me. "He'd shout 'go to the ball, go to the ball. Don't stand still. Keep moving.' And the [Immaculate] Reception is a result of that."

A bronze statue of Franco in his Steelers uniform making that near-impossible catch greets fliers inside the Pittsburgh International Airport and is a must-see for Penn State fans, even if they root for the rival NFL teams.

Of all Paterno's players, none have been as loyal and more outspoken in defending Paterno after his firing and subsequent vilification in the aftermath of the child abuse scandal. It's a long way from Paterno's doghouse in Franco's senior year, when he was benched in the first half of the 1972 Cotton Bowl game for showing up late for practice. Paterno inserted him in the second half and his blocking is credited with helping the Lions come back from a 6–0 deficit to stomp Texas 30–6 in one of the turning-point games in Penn State history.

As of 2014 Harris was still 17th in career rushing at Penn State with 2,002 yards on 380 carries, and his 24 touchdowns still comprise the record for fullbacks.

Dan Radakovich, who coached linebackers at Penn State and the defensive and offensive lines in Pittsburgh when Harris was there, said, "Franco was quick as a cat in my linebacker drills and, when carrying the football, he could make a cut and get turned up field going full speed."

Obviously, offensive linemen like Munchak rarely set records, and their worth to the team is hardly noticed by fans. His teammates and opponents knew.

After playing against Munchak and Farrell, when Penn State upset Nebraska in Lincoln 30–24 in 1981, a Nebraska linebacker said, "I've never seen anyone tougher than those two and I hope I never do again."

What's notable is Munchak and Farrell were defensive linemen until Paterno switched them both in their sophomore years and they quickly became starters. A knee injury forced Munchak to miss his junior season, and that's why he could leave early for the NFL.

Munchak was still an All-NFL player when Franco was inducted into the Pro Football Hall of Fame in 1990, his first year of eligibility. Munchak made it in his second year as a finalist in 2001.

Franco and Munchak. They are Penn State.

51 The Miracle of Adam Taliaferro

Nothing in Penn State's football history will ever match the emotional and electrifying moment when Adam Taliaferro walked and jogged onto the Beaver Stadium field the night of September 1, 2001.

Less than a year earlier, as a true freshman reserve cornerback, Taliaferro had been paralyzed from the neck down at Ohio State and doctors said he had a 3 percent chance of ever walking again.

With a record crowd of 109,313 looking on before the nationally televised season opener against No. 2 Miami in the nighttime glare of a newly expanded Beaver Stadium, Tailiaferro came out of the south end zone tunnel. He walked haltingly at first as the crowd stood and cheered, and when he began jogging slowly past the goal posts, tears streamed down cheeks of thousands of Nittany Lions fans.

"Before the game I was nervous, but once I got out there all the nerves went away," Taliaferro told the media after the game. "I just did what my body told me to do. It was a great moment. The adrenaline was definitely flowing. It took me back to last year. I can't put it into words. The moment just took over. I just went out there and did what my heart told me to do."

A rendering of that moment, with Taliaferro waving at the crowd, is captured in a colorful painting by Johno Prascak that now hangs permanently in the Penn State All-Sports Museum Theater that also serves as the football media room.

Taliaferro credits many people with helping him in his startling recovery, especially his family; team doctor Wayne Sebastianelli and trainer George Salvaterra; his doctors and therapists at Philadelphia's Thomas Jefferson and Magee Rehabilitation

Hospitals; and the support of everyone in Penn State football, starting with head coach Joe Paterno and administrative assistant Joe Sarra (who was with him almost daily in the early weeks after the injury).

"I didn't know I wasn't supposed to walk," he said in the 2001 book *Miracle in the Making*. "I always thought I was. If I knew [I wasn't supposed to], it definitely would have made it tougher. I wouldn't have given up, but it would have been a shock."

The devastating injury happened quickly and the team was already in a gloomy mood. It was late in the fourth quarter on September 23, 2000, and Penn State was on its way to losing its fourth game of the season in the dreary rain of Columbus. Undefeated Ohio State led 38–6 and was driving for another touchdown with two minutes left. Taliaferro, the *Philadelphia Inquirer's* 1999 Player of the Year in southeast Pennsylvania and South Jersey, ran up to tackle Ohio State's reserve 210-pound running back Jerry Westbrooks for no gain at the Penn State 16-yard line.

His head hit Westbrooks' knee and the 5'10", 183-pound Taliaferro went down and didn't move. Doctors and trainers from Penn State and Ohio State dashed onto the field. Later, those first responders and the Ohio State University Medical Center were praised for doing everything right that eventually enabled Taliaferro to recover from his spinal cord injury.

There was 1:42 left in the game and the game was delayed for more than 10 minutes as Taliaferro was cautiously taken off the field and placed into an ambulance. What has galled the Penn State nation ever since is that Ohio State coach John Cooper didn't run out the clock. He allowed his third-string quarterback to pass for another touchdown that made the final score 45–6, which was the worst loss by point differential in Paterno's career. Cooper has insisted he didn't realize the injury was so critical. "It never crossed my mind it was severe," Cooper said in *Miracle in the Making*. "I certainly have a clear conscience."

At the time, Taliaferro remembered the play starting but not the hit that injured him. "I remember waking up on the ground and everything felt numb," he told Marc Narducci of the *Philadelphia Inquirer* shortly after the injury. "I remember seeing everybody over me and telling them I couldn't move. It was a weird feeling. I never thought of being paralyzed…there wasn't any pain at that point. My neck didn't hurt. It was total numbness."

You can see the happiness on the face of Adam Taliaferro as he walks out of the tunnel and across the field at the opening game of the 2001 season less than a year after recovering from a paralyzing injury he suffered at Ohio State.

Taliaferro never played football again. After graduating from Penn State, he went on to get his law degree and win election to the school's board of trustees in the aftermath of the child abuse scandal. Then, in late January 2015, he was sworn in as a newly elected assemblyman from Gloucester, New Jersey. He also established the Adam Taliaferro Foundation to help people with similar injuries and had distributed more than $1 million by 2015.

A special exhibit in the Penn State All-Sports Museum commemorates Taliaferro's miracle. It features a poem titled "When I

Steve Smith and Tim Shaw

Steve Smith and Tim Shaw weren't injured in a football game, but the two former Penn State players haven't been as fortunate as Adam Taliaferro. They are battling the debilitating disease amyotrophic lateral sclerosis, or ALS. It's a progressive neurodegenerative condition affecting nerve cells in the brain and spinal cord.

Smith, a star fullback on the 1986 national championship team, has been confined to a bed since 2002 and can only move his facial muscles and eyes to communicate. That enables him to use a computer, and over the years Smith has written an autobiography about his life and how he has dealt with ALS.

In fact, another diagnosis since 2001 pointed to another progressive degenerative disease, chronic traumatic encephalopathy (CTE), as his problem. Either way, the disease has left him unable to walk but hasn't weakened the spirit and fight he always showed on the football field at Penn State and during nine years in the NFL with the Los Angeles Raiders and Seattle Seahawks.

Shaw was a standout linebacker (2002, 2004–06) who revealed in August 2014 he had ALS just after a seven-year NFL career. He knows what is probably ahead unless a cure is found.

"I have ALS, but I am not letting that dictate my life," he wrote on a website in September 2014.

Neither has Steve Smith. "God is in control of my life," he wrote in his still-to-be published autobiography. "The love of my family keeps me going...I still have much to do with them."

Walk" that he wrote by hand while still partially paralyzed and lists 12 reasons why he would walk again.

This is the beginning and end of his poem:

"When I walk, it will be for those who prayed for me....When I walk it's for Penn State!"

52 Shane Conlan

Shane Conlan will always be remembered for his gutty night in Tempe, Arizona, when he was the Most Valuable Defensive Player in Penn State's Fiesta Bowl upset over Miami for the 1986 national championship.

Despite playing with a gimpy knee and a banged-up ankle he reinjured in the first and third quarters of the game, Conlan was a demon on the field, always in the center of the action. Fans who were there or watched on television can still see him rambling downfield at less than full speed because of his injuries after intercepting a Vinny Testaverde pass at the Miami 44-yard line midway through the fourth quarter with Penn State trailing 10–7. Conlan was tackled at the 5-yard line, but his interception set up Penn State's winning touchdown two plays later.

"To this day, my brothers still think I should have scored," Conlan told Jordan Hyman for the 2006 book *Game of My Life: Penn State*. "[They said] 'why couldn't you jump over him?' I jumped and just flopped...I must have been really tired."

Conlan had intercepted another pass earlier in the game and made several tackles just as Paterno and his assistant coaches had expected when they designed a special defense to stop Testaverde, Miami's prolific Heisman Trophy winner.

"They told me to go tackle the guy with the ball," Conlan wrote for the book *What It Means to Be a Nittany Lion.* "A lot of the times I was out on receivers. But this game, at the beginning anyway, they stacked me behind the two inside linebackers. They would clog up the blockers and I had a chance to run and make plays. I loved that defense."

What's nearly forgotten is that Conlan and Penn State might not have been in that National Championship Game if Paterno had not convinced him to return for this redshirt senior year.

In 1985 Conlan was a first-team All-American on the Lions team that lost to Oklahoma 25–10 on New Year's night in the Orange Bowl. He could have turned pro but wanted another shot at the title and figured the veteran team of 1986 could do it. That 1986 season, Conlan was a consensus All-American and then became the No. 1 draft choice (eighth overall) of the Buffalo Bills. Not bad for a 6'2", 180-pound high school kid from Frewsburg, New York, who had only one scholarship offer.

Within a year at Penn State, Conlan weighed 210 and by 1985 he was a 235-pounder playing with a bit of nastiness. "I was aggressive, but I also was dirty," he admitted. "I got a lot of [personal fouls]."

Conlan is still tied (with John Skorupan) for seventh in career tackles with 274 tackles, 186 solos. Although he led the 1986 team with 79 tackles (63 solos), his best year statistically was 1985 with 91 tackles (57 solos) but fellow linebacker Rogers Alexander had 102. Conlan also caused 10 fumbles, recovered four fumbles, recorded 16 sacks (minus-148 yards), and had 25 tackles for loss (minus-215 yards).

Conlan went on to play nine years in the NFL with the Bills and the Rams, was selected for three Pro Bowls, and made several All-Conference or All-NFL teams. In 2005 he was inducted into the Buffalo Sports Hall of Fame.

Conlan's crowning achievement came in 2014 when he was enshrined in the College Football Hall of Fame. That honor was long overdue, for he had been eligible since 1996. However, even for someone who played for Linebacker U, it is not easy being inducted into the Hall of Fame.

Conlan is just the third Penn State linebacker inducted into the pantheon and the first in 19 years following Jack Ham (1990) and Dennis Onkotz (1995).

Only one other team has three linebackers in the hall—Alabama with Cornelius Bennett (2005), Woodrow Lowe (2009), and Derrick Thomas (who also was inducted with Conlan in 2014). Four schools have two linebackers: Ohio State, Tennessee, Kansas State, and Dartmouth (which is in the lower level NCAA Football Championship Subdivision). In fact, just 49 linebackers have been inducted into the College Football Hall of Fame as of 2015, and only 36 are from the top echelon Football Bowl Subdivision.

When the 2014 class was announced in May, Conlan was chosen to represent all the inductees.

"It's been a tough time the last few years at Penn State," Conlan said as tears came to his eyes. "So most of all I want to thank two people that are most important to me in my life, one being the late, great Joe Paterno. Thank you so much for all you've done. We miss you, Coach. And my defensive coordinator Tom Bradley, who found me at a very small school...and he went to bat for me."

Later Conlan also remembered his two interceptions and three others that Testaverde threw in the 1987 Fiesta Bowl, including the game clincher to Pete Giftopoulos on the last play of the game: "[He] threw it to the wrong team."

53 General Beaver and Old Beaver Field

It could have been named Roberts Field, not Beaver Field.

That was one of the two names suggested by the student newspaper in March 1892 for Penn State's new athletic grounds that would soon include a striking 500-seat grandstand with a blue-and-white roof overlooking the grassy field.

The students were overjoyed with their new playing field. Since 1875, the baseball team had played on a makeshift, poorly kept diamond they had constructed northeast of Old Main, the school's multi-functional building with classrooms, dormitories, and dining facilities.

After the first football game on the Old Main Lawn in 1887, the grouchy, authoritarian faculty banned the team from the lawn and the players moved to a clumpy clearing near the baseball diamond where they practiced and played home games. A running track was added, but the fields were in poor condition and the students began to demand something better. The board of trustees agreed and in March 1891 approved the design of an athletic complex a quarter mile or so away and authorized a miniscule $150 to cover the construction costs.

Led by the monthly school newspaper, the *Free Lance*, the students went looking for a donor to assist in the project. They zeroed in on trustee Charles Roberts, a businessman from West Chester known as Captain Roberts because of his service in the Civil War, who had already helped fund a new academic building and women's residence hall.

Whether Capt. Roberts ever donated is unknown, but that's when the General came to the rescue: James Beaver, a brigadier general in the Civil War who lost a leg in combat and would forever be referred to as General Beaver. He is probably the most important man in the history of the school. A native of the Lewistown area and a Bellefonte lawyer, General Beaver was a Penn State trustee from 1873 until his election as governor of Pennsylvania in 1886. During his last year as governor in 1891 he induced a $3,000 appropriation from the legislature for the athletic venture.

By the spring of 1892 the new area was ready, complete with a cinder track surrounding the football-baseball playing field, and a 500-seat grandstand was being planned for 1893. That March, the *Free Lance* urged the 244-person student body to name the new athletic facility for a past benefactor or someone willing to "donate a liberal sum" to have it named in their honor. (Those young *Free Lance* writers were certainly ahead of the time with this proposal for naming rights!)

"We would like to mention two names that deserve more than passing attention when it comes to the consideration of to whom we should pay honor," the *Free Lance* suggested. "Gen. James A. Beaver and Capt. Chas. W. Roberts are two names so intimately connected with the history and success of our college, that it would be impossible to make a more fitting choice than one of these names."

By then, General Beaver was back on the school's board of trustees. Four months later, the students voted in favor of the General and thus Beaver Field was born.

General Beaver deserved the honor for more than just the funding. The school was struggling and nearly destitute in 1882 when he pushed the selection of George Atherton as the new school president. The two men teamed up to save the college, even fighting back an attempt in 1883 to turn the school into an insane asylum.

The General also had become one of the football team's biggest fans as he and his wife Mary attended games home and away. Often they were on the sideline with the players and coaches. And in an era when open gambling was legal, the General didn't hesitate to bet a few dollars on his favorite team.

The new grandstand was built in the early part of 1893 and it was an instant showcase. The roof was gabled at the center and supported by six columns with three flagpoles. There were 320 chair-type seats in tiered rows with additional bleacher benches in the back. Out of sight and beneath the grandstand was a room with lockers, closets, and a "shower bath."

Dedication was set for the only home game of the five-game 1893 season: Saturday, November 4. Penn State had never played the opponent before, but it was destiny that Western University of Pennsylvania would one day become the school's bitterest foe and familiarly known as Pitt. A severe rainstorm forced the game to be postponed until Monday, and both teams partied away the weekend together at the campus fraternities, maybe the last time that happened, too.

After the pregame dedication ceremonies Monday afternoon, the General and his lady watched with delight as Penn State won 32–0. Just how much money he won betting on the game is not known.

In 1898 the General became board president again and held the position the rest of his life. Then, when Atherton died unexpectedly in 1906, he also became the interim president of the college for two years. Meanwhile, in 1895 he had been appointed one of the judges of the first state superior court and was also still a judge when he died on January 31, 1914.

The original Beaver Field is now a parking lot behind Osmond Lab, not far from the Hetzel Student Union Building. It became known as Old Beaver Field in 1909 when a new athletic complex was constructed northwest of Old Main and also christened Beaver Field. And now you know that Beaver Stadium was not named after an animal.

54 Keith Dorney and Other Grunts

The College Football Hall of Fame has enshrined just 20 Penn State football players as of 2015, two as Nittany Lions coaches, and only one is a pure offensive lineman. That is why Penn State fans need to know about Keith Dorney.

Offensive linemen like Dorney are football's grunts, doing the unglamorous but important work and rarely being recognized for it.

"Offensive linemen are a unique breed," Hall of Fame quarterback Joe Montana wrote in the foreword to Dorney's autobiography, *Black and Blue: In the Trenches of the NFL.* "They are rarely mentioned in the press, they never get to run with the ball (much less even touch it), and the only time they get their names announced over the loudspeaker is when they've committed a holding penalty."

Dorney was a consensus first-team All-American tackle on the 1978 team that was the first in school history to be No. 1 in the nation. Of Penn State's total of 84 first-team All-Americans, only four other offensive linemen were consensus All-Americans—tackle Dave Joyner (1971), guards Sean Farrell (1981) and Jeff Hartings (1995), and center A. Q. Shipley (2008), who is the only Nittany Lion to win the Rimington Trophy as the most outstanding center in college football.

Farrell (1982) and Hartings (1994) were also two-time All-Americans along with guard Steve Wisnewski (1987–88). Five other offensive linemen were also first-team All-Americans—tackles John Nessel (1974), Bill Dugan (1980), and Chris Conlin (1986) and guards Tom Rafferty (1975) and Stephan Wisnewski (2010). These numbers do not count six All-Americans who played

Keith Dorney stands alone as Penn State's only pure offensive interior lineman to be enshrined in the College Football Hall of Fame.

both offense and defense in a different era that ended in 1996 with new unlimited substitution rules.

Dorney, Joyner, Hartings, Stefen Wisnewski, and five other offensive linemen were also examples of Joe Paterno's successful Grand Experiment as first-team Academic All-Americans.

One sportswriter who watched Dorney at Penn State wrote "he just knocked everyone down." In replying to another sportswriter who asked about Farrell, Paterno replied, "If there's a better guard in the country, he's Superman." Hartings' offensive line teammates called him "our best lineman." As for Joyner, at one time Paterno said, "Joyner may be the best tackle we've had at Penn State."

What also sets Dorney, Farrell, and Hartings apart from their fellow Nittany Lions offensive linemates is they were three-year starters at Penn State and went on to have good careers in the NFL after being first-round draft choices. In the autobiography that Dorney wrote he tells about his nine years of frustration with the Detroit Lions. Farrell spent 11 years in the NFL, mostly with Tampa Bay, and Hartings played 11 years with Detroit and Pittsburgh.

Steve Wisnewski and guard Mike Munchak had the most distinguished pro careers of all Penn State offensive linemen who were All-Americans. Wisnewski was an eight-time Pro Bowler and is probably headed to the Pro Football Hall of Fame. Munchak, a second-team All-American in 1981, is already there, the first Lion offensive lineman to be inducted after 12 years with the Houston Oilers.

Tom Rafferty was another first-team All-American at guard (1975) who had one of the best pro careers. In his 14 years with the Dallas Cowboys, he started in two Super Bowls. Tackle Irv Pankey was a third-team All-American in 1979 and a starter for the Rams in nine of his 12 pro years.

Some of Penn State's grunts never were more than honorable-mention All-Americans but they also had fine NFL careers.

Bill Lenkaitis, the center on Paterno's first two teams in 1966–67, spent three years with San Diego and 11 years as a starter in New England. Tackle Brad Benson started for the New York Giants winning Super Bowl team in 1986 in the ninth of his 10 years with the Giants. Marco Rivera, the tackle alongside Hartings on the undefeated Rose Bowl champions in 1994, was a three-time Pro Bowler in his eight years with Green Bay and two years in Dallas, playing on a Super Bowl runner-up in his rookie season. Nose tackle Pete Kugler was on three of San Francisco's Super Bowl champions in his eight years with the 49ers and Roger Duffy was a guard and center from 1990 to 2001 with the Jets and Steelers. Hartings also started on the Steelers 2005 Super Bowl–winning team.

One cannot forget about the old-time All-American offensive linemen who also played defense. Mother Dunn, Penn State's initial first-team All-American in 1906, was a center and linebacker, as was Leon Gajecki in 1940, while Sam Valentine was a guard and linebacker in 1956. Red Griffiths in 1920, Joe Bedenk in 1923, and Steve Suhey in 1947 were two-way guards and Glenn Ressler in 1964 was a center guard and nose guard.

Then there were second team All-Americans guards Stan Czarnecki (1920), Ray Baer (1921), and John Jaffurs (1943), and tackle Jules Prevost in 1924—some historians believe Prevost was Penn State's best lineman of the 1920s. And one can't forget the Lions' first-ever All-American, third-team guard Brute Randolph in 1898, and two centers who never became All-Americans, Newsh Bentz (1920–22) and Bas Gray (1923–25).

All grunts like Keith Dorney.

The Would-Be Heisman Trophy Quarterbacks

Richie Lucas and Chuck Fusina were consensus All-American quarterbacks whose names should be as familiar to Penn State fans as John Cappelletti's. Cappelletti continues to be the only Nittany Lion to win the Heisman Trophy, the most prestigious annual award in college football.

Lucas and Fusina finished second in voting in 1959 and 1978, respectively. So did Ki-Jana Carter in 1994. "Nobody remembers who finishes second," Fusina said, using a familiar quote.

That's not quite true. The College Football Hall of Fame remembered and inducted Lucas in 1986, the only Penn State quarterback so honored. Fusina has not been as fortunate, even though, like Lucas and Cappelletti, he won the Maxwell Award in 1978 as the most outstanding player in collegiate football.

Fusina doesn't think his statistics in his senior year were good enough to beat out Oklahoma's junior tailback Billy Sims. It was then the fifth-closest competition since the creation of the Heisman Trophy in 1935.

Sims led the nation in rushing while setting a Big 8 rushing record with 1,896 yards and 22 touchdowns on 275 carries that helped thrust the once-beaten Sooners into the Orange Bowl. At the same time, Fusina's passing artistry and leadership led Penn State to its first No. 1 ranking in history and the National Championship Game in the Sugar Bowl.

The voting margin for the Heisman was a mere 77 points, 827 to 750. Fusina actually received more votes for first place (163 to 151) and third (83 to 70) than Sims, who had the most second-place points (152 to 89). Michigan quarterback Rick Leach was a far third with 435 points.

Lucas was a distant second choice in the 1959 Heisman voting as LSU's halfback Billy Cannon won with 1,929 points to Lucas' 613. Cannon had more first- and second-place votes than Lucas. Don Meredith, who became more famous as a sports broadcaster and actor, was third with 286 points.

Lucas' fate as the runner-up was probably sealed in an eight-day period starting on Halloween night in Baton Rouge. No. 1 LSU was trailing No. 3 Mississippi 3–0 in the second half when Cannon electrified the crowd with a brilliant 89-yard touchdown run that won the game and was seen throughout the next week in black-and-white film on local television newscasts. The following Saturday afternoon at Beaver Field in a game between unbeaten teams, No. 4 Syracuse squeaked out a 20–18 win over No. 7 Penn State despite the steady quarterbacking and leadership of Lucas.

Nowadays, there is a season-long buildup to the Heisman Trophy and the top candidates are flown to New York for an elaborate prime-time television announcement and ceremony. It wasn't that way for Lucas and Fusina.

"I found out I came in second…when I was at an airport going someplace," Lucas recalled in the book *What It Means to Be a Nittany Lion*. "It was in the paper. I actually had no idea what the Heisman was."

Fusina remembered seeing his name mentioned in the newspapers late in the season but "didn't give it much thought." He was getting ready to go to dinner with roommate Tony Petruccio when he had a telephone call telling him he finished second. "I was sort of surprised because I did not have a very good year statistically," he wrote. "But our team did well."

Fusina actually had a pretty good year in 1978, passing for 1,859 yards and 11 touchdowns. But the previous year he had broken the record for single-season passing yardage with 2,221 yards and tied the team record with 12 touchdown passes. He is still fifth in career passing with 5,382 yards and 37 touchdowns, completing 371 of 665 attempts with 32 interceptions. When he graduated, Coach Joe Paterno said Fusina was "without question the best quarterback we've had in my 29 years at Penn State."

Although Lucas led the 1958 and 1959 teams in passing, it wasn't his specialty. He was an exceptional ball handler and runner who called his own plays and, with the assistance of sports information director Jim Tarman, earned the nickname Riverboat Richie for his daring, gambler-like instincts on the field. Coach Rip Engle called Lucas "the modern version of the old triple threat player. He runs, passes, punts, blocks, holds the ball on extra point attempts. and is an excellent defensive player both against running and passing....he's the complete man, the player who does it all."

Nether Lucas nor Fusina fared well in the pros. Lucas was the first draft choice of both Washington in the NFL and Buffalo of the new AFL, but injuries at Buffalo ended his career after two years. Fusina led Philadelphia/Baltimore of the fledgling United States Football League to two championships in his three USFL years, but his four years in the NFL were spent as a backup.

As for Carter, he finished 842 points behind Colorado's Rashaan Salaam and even with the votes of his teammate, Kerry Collins, who was fourth, Carter would not have won the trophy.

"Nobody remembers who finishes second," eh? Now you do for the Heisman Trophy: Lucas, Fusina, and Carter.

56 Ride the Blue Buses

They are ordinary school buses painted dark blue instead of yellow. Before they became a Penn State football tradition, they were a necessity.

It all goes back to the opening of Beaver Stadium in 1960 in what had been an isolated area on the far western edge of the campus. Cows used to graze there during the day and student lovers parked there late at night. With the move from New Beaver Field to the stadium, a new football building and practice fields were constructed about an eighth of a mile south of the stadium along University Drive.

Penn State's Beaver Stadium dressing room under the northwest corner grandstands was small and dank with limited showers, almost a carbon copy of the one at Beaver Field. The football staff decided to utilize the expansive locker room in the football facility, now known as the East Area Locker Room Building, before and after the game. The stadium dressing room was used primarily for pregame and halftime.

So on September 17, 1960, the blue buses began carrying the players in their full uniforms up to the stadium and back to the East Area Locker Room, with a police escort to move quickly through the crowds and traffic. No one could have believed the rickety old blue school buses would become tradition involving the fans.

"We didn't think much about riding the buses at the time," the captain of the 1960 team, Hank Opperman, told me recently. "We had to do it because we no longer had the locker room in the water tower outside Beaver Field. I don't even remember the color of the buses. It certainly has become a phenomenal tradition."

It's a tradition now, but it actually took four decades to evolve.

In the early years, a small contingent of fans, mostly parents and relatives of players, would greet the buses outside the stadium locker room entrance underneath the press box. There would be some cheers as the players departed, but it was so low-key that most of the fans who went to games back then hardly paid attention.

All-American linebacker Greg Buttle, one of the Nittany Lions' true characters, described in his own waggish style what it was like to ride those "ugly, blue 'only at Penn State' buses" when he played from 1972 to 1975: "The 'Very Serious Defense' and coaches were always on bus No. 1, 'Serious Offense' and coaches on bus No. 2, 'Mildly Serious Backups' on bus No. 3, and the rest of the team and the 'Not Quite Really Serious At All Guys' on bus No. 4. Now, bus No. 4, affectionately known by us all as the 'Mops Bus,' was a perfect hiding place for the not-so-serious-until-kickoff-but-ready-to-play guys [like me]."

As part of a major Beaver Stadium expansion before the 1978 season, Penn State constructed a new locker room in a separate building straddling a fence at the south gate. The players were able to dress there, but the buses were still used to transport the players from either the football building or the hotel where they had stayed overnight. It was still rather subdued.

It wasn't until the last major stadium reconstruction and expansion project before the 2001 season that the tradition of welcoming the buses really took hold. New locker and media rooms were built at the south end separated by a tunnel entrance that led directly to the locker room door. Hundreds of fans began congregating to cheer the team three hours before kickoff, with Paterno and the starting quarterback being the first ones off bus No. 1.

Coach James Franklin altered the tradition in 2014 by having the buses stop a half block before the tunnel entrance. Now the players get off near the student gate, where hundreds of students who camped out overnight for three days are lined up to get the best seats. From there, the players walk to the tunnel entrance through a roped-off area between a phalanx of cheering fans on both sides. Such "walks" are a tradition at many colleges, particularly in the SEC. The Penn State fans love the new twist so much they start lining up along Curtin Road hours before the buses arrive.

Fans can ride those fabled blue buses just like the players and coaches. In cooperation with the football staff, the Penn State All-Sports Museum began special Blue Bus excursions in 2015. The tours start at the Lasch Building football facility—across from the East Area Locker Room, which is still used by other varsity teams—and includes various player meeting rooms, the weight room, and practice fields. Then the buses take the participants to Beaver Stadium on the same route they travel in the fall, unloading near the tunnel entrance. The itinerary continues into the home-team locker room, a walk through the inside tunnel onto the field, and a final stop at the media room. There is a fee, and tours are limited to a few times annually during February, May, and July.

Riding the blue buses: a must-do for Penn State fans.

57 Joe, Bobby, and the Bear

Joe Paterno, Bobby Bowden, and Paul "Bear" Bryant: they are the winningest coaches in major college football and their lives were intertwined over decades. They were rivals on the field but friends off it.

Bryant was already a successful head coach when Paterno and Bowden met him, and it was Bryant who broke the 35-year victory record of Amos Alonzo Stagg in 1981 by beating Paterno's Penn State team 31–16 at Beaver Stadium. Paterno surpassed Bear's 323 wins in 2001 with a 29–27 victory over Ohio State at Beaver

Penn State's Joe Paterno shakes hands with Alabama's Bear Bryant after Alabama beat Penn State 31–16 at Beaver Stadium, tying Bryant with Amos Alonzo Stagg's all-time coaching record of 314 wins. This was Bryant's only visit to Penn State.

Stadium. Bowden officially passed Paterno in 2003, but when Paterno's career ended in November 2011 he was on top again with 409 victories and the retired Bowden was a far second at 346. (Since Paterno's 324th victory, the NCAA revised the official coaching records and moved Glenn "Pop" Warner ahead of Stagg with 319 victories.)

Go behind the numbers and you find intense on-field competition with the older coach besting his younger rival. Paterno couldn't beat Bryant in four games but lost only one of eight to Bowden. Paterno's most devastating defeat was against Bryant for the 1978 national championship in the Sugar Bowl.

"It got to me," Paterno later wrote in his autobiography. "It hammered at my ego. When I stood toe to toe with Bear Bryant, he outcoached me."

Bowden was equally frustrated with his record against Paterno, six defeats while coaching at West Virginia, and the most disheartening loss of all in Florida State's 26–23 triple-overtime defeat at the 2006 Orange Bowl. "If you play Joe, you better get ready for a great defense, an offense that doesn't beat itself and a solid kicking," Bowden wrote in *State College* magazine in 2008. "He finds a way to beat you."

Paterno was still an assistant coach for Rip Engle when he met both Bryant and Bowden. He was introduced to Bryant at a coaches' clinic in the 1950s and then was on the sidelines at the 1959 Liberty Bowl when Penn State beat Bear's second Alabama team 7–0.

In 1968 Paterno won his first Coach of the Year Award, and at the banquet, he was seated next to Bryant, "the nearest thing we had to a god in football," Paterno wrote later. The conversation was an eye-opener for the 41-year-old Paterno about a different college football world than Paterno lived in, one that would never fit him.

The Winningest Major College Coaches

Joe Paterno (Penn State): 1966–2011 Record: 409–136–3

Bobby Bowden (Samford, West Virginia, Florida State): 1959–62, 1970–2009 Record: 377–129–4

Paul "Bear" Bryant (Maryland, Kentucky, Texas A&M, Alabama): 1945–82 Record: 323–85–17

Glenn "Pop" Warner (Cornell, Georgia, Carlisle Indians, Pittsburgh, Stanford, Temple): 1895–1938 Record: 319–106–32

Amos Alonzo Stagg (Yale, Springfield, Chicago, Pacific): 1890–1946 Record: 314–199–35

Roy Kidd (Eastern Kentucky): 1964–2002 Record: 314–124–8

Despite their diverse styles, Bryant and Paterno became friends, almost like the relationship of an older uncle to a nephew. Bryant's untimely death at age 69 a month after his retirement at the end of the 1982 season was an unspoken influence on Paterno's adamant desire to continue coaching into his eighties. "What would I do? I'm enjoying what I'm doing," Paterno often replied when asked why he was still coaching.

Bowden was the head coach at little Howard College in Birmingham, now known as Samford, when he watched the Lions beat Georgia Tech in the 1961 Gator Bowl. In the spring of 1963 Bowden asked head coach Rip Engle if he could visit Penn State and Engle said yes. Bowden took a train to Pittsburgh and Lewistown and hitchhiked into State College to watch Penn State practice for a few days. "When Coach Engle went to buy Joe a wedding present, he took me with him," Bowden wrote. "He picked out a beautiful lamp for Joe and Sue. The owner of the shop gave me a silver dollar and I [still] have it...."

Over the years, Bowden said he often called Paterno for advice about his team. He and his wife, Ann, became friends of Joe and Sue, spending five days together at the annual NIKE gatherings. "I'm proud to say that he is my compatriot and friend," Bowden wrote.

"Bobby Bowden is one of the great coaches, if not the greatest that's ever coached," Paterno told the media before the 2006 Orange Bowl. "Bobby's been a friend."

There is an underlying controversy among the fans and media of Penn State, Alabama, and Florida State concerning the victories of the three winningest coaches. It stems primarily from the Penn State child abuse scandal and the NCAA's decision to vacate 12 of Bowden's FSU victories for rule violations while officially including 31 of his wins at Howard. Even adding Bowden's 12 vacated victories would not pass Paterno.

However, many fans and media in the Alabama and FSU camps believe Paterno's involvement in the child abuse case, no matter how deep or how inconsequential, is reason to exclude 111 victories as the NCAA initially did for three years before admitting in 2014 it had no jurisdiction to do so. This controversy may not be resolved until the full truth emerges about Paterno and the Penn State scandal, and that may take years, if not decades.

So right now it is Joe, Bear, and Bobby, and no one else is even close.

58 1978: Losing the National Championship

Penn State's 1978 football team may have had the most overall talent on offense and defense of any in school history. It was the first one to reach No. 1 and the first to play for the national championship on the field, just like Joe Paterno had wanted since becoming the head coach in 1966.

Unfortunately, it lost the title game to Alabama at the Sugar Bowl in one of those historic "battles of inches." Nowadays, the accomplishments of that 1978 squad are mostly the fodder of trivial questions.

"Nobody remembers who finishes second," said quarterback Chuck Fusina, who finished a close second himself by just 87 total votes in the Heisman Trophy balloting that year. "I don't care what it is. Nobody remembers who finishes second in the Super Bowl either, but that's just how it is."

What people especially remember, however, is Alabama's climatic fourth-quarter goal-line stand: Mike Guman's unsuccessful fourth-and-inches plunge up the middle that was immortalized forever on the cover of *Sports Illustrated*. That moment (and that photo) is almost like the Holy Grail for Alabama fans. That's why a large blowup of the *SI* cover photo is displayed prominently in the Bryant Museum in Tuscaloosa, and why this game is No. 22 in *100 Things Crimson Tide Fans Should Know & Do Before They Die*. What's mostly forgotten by nearly everyone except the Penn State players nowadays are the half dozen or so other plays that could have changed the outcome, such as:

- The Scott Fitzkee pass reception that ended on the Alabama 1-yard line instead of the end zone two plays before the fateful Guman dive;
- The 61-yard Alabama punt return against the Lions' outstanding special teams unit that set up the winning touchdown;
- The controversial second-quarter touchdown catch by an Alabama receiver who dropped the ball but was given the touchdown by an official despite what a TV replay showed;
- The obvious interference that wasn't called on a pass to tight end Brad Scovill at the Alabama goal line late in the game;
- The 12-men-on-the-field penalty that negated a fourth-quarter PSU scoring opportunity following a shanked Alabama punt at the Alabama 20-yard line.

The failure at the goal line was the worst and one of the players in the middle of the pile is still bothered by it.

"To lose like that—to be that close and then be denied—was devastating," tackle Keith Dorney wrote in *What It Means to Be a Nittany Lion*. "How could it have slipped away?"

Fusina and Dorney were consensus All-Americans, and so was defensive tackle Bruce Clark. Fusina won the Maxwell Award as the most outstanding player in college football, and Clark is the only Nittany Lion to win the Lombardi Award presented to the nation's best defensive lineman or linebacker. Dorney is the only member of the team enshrined in the College Football Hall of Fame.

Defensive tackle Matt Millen, defensive back Pete Harris, and kicker Matt Bahr also were selected to various first-team All-American squads, making a total of six, the most of any team in Penn State's history. Except for Harris, they all played in the NFL along with such teammates as Guman, Fitzkee, linebackers Lance Mehl and Rich Milot, defensive end Larry Kubin, and offensive linemen Irv Pankey, Chuck Correal, and Pete Kugler.

The eventual showdown with No. 2 Alabama may have been preordained by the stars. Alabama had been the consensus preseason No. 1 and Penn State the consensus No. 3. However, in late September, USC upset Alabama, dropping the Crimson Tide to No 7. Meanwhile, the Nittany Lions were methodically working their way up to the top of the mountain, after avoiding an opening game upset against underdog Temple, winning 10–7 on a last-minute 23-yard field goal by Bahr. Two weeks later, the Lions proved their worth by shutting out then–No. 6 Ohio State 19–0 in Columbus.

The crucial game in their climb to No. 1 was against Maryland in the ninth game of the season. It was another of those Battle of Unbeatens with the Lions ranked No. 2 and the Terrapins No. 5. With a record crowd of 78,019 looking on in recently expanded Beaver Stadium, Penn State overwhelmed Maryland 27–3 as the star-studded Lions defense limited the high-powered Terps offense to minus-32 yards on 43 carries while picking up five sacks and five interceptions.

After coming from behind the following week to beat North Carolina State 19–10 at Beaver Stadium, the 1978 team made history when the Associated Press and United Press International coaches polls were released on November 18 and Penn State was No. 1 for the first time.

In those days, the bowl matchups were still being finalized before the end of the regular season. Penn State seemed to be headed toward the Orange Bowl and a meeting with No. 2

Nebraska until Missouri upset the Cornhuskers. That set up Penn State against Alabama and both won their last games of the regular season to make it the National Championship Game.

Despite its 14–7 win over Penn State, Alabama had to share the 1978 AP title with UPI champion USC.

"It would take me years—decades to shed the bad memories of that last damn game," Dorney wrote. "It still hurts when I think about it."

59 Attend Lift for Life

Nothing epitomizes the true Penn State football culture, and not the false narrative of the critics since November 2011, than Lift for Life.

What started at Penn State in 2003 as a strength-training and exercise competition to raise money for the Kidney Cancer Association has spread to other college football teams nationwide. One year after the first Lift for Life, the Penn State players who created it formed a nonprofit corporation called Uplifting Athletes to expand the fund-raising beyond a single annual event.

In 2007 Uplifting Athletes went national with Penn State as the model for other programs. As of the spring of 2015, Uplifting Athletes had a network of more than 25 chapters with at least one chapter in every major conference, including half the Big Ten and ACC.

"Each of the football student-athlete led chapters raises aware-ness and research dollars for their individual chosen rare disease by holding a Lift For Life or an alternative event each year," states the Uplifting Athletes website, http://www.upliftingathletes.org.

For example, 2014 national champion Ohio State raises money for research of Charcot-Marie Tooth Disease and 2013 national champion Florida State supports research for Fanconi anemia, while Notre Dame funds osteosarcoma research and Baylor helps fight cerebral palsy. At least half the chapter schools hold annual Lift for Life events. Other projects include golf tournaments, tailgate barbecue challenges, 5K road races, and touchdown pledge drives with money donated for each touchdown a team scores in a specific game.

Since 2012 Penn State's Uplifting Athletes have held a fundraising black-tie Gridiron Gala in mid-March in Harrisburg featuring many former Nittany Lions players and a silent auction. The gala is a long way from the first Lift for Life event inside Holuba Hall, the football team's indoor facility, on July 3, 2003.

It all started with Scott Shirley, who was a senior walk-on wide receiver from Mechanicsburg in the fall of 2002 when he learned that his father, Don, had incurable kidney cancer and was given six months to live. Shirley and teammates Damone Jones and Dave Costlow came up with the concept of strength training and conditioning and coach Joe Paterno and his staff bought into it.

Fifteen teams of four showed up at 6:00 AM to begin competing in various exercises from traditional weight lifting to a 200-yard sprint while carrying 100-pound plates in either hand. Some 200 people, mostly families and friends of players, were there throughout the morning and early afternoon on that Fourth of July weekend and Lift for Life raised just less than $13,000.

The next year, the players moved the event permanently to the four-day weekend of the popular State College Arts Festival that attracts exhibitors and visitors from throughout the nation. Over time, the players tweaked the format, and when the new strength coach Craig Fitzgerald devised new and unique exercises in 2012, Lift for Life moved outdoors to the lacrosse field across the street.

Instead of two-man teams then in vogue, Fitzgerald matched the offense against the defense in such exercises as heaving a 20-pound medicine ball over their heads over goal posts, pushing a 6,400-pound van across the field, and shuttling 100-pound sandbags. The day climaxed with a crowd-pleasing tug-of-war and the defense was declared the winner in Fitzgerald's point-scoring system, 176–146. A record crowd of more than 2,500 helped Lift for Life raise a record amount in excess of $110,000.

The money and the crowds have continued to increase in the outdoor format with $133,500 raised in 2013 and more than $140,000 generated in 2014. Money from ancillary projects pushed the chapter's total fund-raising for kidney cancer research to nearly $1 million.

Coaches vs. Cancer and the Pink Zone

Penn State's men's and women's basketball teams support two of the more notable fund-raising efforts emanating from the athletic department.

The prime events for the men's Coaches vs. Cancer effort are the spring golf tournament, winter game day silent auction, and car raffle. The women's main events are the Pink Zone game in March and a one-mile run in April.

The men's team raises money for the American Cancer Society and two local groups. Since the start of its celebrity golf tournament in 1997, more than $2 million has gone to fight cancer.

"It takes a team effort to make a difference in the fight against cancer in our community and beyond, and that's our goal," said men's coach Patrick Chambers.

The women's team has contributed more than $1.3 million on behalf of breast cancer victims to several organizations, including the Pennsylvania Breast Cancer Coalition.

"Pink Zone is a day where we get to be inspired by what we see," said women's coach Coquese Washington after more than 650 cancer survivors all dressed in pink were honored at halftime of the 2015 game. "It's just a big celebration of surviving and fighting."

"The first Lift for Life was inspiring for many reasons," Shirley told me. "The most important lesson that we learned, though, was that we truly were in a position to inspire rare disease patients with hope. We really were just a couple of naive college kids when this all started. From the very first conversation with Damone, we envisioned this as a national movement. We just had no idea how challenging it would be or a plan for how to actually accomplish it."

From its humble beginning with Shirley, Jones, and Costlow, the Penn State chapter has evolved into a nine-man leadership council with a president, vice president, and secretary at the top. They continually try to create new ways to raise funds. During the 2015 NFL Combine in Indianapolis, tight end Jesse James, the chapter erstwhile director of marketing, raised $5,461 by completing 26 260-pound bench-press repetitions.

Shirley wanted to do more for cancer research after he graduated in 2004, and that's why he led the creation of Uplifting Athletes in 2004. Three years later he left his job as mechanical engineer to be the executive director of the organization, which has a six-man board of directors. Shirley is the only former Penn State football player on it.

"I'm amazed every time I take a step back and reflect on the progress we've made," Shirley said. "Seeing [Coach] Jimbo Fisher raising the national championship trophy for Florida State [in 2013] with our wristband in plain sight was very gratifying. We've had over a $400 million impact on the rare disease community. I believe in the power of sport for social good and I am not alone. The future looks brighter every day."

Uplifting Athletes and Lift for Life. That's the true culture of Penn State football.

60 Watch the Homecoming Parade

You don't have to be a football fan to enjoy one of the most enduring and popular Penn State traditions. Watching the homecoming parade on campus or downtown State College the Friday night before the annual homecoming football game is a must-do for everyone, not just returning alumni.

It's been going on since October 8, 1920, rain or shine. There are the usual bands, floats, student military contingents marching in cadence, clowns, fire trucks, magicians, dance teams, specialty performers, celebrities, and other groups, all led by a grand marshal selected by the student-run Homecoming Committee. Over the years the grand marshals have included some famous alumni such as ABC-TV's Lara Spencer, Olympic skating medalist Allison Baver, and astronaut Guion Bluford.

Individual fraternities and sororities join forces to build the most attractive themed floats like pirate ships, tropical islands, and farms. Penn State alumni chapters from around the world send members to march behind special chapter banners. Awards are given to the best floats and the best-looking banners that are carried ahead of each parade entry. Sometimes football players ride in vehicles or flat beds. Clowns roam up and down the street passing out candy and trinkets while T-shirts are thrown by other marchers.

John Black, who writes the popular football alumni *Football Newsletter*, has seen 49 parades as of 2014.

"Homecoming is one the great traditions at Penn State and one of the highlights is the Homecoming Parade, which is the largest in the nation, featuring hundreds of marching units," he told me. "It's watched by thousands as it winds its way for two miles across campus and through downtown State College."

The parade route takes two to three hours from start to finish. After the parade, there's now a candlelight rally on the steps of Old Main, featuring various campus singing groups and the parade's grand marshal.

At around the same time, some alumni gather with the student service group, the Lion Ambassadors, and dozens of others at the Nittany Lion Shrine across from Rec Hall for the annual Guarding the Shrine event.

The roots of Penn State's homecoming weekend go all the way back to 1869. In his book, *Penn State: An Illustrated History*, Mike Bezilla details President Thomas Burrows believing graduates and former students would return for "a kind of open house" aimed at parents, perspective students, farmers, and others to "inspect the College."

Burrows called it Harvest Home and the first one in July 1869 was a bust, but the next year it drew 2,000 people. The old grads who showed up held an organizational meeting that four years later resulted in the official formation of the Penn State Alumni Association. However, when Burrows died the following February, the Harvest Home event did too.

In the early 1900s, Penn State began holding an annual Pennsylvania Day at one home football game to honor the governor, legislators, and other dignitaries and to attract out-of-town visitors. In addition to speeches, the football game, and partying, the VIPs also reviewed the parade of the college cadet corps and band. "Pennsylvania Day has become second only to Commencement…because of the large assemblage of visitors at the college on this day," read an editorial in the student newspaper on November 12, 1914.

Many alumni would return for the Pennsylvania Day activities, but it wasn't until 1920 that administrators in Old Main decided to honor past graduates with a special weekend. They called it Alumni Home-Coming.

A series of parties, rallies, and other events were planned around the Saturday afternoon football game against Dartmouth on October 9. The alums began streaming into town Thursday afternoon by car, train, and buggy. By Friday evening, the town and campus were jumping and the Penn State marching band paraded around town. On Saturday morning, some 4,000 people congregated in front of Old Main for a welcoming speech by the governor.

Afterward, many in the crowd went to Beaver Field to watch the football and soccer games, and both teams made the alumni happy with victories. The football Lions beat Dartmouth 14–7, and the soccer team beat Haverford 3–1. Saturday night was filled with fraternity parties and a special reception at the Armory featuring the glee club, speeches by football coach Hugo Bezdek and President Sparks, and alumni secretary Mike Sullivan, as well as "cider, pretzels, and smokes."

The *Penn State Collegian* was ecstatic in its editorial of October 12: "What a memorable week-end has just been passed!, What a glorious period in the annals of this college…Penn State alumni who were able to return for the great event will ever remember these glorious days at the old college…It is our sincere wish that all alumni might 'come home' sometime each college year."

Shortly after the weekend, the president, football coach, and alumni secretary decided to make "Home-Coming" an annual event "set aside purely for alumni and everything turned over in the advancement of their interests."

So, watch the homecoming parade, applaud the homecoming king and queen when they are introduced at halftime of the homecoming football game, and enjoy the cider, pretzels and other food and drinks that weekend, but forget about those "smokes." They're no longer part of the tradition.

61 Salt and Pepper

Matt Millen was not the best defensive tackle who ever played for Penn State, but he was, and still is, the most controversial.

Millen was the "bad boy" of coach Joe Paterno's teams in the late 1970s. He was a first-team All-American in his junior year when chosen by United Press International and Walter Camp. But his teammate at the other defensive tackle spot, Bruce Clark, was a consensus All-American in 1978 and 1979, and as a junior won the Lombardi Award, still the only Penn State player to win the award. Clark was a finalist in 1979 and so was Millen.

The Lombardi Award, named after legendary coach Vince Lombardi, is presented to the offensive or defensive lineman or linebacker, who, in addition to outstanding performance best exemplifies the discipline of Lombardi.

It's that word *discipline* that didn't quite equate with Millen's character back then. The most glaring example is now legendary when talking about Millen. He had been elected a co-captain before his senior year, but when he refused to run two half-mile drills in preseason practice Coach Joe Paterno stripped him of his captain. When that 1979 team did not play well, finishing with a disappointing 8–4 record, Paterno traced part of the reason back to Millen's running revolt.

"Two days later, Matt made the run with no problem," the coach wrote in his autobiography, *Paterno: By the Book*, "but the morale and concentration of the team were severely shaken."

Millen apologized shortly afterward, but the incident has continued to follow him. "I wasn't a real leader like I should have been on the field," he said years later. "I think it set the tone for the team, and, psychologically, it hurt the team."

Millen has been a bit of a rebel all his life. He makes no apologies for being outspoken, even today as a well-known football analyst on TV and former president and general manager of the Detroit Lions. He certainly was different from Bruce Clark.

First of all, Millen was white and Clark was African American. That had absolutely no impact on how they played. They first teamed up as freshmen inside linebackers, starting six games, and then moved to the starting two defensive tackle spots in 1977.

Matt Millen (Salt) and Bruce Clark (Pepper) pose with assistant coach J. T. White in 1978. Millen and Clark were one of the two best defensive tackle tandems of the Joe Paterno coaching era, rivaling Mike Reid and Steve Smear of the late 1960s.

They were so compatible that they eventually gave themselves their lasting nickname of Salt and Pepper.

The only tandem of Penn State defensive tackles that rivaled Clark and Millen on the field in the Paterno era were Mike Reid

The Best Defensive Linemen

Only one pure Penn State defensive lineman is in the College Football Hall of Fame: Mike Reid.

Twenty-five other defensive linemen were first-team All-Americans, dating back to end Bob Higgins in 1915 and 1919. That's when players had to play both offense and defense, an epoch that lasted until 1966. Before Higgins, end Dex Very was picked as a second-team All-American (1911–12) and he's also in the College Football Hall of Fame. Long after, Higgins, Sam Tamburo (1948), Bob Mitinger (1961), and Dave Robinson (1962) were also two-way ends.

Middle guard Glenn Ressler (1964) is in the Hall of Fame too. Some guards in that two-way era were linebackers, but most were on the defensive line like Red Griffiths (1920), Joe Bedenk (1923), and Steve Suhey (1947).

Since Reid, the first team All-American defensive tackles were Randy Crowder (1973), Randy Sidler (1977), Millen and Clark, Tim Johnson (1986), Lou Benfatti (1993), Jimmy Kennedy (2002), Jared Odrick (2009), and Devon Still (2011). The first-team All-American ends since 1966 were Bruce Bannon (1972), Mike Hartenstine (1974), Walker Lee Ashley (1982), Courtney Brown (1999), Michael Haynes (2002), Tamba Hali (2005), and Aaron Maybin (2008).

Still, there have been other players in that two-way era who were among Penn State's best in history. Some were chosen second-team All-Americans like guards Stan Czarnecki (1920), Ray Baer (1922), and John Jaffurs (1943), tackle Jules Provost (1924), and end Stan McCollum (1921). Guard Brute Randolph, the school's first All-American was a third-team pick in 1894. John Potsklan is considered one of the all-time ends on defense, but his prime football years were spent in World War II after playing on Penn State's best-ever freshman team in 1941. He survived heavy combat and a German prison camp to become the co-captain of Penn State's great Cotton Bowl team of 1947.

Defensive Line U, anyone?

and Steve Smear, co-captains of the great 1968–69 teams. Clark and Millen are still among the career leaders in career quarterback sacks and tackles for loss. Millen is fifth in sacks with 22 while Clark is tied for ninth with 19. Clark is tied for fourth in tackles for loss with 43 and Millen is tied for eighth with 36. As sophomores on the 1977 team that lost only one game and was ranked fifth in the country, they led the defense in sacks with six apiece.

Salt and Pepper also were prime factors in the 1978 team becoming the first in Penn State history to be ranked No. 1, and Millen is still upset at losing the National Championship Game to Alabama in the Sugar Bowl.

"I never took a shower," Millen remembered. "I just changed and walked back to the hotel. I was disgusted."

Before Millen's running incident in 1979, Paterno said, "Bruce and Matt may be the two best players in the country and they certainly are the best pair of defensive linemen…." And then, everything went sour.

When the 1979 season ended, Clark seemed headed for pro football glory with Millen a question mark. It went the other way.

Clark was the fourth player chosen in the 1980 NFL draft, but when Green Bay wanted its No. 1 choice to play nose guard he bolted for the Canadian Football League. He returned in 1982 and played seven years with New Orleans and one year with Kansas City, playing in the 1985 Pro Bowl.

Millen was taken in the second round by Oakland, moved to inside linebacker, and went on to play in four Super Bowls with three different teams. He was a starter his entire 12-year career, nine with the Raiders, two with San Francisco, and his last season with Washington.

You can see Pepper's Lombardi Trophy in the Penn State All-Sports Museum. You can watch Salt on television.

62 Kickin' with Ficken and the Bahr Brothers

If you want to start a good argument, ask any Penn Stater who is the team's best-ever field goal and extra point kicker.

You should get a lot of answers. The Bahr brothers, Chris and Matt, will top many lists. Kevin Kelly, Robbie Gould, Craig Fayak, and Brett Conway will be up there, too. So will Travis Forney, Massimo Manca, and Nick Gancitano. And if you ask historians, Pete Mauthe from the early 1900s is also in the mix.

Great kickers all. But none encountered what Sam Ficken did from 2012 to 2014. Kicking is mental as much as athletic. That's why opposing teams sometimes call timeouts moments before kicks. They're trying to get into the kicker's psyche. Ficken not only had to survive one of the worst debuts of a kicker in Penn State history, but also three years of the debilitating NCAA sanctions and adversity in the aftermath of the child abuse scandal.

Kicking specialists were not an integral part of Penn State football until 1971, when Italian native Albert Vitiello of Nassau (NY) Community College became the school's first junior college player transfer. He also was the team's first soccer-style kicker, and was left-footed, too. Vitiello broke most school kicking records in his two years, but all have been surpassed.

Chris Bahr took over in 1973 and he was already a junior star on the Penn State soccer team, which had originally recruited him. He wasn't on a football scholarship until his soccer eligibility ran out, and in his first two seasons he hardly practiced with the football team.

"More than once I played soccer on Friday night and then caught a plane for a football game," Chris told this writer.

Matt Bahr was on a football scholarship when he succeed his brother in 1976, but also was a star on the soccer team, then being coached by his father, Walter. The Bahr brothers remain the only two Penn State kickers selected as first-team All-Americans. Before Matt was done after 1978, he and Chris held most of Penn State's kicking records. Matt is still tied for seventh in career field goals (39) and Chris is 10th (35). With his 22 field goals in 1978, Matt is tied with Kevin Kelly for second in most field goals in a season behind Ficken's record 24, and Chris is tied with Brett Conway for sixth with his 18 in 1975.

Chris continues to hold the record for the longest field goal, making three 55-yard kicks in 1975. Matt is tied with Manca for the most field goals in four games (four). However, the record for most field goals in a game is five, and that's held by Manca, Forney, Brian Franco, and Colin Wagner.

When you count their success in the NFL, the Bahr brothers lead the pack, although Robbie Gould is coming on fast after his first 10 years with Chicago. In his 14-year career with the Oakland/Los Angeles Raiders, Cincinnati, and San Diego, Chris kicked in two Super Bowls (winning in 1981 and 1984). Matt played in the NFL longer than any Penn State player. His 17 years with six different teams included Super Bowl victories in Pittsburgh (1979–80) and New York (Giants, 1991).

"Without question, playing for Penn State helped me have a long career in the NFL," Matt said. "The average lifetime in the NFL is 3.2 years, and a kicker's average life is less."

Of Penn State's top 10 career field goal kickers, only the Bahr brothers, Gould, Conway, and Manca played in the NFL. Conway kicked four-plus years for Washington and two other years for four different teams while Manca was briefly with Cincinnati. Sixteen years later Manca helped save the 2012 season when he reached out to help Ficken make it through his early struggles.

Ficken, then a sophomore, unexpectedly became the Lions' place kicker when Anthony Fera left for Texas under the special eligibility rules included in the NCAA's 2012 sanctions. In Penn State's second game at Virginia, Ficken missed four field goals, including a 42-yard attempt with one second left, and was blamed

Joe Colone

Jeremy Boone holds the Penn State career record for punting based on his three-year average of 43.1 on 151 punts from 2007 to 2009. Jeremy Kapinos' 251 punts from 2003 to 2006 are the most for any Lions punter in the record books. But old-timer Joe Colone may have been the best of all, statistics be damned.

Colone kicked some great ones and his freshman year punting in 1942 before he left for World War I isn't even counted in the record book. His three year average from 1946–48 of 37.15 yards per punt (79) is just short of Penn State's top 12 career punters.

Colone may have been Penn State's most versatile and accurate punter of all time. The weather never bothered him and some of his best punts were with a wet ball. He could place the ball wherever he wanted to, whether it was for a long distance or a short one. And he was a master at quick-kicks, then in vogue in that period of power-running single-wing football, often kicking 50–60 yards with his powerful leg.

Look at the Penn State record books and you'll see that he is tied with just Boone and Kapinos as the only punters with three kicks greater than 65 yards. His 71-yard punt in a driving rain that helped beat Syracuse 9–0 at Archbold Stadium in 1946 is the sixth-longest of all time. He also had a 66-yard quick-kick in that same game.

Unlike 11 of the 12 men at the top of Penn State's career punt leaders, Colone was not a punting specialist. He was a fullback on offense and linebacker-guard on defense and had no fear of crashing into the line with his 5'11", 200-pound body. None of the other career punting leaders ever became captain of the team, but Colone was the single captain of the 1948 team that posted an 8–1–1 record and almost went back to the Cotton Bowl.

The next time you see a Penn State player drop back in punt formation, think of Joe Colone, the greatest punter in team history.

by many fans for the 17–16 loss. With fans calling for Ficken to be replaced, his troubles continued through the next six games, failing on four of his first seven field goal attempts in that stretch and even having an extra point blocked. His slump finally ended with a 2-for-2 day in field goals and four perfect extra points in a 34–9 win at Purdue. Then he topped off his comeback with a 37-yard field goal in overtime that proved to be the game winner against Wisconsin in the last game of the season.

As Ficken continued to improve during his last two seasons, he became a darling of the fans. He topped off his career with a 45-yard field goal with 20 seconds left to tie Boston College in the 2014 Pinstripe Bowl that enabled the Lions to win 31–30 in overtime, and he left for the NFL as Penn State's fourth-leading scorer of all time.

Kickin' with Ficken and the Bahr Brothers will always be part of Penn State football.

63 Rosey and Charlie

Visitors to the Penn State All-Sports Museum are surprised when they see two photographs of Rosey Grier, one in his football crouch and another throwing the discus. They're surprised the former pro football player, actor, musician, and civil rights humanitarian played for Penn State.

There's no photo of his early 1950s teammate, Charlie Blockson, in the museum. There should be. Dr. Charles Blockson, a fullback who opened holes for Penn State's great Lenny Moore, is not a famous celebrity like Roosevelt Grier, but he is one of the world's foremost authorities on African American culture.

Both Grier and Blockson have been given Penn State's highest honor as Distinguished Alumni for their achievements after graduation, Grier in 1974 and Blockson in 2007. Neither came close to being chosen an All-American on the football field, not because of how they played. They were on teams in the early years of Coach Rip Engle that were struggling for recognition in the college football fraternity.

Grier and Blockson were part of a group of Penn State football's racial pioneers recruited by Engle that included Moore, Jesse Arnelle, and several others shortly after Engle became the head coach in 1950. Grier and Blockson were first given scholarships in track, knowing they would also play football, and Arnelle was brought in to also play basketball. Moore also ran track for two years before concentrating on football.

Track coaches Chick Werner and Norm Gordon recruited Grier. "I didn't meet the football coaches until I went there in the fall," Grier wrote in the book *What It Means to Be a Nittany Lion*.

Blockson and Moore were rivals in high school football and track. Blockson lived in Norristown and Moore in Reading, 40 miles away. Blockson also knew about Grier, a New Jersey state champion, from Roselle.

"Lenny ran on the mile relay team and was the greatest broad jumper in Pennsylvania," Blockson told this writer a few years ago. "Chick Werner told me in my senior year I had a rival in New Jersey. That was Rosey. I also saw Jesse running on a relay team for New Rochelle High School at the Penn Relays."

With very few African Americans on campus, the four quickly bonded, but Arnelle was different. He became more involved in student government. All of them faced racism off the field but rarely on the field.

"We had more blacks than any other teams outside the Big Ten," Blockson remembered. "Some of the same people that were cheering for you an hour or two hours before were walking the street downtown and they didn't even know you. We couldn't go to the fraternities. The only place we could really go was the Rathskeller, the Corner Room, and the Penn State Diner, which was open all night."

Most of their white teammates didn't socialize with them, but there was little overt racism. They all credit Engle and his staff. "Rip Engle was a fair man," Blockson said. Grier added, "Rip spoke gently…he wouldn't scream and yell at you and make you feel like nothing."

While Grier and Blockson were setting school records in track-and-field, Moore was doing the same in football and Arnelle in basketball.

They went their separate ways after graduation but remain close friends to this day. "Charlie was probably the biggest influence for me [in college] because we could talk and work through our problems," Moore said.

Grier was drafted in the third round (31st overall) by the New York Giants in 1955 and started at defensive tackle for seven years before moving to the Los Angeles Rams in 1963 and becoming part of the Rams' famous Fearsome Foursome until his retirement in 1967. Soon after he was acting in television and performing in nightclubs on the road. At the same time, Grier also became involved in civil rights and campaigning for Bobby Kennedy. He was with Kennedy the night Kennedy was assassinated in a Los Angeles hotel kitchen in 1968. For years Grier has been involved in community service working out of California.

Blockson turned down a chance to play pro football with the New York Giants and after two years in the air force went into education, teaching multiculturalism and diversity in his hometown. With roots that trace to his family escaping slavery via the Underground Railroad, he became a learned scholar in African American culture throughout the world.

Blockson is one of the leading African American bibliophiles and private collectors, lecturing and teaching all over the world. In 1982, Temple University set up the Charles L. Blockson Afro-American Collection with Blockson as curator. According to his online biography, his extensive collection includes some 1,500 items such as rare books, prints, photographs, slave narratives, manuscripts, letters, sheet music, and foreign language publications from the 1600s.

"I have spent more than 40 years amassing one of the nation's largest private collections of items relating to black history and traditions," Blockson said.

Rosey and Charlie. Not just two great Penn Staters but two great Americans.

64 Mother Dunn and Brute Randolph

Mother Dunn may be a familiar name because he is Penn State's original first-team All-American.

What you may not know is how difficult it was to be a first-team All-American in 1906, when only the selections of two men were deemed All-Americans. Any other writer, newspaper, or magazine that picked All-American teams were blithely ignored.

Today, there are more than two dozen bona fide organizations that choose All-American teams, according to the NCAA, which began keeping track of all the All-American teams in 1950. Just being on one of those teams is enough for a college to designate that player as an All-American. Get on most of those various legitimate All-American teams, and you can become a consensus All-American.

William "Mother" Dunn was named the All-American center in 1906 by Walter Camp, the official "father of American football," who also was a coach and sportswriter. While in his second year of coaching at Yale in 1889, Camp teamed up with editor-writer Casper Whitney, who is credited with originating the All-American team concept that year. Their 11-man team of all Ivy League players included two historic football figures, end Amos Alonzo Stagg and guard Pudge Heffelfinger of Yale, and a Princeton end who would become a famous writer, Edgar Allen Poe.

Whitney's All-American teams were published in various magazines until they ended in 1908. Camp started his own All-American teams in 1898 and they were released in *Collier's* magazine until Camp's death in March 1925. The International New Services began selecting All-American teams in 1913, but it wasn't until the mid-1920s that some half dozen other groups were recognized for their All-American teams.

In the first 30 years, the All-American teams were dominated by the Ivy League. It wasn't until the 10th team in 1898 that outsiders were selected from Army, Michigan, and Chicago.

Mother Dunn wasn't the first Penn State player to be on an All-American team. In Camp's inaugural team of 1898, he selected guard Carlton "Brute" Randolph to his third team. Randolph has been forgotten over the decades.

Randolph was a 6'1", 199-pounder from Lewisberry, described as a good runner who earned his nickname for his brute strength. One sportswriter said Randolph could "hit like a sledgehammer." Randolph was a junior when chosen by Camp. The next season he was captain of the team but not a Camp All-American.

Camp must have seen Randolph play in both 1898 and 1899 when two to three Ivy League schools were on Penn State's schedule. Maybe Randolph missed Camp's 1899 team after thrashings at Yale (42–0) and Penn (47–0) in back-to-back games in late November.

William "Mother" Dunn was Penn State's pioneering first-team All-American as a center-linebacker in 1906 when chosen by the "father of American football" Walter Camp.

Camp did see Dunn at least once in 1906, if not more. With Camp watching in the rain on October 20 in New Haven, unbeaten Penn State was outplaying powerful Yale late in the first half. Yale was leading 6–0 after returning a fumbled punt by Penn State for a touchdown five minutes into the game.

As the clock was winding down, Dunn blocked a Yale punt at midfield. Sophomore guard Cy Cyphers grabbed the ball and ran toward the end zone. Unfortunately, it was the wrong end zone. By the time Cyphers realized it, he was tackled at Penn State's 20-yard line. Cyphers' foul-up resulted in a field goal and eventually a 10–0 victory. "Yale's proverbial luck saved the day," one sportswriter wrote.

Dunn, a 6'1", 190-pound four-year veteran, certainly impressed Camp as a center and linebacker. In his *Collier's* magazine All-American selections, Camp wrote:

> Dunn of Penn State was the best center of the season, and it was he who led his team to such a remarkable record (8–1–1), a good deal of it depending on Dunn himself. He...is absolutely reliable in his passing, secure in blocking, active in breaking through and in diagnosing plays.... He persistently broke through and blocked kicks. Able to run the 100 in 11 seconds, he was down under his own side's kicks with the ends. Beyond all and giving him added worth was his earnestness of purpose and character.

Blocking kicks was Dunn's specialty. Newspaper summaries of games in those early decades of Penn State football document that he blocked more kicks than any State player in history, but no official records of blocked kicks were kept back then.

Dunn was 29 years old when selected by Camp. He had worked in Youngstown steel mills a few years to earn enough money to pay for college before enrolling at Penn State in 1903. Because of his maturity, he was the leader of his freshman class and that led to his nickname. He was leading fellow frosh across campus one day when an upperclassman joked, "There goes Mother Dunn leading his chickens." His nickname has lasted longer in Penn State history than his given first name.

Dunn had great personal qualities and integrity and never swore, smoked, or drank. He went to University of Pennsylvania Medical School intent on becoming a doctor in China. After interning in Hawaii, he stayed there the rest of his life as a physician and surgeon in Maui until his death in 1962.

What happened to Brute Randolph is not known.

65 Watch Wrestling's National Champions

Penn State football was known as the Beast of the East from the late 1960s until the early 1990s, when Coach Joe Paterno's teams dominated the region. Nowadays, that's the perfect appellation for Coach Cael Sanderson's wrestling teams, but their supremacy covers the entire nation, not just the region.

Four back-to-back NCAA championships from 2011 to 2014 will do that.

Since being hired away from his alma mater, Iowa State, in April 2009, Sanderson has turned the Nittany Lions into a potent force rivaling the longtime college wrestling czars, Iowa and Oklahoma State. In the process, Penn State wrestling has become a red-hot ticket with sellout, standing-room-only crowds of some 7,640 for dual meets in the intimate setting of Rec Hall.

When the match on December 8, 2013, with longtime rival Pitt was moved to the expansive Bryce Jordan Center, which is primarily a basketball and concert arena, a crowd of 15,996 set a new NCAA record for attendance at a dual meet. During the 2015 season, another dual meet with Big Ten peer Iowa almost broke that record as 15,967 fans turned out.

Penn State beat Pitt in 2013 18–12, but lost to Iowa 18–2 in 2015, making the Hawkeyes the only team to defeat the Lions three times during Sanderson's tenure. In his first four seasons, Penn State lost just one dual meet a year while posting a record of 54–4–1 with two Big Ten regular-season titles and four postseason tournament championships.

Sanderson is not the boastful type. He told the *Pittsburgh Tribune-Review* he simply likes "building stuff."

"It's about being able to put a team together and try to be the best team in the country or the best program you can be," Sanderson said. "That's exciting to me."

While winning the four NCAA team championships, Sanderson's wrestlers have won eight individual national titles through the 2015 season. That's the most ever for Penn State in a four-year period dating back to the first of 29 championships won by Howard Johnson in 1935.

Until Sanderson's arrival after four years of coaching Iowa State to three Big Ten titles and runner-up in the 2007 NCAA tournament, Penn State's venerable wrestling program was struggling. Legendary coaches Charlie Speidel (1927–42, 1947–64) and Bill Koll (1965–78) had made Nittany Lions wrestling an eastern power, winning a combined 30 EIAW/EWL team titles. Speidel's 1953 team became the first eastern team to win the NCAA tournament championship, and no other eastern team but Sanderson's four titlists have been able to duplicate that feat.

Since the NCAA tournament began in 1928, Oklahoma State has won 33 titles with 10 runners-up while Iowa has captured 23 crowns with five second-place finishes. Only Iowa State and Oklahoma with seven championships each have more than Penn State's five.

Pennsylvania has been a hotbed for scholastic wrestling for decades, and Penn State thrived on homegrown standouts in the competitive East against such schools as Pitt, Cornell, and Lehigh. The Big Ten was another matter until Sanderson. In the Lions' first Big Ten season of 1992–93 under John Fritz, they were 20–0–1 and finished second in the NCAA and Big Ten tournaments, but gradually things went awry.

In the 10 years before Sanderson was hired, the best Penn State could do in the NCAA tournament was third in 2008 and sixth in 2003 with four losing dual meet seasons and at least four defeats in each of those 10 seasons.

Penn State made Sanderson the highest-paid coach in collegiate wrestling at a base salary of $175,000 annually. With the help of donors, Sanderson immediately upgraded the wrestling facilities that now include a state-of-the-art weight room and flat-screen TVs.

Sanderson is still an active wrestler himself, and he likes to mix it up with his protégés.

"You have to do the same things you ask your kids to do," Sanderson said. "If you're telling your kids they have to believe in themselves, I have to believe in them first…If I'm telling them to work hard, then I need to work hard…It's real easy to share theory. It's another thing to practice it."

Sanderson is arguably the greatest collegiate wrestler ever. He was undefeated in 159 matches at Iowa State, a streak *Sports Illustrated* rated the No. 2 "outstanding achievement in college history." Wrestling at 184 or 197 pounds, Sanderson won three Hodge Trophies—the Heisman of collegiate wrestling—four NCAA titles, and an Olympic gold medal in 2004.

The 2015 season that ended the four-year championship streak was a rebuilding year for Sanderson and Penn State. The 11–4 dual meet record that included losses to Iowa and Oklahoma State was the Nittany Lions' worst since Sanderson's first season, but his 2015 team still finished sixth in the NCAA tournament.

A contract extension in 2012 keeps Sanderson the coach through the 2017 season. What happens after that is unknown. That's why watching wrestling at Rec Hall or the BJC is a must right now for Penn State fans.

Dick Harlow: Paterno's Godfather

Joe Paterno might never have become Penn State's famous head coach but for a pugnacious tackle on the undefeated 1911 football team who decked an Ohio State fan as an assistant coach in 1912.

Dick Harlow was a Hall of Fame coach himself after a 29-year head coaching career at Penn State, Colgate, Western Maryland, and Harvard. One of his players at Western Maryland in 1929 was an All-Maryland end named Charles "Rip" Engle, and when Engle became the new head coach at Penn State, he brought Paterno with him from Brown.

Harlow could have persuaded Engle not to take the job.

Although Harlow had been a highly regarded starting tackle for Penn State from 1910 to 1911 and a successful Nittany Lion head coach from 1915 to 1917 with a 20–8 record, he left the school in 1922 with bitterness and anger in his heart. His coaching tenure was marked by backstabbing, demeaning demands and duplicity within the Penn State athletic department and alumni.

It didn't start out that way in 1912, when Harlow became the only assistant coach for his own head coach, Bill Hollenback. Harlow was an astute scout and compelling recruiter, whose biggest coup was a New Jersey prep star, Bob Higgins, who would become a two-time All-American and another of Penn State's Hall of Fame coaches. When Hollenback left after the 1914 season Harlow was the natural successor. But the people doing the hiring wondered about his on-field coaching skills and his temper.

They reluctantly gave him the job, initially with just a one-year contract, and required him to have an assistant not connected with Penn State to help him. Harlow was well liked by his players, but his three years as head coach were contentious ones, marked by end-of-season losses to rival Pitt that upset the influential Pittsburgh alumni, who turned against him.

In July 1918 Harlow resigned to join the army in World War I. Returning the next year, he agreed to go back and be an assistant for new head coach Hugo Bezdek. It was during his second stint that Harlow started a varsity boxing team, and he is credited with helping to create intercollegiate boxing.

Harlow constantly clashed with Bezdek's abrasive personality, usually over the treatment of players. Finally, he had enough, and before the 1922 season Harlow left for the head coaching job at Colgate, taking six players with him.

After four years of winning seasons at Colgate, Harlow turned little Western Maryland (now McDaniel College) into a power, consistently beating bigger nationally known schools. His 1929 team with Engle as one of the leaders was 11–0 and two other teams were undefeated with one tie, including 1934.

That earned an invitation to play in a new postseason bowl game in Miami, but Harlow turned down the Orange Bowl so that his players could participate in the then-more-prestigious East-West Shrine Game. It also brought Harlow an offer from a more prestigious college, Harvard. Harlow was named Coach of the Year at Harvard in 1936, but he had four losing seasons in his 11 years there.

Harlow had encouraged Engle to go into coaching and they had remained friends, with Engle often seeking advice from Harlow. In six years at Brown, Engle had turned around a struggling program with back-to-back winning records in 1948 (7–2) and 1949 (8–1) led by quarterback Joe Paterno.

Penn State's coaching offer was tempting, especially for a onetime teenage coal mine mule driver from southwestern-central Pennsylvania. Engle knew all about his mentor's problems at Penn State, not only from hearing about them from Harlow but also from Engle's Uncle Lloyd, who had been Harlow's Penn State teammate.

Engle wasn't sure the internal politics had changed much at Penn State. The head coaching job was open because longtime assistant Joe Bedenk was stepping down, only one year after winning a power struggle with another longtime assistant, Earle Edwards, to succeed Higgins.

Harlow still had friends at Penn State. Both he and Uncle Lloyd believed it was a great opportunity for Rip and that he could overcome any problems that popped up. The first one occurred as soon as Rip accepted the job. There was one last caveat. He had to retain the 1949 coaching staff, including Bedenk, but could hire one new assistant.

Engle agreed. None of his Brown assistants wanted to go with him. So Engle convinced his quarterback from the streets of Brooklyn to delay law school for one year and follow him to the woods and farms of central Pennsylvania.

It wasn't quite a Don Corleone offer that Paterno couldn't refuse. But a Penn State godfather made it happen.

One more historic note: except for Bedenk, Penn State's coaches from 1909 to 2012 could have their own wing at the College Football Hall of Fame. Hollenbeck was inducted as a player from Penn in 1954 and the others as coaches: Harlow (1954), Higgins (1954), Bezdek (1960), Engle (1974), and Paterno (2007 but vacated in 2012).

67 Attend the Blue-White Game

There are two football seasons each year at Penn State, the normal one from late summer through late fall and the Blue-White Game at Beaver Stadium in the spring.

Just like the six to seven home games in the regular season, the weekend and the tailgating start early with the fans and the RVs starting to arrive Thursday. For a number of years until 2014, a carnival complete with a small Ferris wheel and merry-go-round was operating Friday and Saturday out of a parking lot behind the press box.

Parking is free and the game is free. If the weather cooperates, and it usually has, 70,000 will be inside the stadium to witness what is simply a glorified intrasquad scrimmage game. Unlike in the fall, tailgating continues even while the scrimmage is in progress and there are times after the game's intermission when there are more fans partying outside than watching inside.

The night before the game, the past lettermen gather to socialize and reminisce. Before the game, there is an autograph session with the players and a special breakfast for major donors. During the Joe Paterno era, a popular breakfast open to season-ticket holders from the Nittany Lion Club featured Paterno introducing each of his seniors and answering questions for 15–20 minutes.

Inside the stadium or out, the fans will yell the famous "We Are—Penn State!" cheer and do the wave many times. The Blue Band, Lion Mascot, and the cheerleaders will be there. Who cares who wins? Who cares if the stars of the game will be an unknown walk-on running back or the fourth-string quarterback? It's Penn State football! That's all that matters, even though the game simply marks the unofficial end of spring practice.

The Penn State football nation treats the affair as the true start of the upcoming fall season. They're like the nearby fabled Punxsutawney Groundhog, awakened from his winter slumber to see if it's time to enjoy life again. The fans will have to wait another four or five months, but the Blue-White game will tide them over.

And if fans can't be there in person, they can listen to it on the Penn State radio network as they have for decades, or watch it on television, sometimes live, and in recent years streamed over the Internet.

Until the coaching change in 2012, the game was almost like an actual game in the fall, with four quarters, halftime, and college referees, but without kickoffs and punts and using a clock that continued to run except for timeouts. The traditional format has continued to be altered every year, and in 2015, the game started at 4:00 PM instead of three hours earlier.

Still, the Blue-White Game has come a long way from its start in 1951 to raise money for an alumni association scholarship fund. The first game had to be played at the State College High School field because new grass had just been planted at Beaver Field. Admission was $1.00 and half off for students.

From the beginning, it was referred to as the Blue-White Game by the only two newspapers that covered the original game, the *Centre Daily Times* and the *Daily Collegian*.

"Blues Eleven Defeats Whites, 7–0; Anders Tallies Touchdown," read the headline in the *Centre Daily Times*. Sophomore Paul Anders scored the only touchdown on a 15-yard run in the second quarter to cap a 92-yard drive in eight plays, and Bill Hockersmith kicked the extra point. The winning coach, assistant coach Al Michaels, was carried off the field at the end.

However, it was a financial dud as a disappointing crowd of 500 showed up on a cloudy mid-50s afternoon. They tried to raise money for the scholarship fund again the next year. That also failed with a small turnout of fans competing against a Penn State baseball game on an adjoining field and Olympic gym tryouts inside nearby Rec Hall, which drew 4,000 to 4,500 fans for Saturday afternoon and evening competition.

That brought an end to the fund-raising for scholarships. From then on, Blue-White Games have been free.

The White team did not win until 1955, ending the losing streak for one particular young assistant helping coach the White team. The Whites broke the scoring record with a 24–12 victory and, finally, 28-year-old assistant Joe Paterno was on the winning side.

Just who came up with the idea to turn a glorified scrimmage into an actual game that would delight the team's fans five months before the first game of the next season is lost somewhere in the Penn State sports archives. Too bad. The guy deserves an award in his name as the MVP of the annual Blue-White Game.

68 The Penn State Way

It didn't have a name at the beginning, more than a century ago. After a few years, the former players and sportswriters referred to it as the Penn State Way.

There was a double meaning melded into the moniker. Philosophically, the name described a way of doing things in football, from the way players were coached in practice to the tactics and strategy during a game. But it also defined the ritual of former players returning after graduation to help coach the team.

Charlie Hildebrand, the co-founder of Penn State's football team in 1887, is believed to be the first in the long line of such former players starting in 1893 and continuing today. Another of the early returnees was Earl Hewitt, a star running back best known in Penn State history for his 65-yard punt return that upset Army in 1899.

Neither Hildebrand nor Hewitt or several others from that time period are among the official 46 assistant coaches listed in the Penn State football yearbook who once played for the Nittany Lions. Andy Moscrip, a tackle and place kicker on the 1903–04 teams, is the first ex-player to officially become an assistant coach in 1905.

Since then, there has been at least one former player on the Penn State coaching staff every year except for 1916 and 2012–13. However, there is evidence that at least two of the Lions' star players from the great undefeated 1911–12 teams did help out the team in 1916—Pete Mauthe and Dex Very, both now enshrined in the College Football Hall of Fame.

Before the second game of the 1916 season, the *Penn State Collegian* reported that Mauthe (who was officially an assistant coach the previous year) and Very were returning:

In her preparation of the balance of the season, the State team will be benefitted to a great extent by the volunteer assistance of some of the old stars who are drifting back one at a time to aid Head Coach Harlow in rounding the team into undefeatable form. 'Pete' Mauthe…is spending this week with the squad helping [assistant coach] Bud Whitney with the backfield men. 'Dex' Very will drift into camp about next Monday to do his share with the linemen and from now on some one [sic] or other of the old stars will be on hand nearly all the time to aid in the work of building a first class combination.

Regardless, there were 96 years straight with at least one former player officially on the coaching staff until Bill O'Brien ended it in the aftermath of the child abuse scandal. But Penn State's newest head coach, James Franklin, unknowingly resurrected one aspect of the Penn State Way in 2014 with the hiring of Terry Smith, a standout wide receiver (1988–91), to coach cornerbacks.

It's noteworthy that Penn State's initial first-team All-American, Mother Dunn in 1906, was an assistant for one year (1907).

And here's a figure that proves the Penn State Way can be credited for the success of the team over the years. Of the 101 assistant coaches on the all-time roster, 45.5 percent are former players, even with an influx of 17 new assistants since 2012. That includes five assistants who were there for Joe Paterno's historic 409th victory on October 29, 2011: Dick Anderson, Tom Bradley, Galen Hall, Jay Paterno, and Mike McQueary. (The disgraced Jerry Sandusky (1969–99) has been eradicated from the official list.)

Four of the all-time assistants eventually became the head coach—Dick Harlow (1915–17), Bob Higgins (1930–48), Joe Bedenk (1949), and Joe Paterno (1966–2011), and only Paterno was not a former Penn State player.

Higgins was an assistant under his head coach, Hugo Bezdek, for two years in 1928–29. Bezdek started the movement of having at least two ex-players on his staff and Higgins continued it with Bedenk (1929–48, 1950–52), Larry Conover (1926–30), Earle Edwards (1936–48), Al Michaels (1935–52), Marv McAndrew (1936, 1941–45), and Jim O'Hora (1946–76).

When Rip Engle took over in 1950 with the stipulation that he had to keep the previous staff, he inherited ex-players Bedenk, Michaels, O'Hora, and Tor Toretti (hired by Bedenk). One of Engle's linebackers, Dan Radakovich, would join the staff in 1960. When Paterno succeeded Engle in 1966, O'Hora, Toretti, and Radakovich were still there.

Paterno elevated the Penn State Way to another level with multiple ex-players as assistant coaches. In the latter years of his career, he was often criticized by the media, right or wrong, for not hiring more outsiders to give the program new life.

The Penn State Way is now just a scintilla of what it once was. Don't count it out in the future.

69 A Camping Trip

Bobby Knight called it a camping trip.

The onetime Indiana basketball coach was jesting when he uttered those three words now legendary in Penn State history upon learning in 1989 that the Big Ten had admitted Penn State into the conference. Or was he?

Even in the modern-day world with jet passenger planes flying in and out of the airport two miles from Beaver Stadium and interstate highways going north-south on the edge of campus and east-west about nine miles away, it is not easy for everyone to get to Penn State. Two-lane highways are sometimes still needed. University Park is about four hours from New York City, Philadelphia, and Washington, DC, Pittsburgh, and Erie are some two to three hours to the west and Harrisburg about 90 minutes to the east.

The only direct flights beyond charters in recent years have been from Philadelphia, Washington, and Detroit. Occasionally another city is added, like Chicago, Atlanta, or Charlotte, but later eliminated. The jets or propeller planes have limited capacity and the number of flights daily is not large, and is less on weekends. Bad weather at University Park and destination cities occurs often and it's not unusual anymore for frustrated airline passengers delayed by the weather to take a special bus or rent a car to get here.

Except for some improved roads and a few more flights on some larger puddle jumpers, not much has changed from December 31, 1986, when the *Washington Post* published this headline on a story about the football team's upcoming National Championship Game in Arizona: "Isolated, Bucolic Penn State Makes the Most of a Liability."

"Paterno and several former Penn State players," wrote Michael Wilbon, "said the school's isolation—at least three hours' driving time from any major city—has turned into a major plus [in recruiting]…[Former linebacker Rogers] Alexander describes it as "a place in the middle of the sticks with one [nightclub] and 40 local hangout bars that you can do all within a week without a car."

Okay, Alexander was joking a bit, too, but not by much.

With the opening of the Bryce Jordan Center in 1996, big-time concerts are the norm now, with such performers as Billy Joel, Elton John, and the hottest rock or country performer. Touring stage plays make the Performing Arts Center a regular stop and celebrity lectures occur on campus throughout the academic year. There are some good non-chain restaurants and a couple luxury hotels.

Just what you might expect for a rural college town of 45,000 students near the middle of Pennsylvania's geographical gravity center and surrounded by miles and miles of woods, small mountains, and farmland.

Certainly, Penn State is not as isolated as it was in 1953 when the TCU football team flew into Harrisburg thinking Penn State was there. They didn't realize it until their plane landed and they were told by snickering airport employees that they were still 90 miles away.

And Penn State still gets confused with Penn—the University of Pennsylvania—which is in Philadelphia, while others mix up the campus' University Park post office location with College Park, the home turf of the University of Maryland.

In the late 1940s and 1950s, Stanley Woodward, the great sportswriter of the *New York Herald Tribune*, wrote that he was often asked by his New York colleagues how to get to Penn State to cover a game. "You drive to Harrisburg," he would tell them, "then swing through the trees."

Anyone who thinks Penn State is isolated now should have been around in the first 60 years or so of Nittany Lions football.

In the early decades, Penn State had difficulty getting opponents to travel to State College for a game, and most of the team's big games were on the road. The teams had to travel by train. The closest train station was about five miles from the playing field, and until automobiles were invented, horse-and-buggy was the mode of transportation to and from that train station.

The first big-time team to play at Beaver Field was Notre Dame in 1913, but that's because, at that time, the Irish were trying to make a name for themselves by playing teams in the East. Michigan Agricultural College, now known as Michigan State, visited the next year and Dartmouth, North Carolina State, and Nebraska were all at Beaver Field in 1920. The big breakthrough didn't come until the roads started improving, and by the 1950s Big Ten teams began showing up regularly.

Still, opposing teams had to fly first to Harrisburg or Pittsburgh and then bus up to Penn State until the mid-1990s. From 1953 to 1978 there was limited commercial service by one airline flying out of a mountainous airport about 25 miles away near Phillipsburg. The State College airport opened near Beaver Stadium in 1972, but it was almost two decades before the runways were big enough to allow bigger planes with football teams to fly in and out.

Yes, Bobby, to many outsiders Penn State is still a camping trip. But what a campground, Bobby!

70 Joe Bedenk and the College Baseball World Series

Like many of the nation's historical figures of the past whose accomplishments have faded into oblivion over time, what Joe Bedenk did for Penn State football and baseball and for college baseball teams throughout the nation is virtually unknown today.

Nowadays, those Penn State fans who have heard of Bedenk probably have read about how his unhappy one year as the head football coach in 1949 triggered the arrival of Joe Paterno on campus in 1950. Or perhaps they've simply seen his name in the football media guide as Penn State's seventh first-team All-American at guard in 1923 or in the list of assistant coaches (1929–48, 1950–52).

An older generation of Penn State alumni may remember Bedenk as the school's head baseball coach for decades, from 1931 to 1962, but even they are probably unaware that he was one of the founders of the now-famous NCAA College World Series.

Heck, his name isn't even associated with Penn State's modern baseball stadium, despite being the team's winningest baseball coach from 1931 to 1962 with a record of 380–159–3. Bedenk also took three teams to the College World Series in Omaha in 1952, 1957, and 1959, and his 1957 squad, the best in Penn State history, made it all the way to the championship game.

Yet it is Bedenk's longtime assistant and successor, Chuck Medlar, who was honored when one of his players, Anthony Lubrano, donated money to have the baseball stadium named Medlar Field at Lubrano Park. Medlar also was a big success in his 19 years as head coach, posting a 312–14–6 record with his 1963 and 1973 teams making it to Omaha.

If not for Bedenk and his colleague at Colgate, Eppy Barnes, there might not be a College World Series in Omaha. In the latter years of World War II, Bedenk and Barnes decided college baseball needed to do something to counter the popularity of football and basketball and the continuing loss of undergraduate talent to professional baseball. So, in early 1945, they surveyed some 200 of their peers.

On June 29, 1945, more than 25 of the coaches met in New York and voted to organize the American Association of College Baseball Coaches, now known as the American Baseball Coaches Association. Within months, Major League Baseball agreed to host a post-season college All-Star Game at Fenway Park in June of 1946. During the next year, the coaches convinced the NCAA to sponsor an official championship tournament. The final championship games were in Kalamazoo, Michigan, and featured just two teams in a three-game series. California beat Yale that year and Southern Cal defeated Yale the next season. In 1949 the championship series expanded to four teams and the games were moved to Wichita, Kansas. Texas went undefeated in three games to win the title.

One year later, the series found its permanent home in Omaha. The format was revised to feature eight teams in a double-elimination structure. Then in 1987 the format was altered again, with the eight teams divided into two four-team double-elimination brackets and the winner of each bracket meeting in a single championship game. That has remained the format ever since.

However, it wasn't until the late 1960s that the tournament became officially known as the College World Series. And from its humble beginning in 1947 when 1,896 fans watched in Kalamazoo, the College World Series now attracts upward of 25,000 annually.

Just before Bedenk's death in 1978, the Penn State Paterno-Pattee Library Archives asked him to write about his involvement in the coaches' organization and College World Series. His hastily scrawled reply at the bottom of the archives inquiry simply noted: "E.D. Barnes and I organized the association behind closed doors before it was made public. —F. Joe Bedenk."

You need to see the two photos of Joe Bedenk and some of his memorabilia, including a football playbook from the 1920s, in the Penn State All-Sports Museum. There is a large photo at the entrance of the football exhibit showing Bedenk in his football uniform shaking hands with the Syracuse captain before the first game the two teams played in 1922. The steel-like, hardened look on Bedenk's face is classic. He was a take-no-prisoners type of warrior on the football field.

Back in the baseball trophy case, you'll find a smaller photo of Bedenk relaxing on a bench at the baseball field. That's the easygoing baseball coach Joe Bedenk who made history, and now you understand why you needed to know about him.

71 John Urschel and the Scholar-Athletes

John Urschel is the smartest athlete in Penn State history, and there's no one who comes close.

In 2013 Urschel was the premier scholar-athlete in the country and not just in college football. It's not just the numerous awards he won at the end of the year but also what he did off and on the field during those 365 days.

Seven months before the year started and in less than three years since he stepped on campus, Urschel earned his undergraduate degree in mathematics with a 4.0 grade-point average (GPA). That was just the beginning. He immediately began working on a master's degree in math, and before his academic endeavors concluded in 2014 he had two master's, in math and math education, with an amazing 4.0 GPA all the way.

During the spring of 2013, he also taught a 9:00 AM undergraduate class in trigonometry and analytic geometry three days a week while continuing research. An earlier research project took a year and was published in the international journal *Celestial Mechanics*

John Urschel taught an undergraduate course in mathematics while earning an undergraduate and two master's degrees with a perfect 4.0 grade-point average and honors on the football field as a two-time All–Big Ten guard and second-team All-American.

and Dynamical Astronomy, titled, "Instabilities of the Sun-Jupiter-Asteroid Three Body Problem." Got that?

"With football and math, I'm very precise," Urschel told *USA Today*. "With everything else, I'm a simple guy."

Yeah, sure. On the football field he was a two-time All–Big Ten starting guard and a second-team All-American in 2013 when he also was a co-captain. Many people outside Penn State wonder how this math genius wound up at Penn State instead of, say, MIT, Harvard, or Stanford, and even why he stayed after the 2012 NCAA sanctions allowed all players to transfer without losing eligibility.

A Canadian by birth, Urschel grew up in suburban Buffalo and his parents sent him to a Jesuit prep school, Canisius, where he fell in love with football.

"My mother wanted me to go to MIT," Urschel told *USA Today*. "I wanted bigger football. We settled on Princeton."

Then he received football scholarship offers from Penn State, Stanford, and Boston College. He says he fell in love with Penn State while touring the campus on a recruiting visit and listening to Coach Joe Paterno expound about the mix of academics and big-time football. That didn't change with the NCAA sanctions.

Bill O'Brien, Urschel's coach in 2012 and 2013, said Urschel is the "embodiment of what Penn State's all about." That also means Urschel was the ultimate success story of Paterno's Grand Experiment. It was O'Brien and his staff that brought out the best of Urschel on the field and helped him get drafted in the fifth round by the Baltimore Ravens.

Before joining the Ravens, there were his numerous honors, starting in August 2013 when Urschel was the keynote speaker at the popular Big Ten Kickoff Luncheon in Chicago. At the end of the season, he became a two-time first-team Academic All-American and a four-time Academic All–Big Ten.

Then on December 9, Urschel received the William V. Campbell Trophy, presented to the nation's premier college football scholar-athlete by the National Football Foundation and College Hall of Fame at its annual black-tie dinner at New York's Waldorf-Astoria. The award added $7,000 to the $18,000 post-graduate fellowships each of the 16 finalists received. It was the first time a Penn State player won the award.

"Words cannot describe how much this means to me," Urschel said in his thank-you speech. "I want to thank my coaches, team-mates, and fans for their love and support while at Penn State. I am grateful for playing in front of 108,000 fans; the best fans in college football."

Two weeks later, Urschel became Penn State's first recipient of the 2013 Senior CLASS Award, given annually to the most outstanding senior student-athlete in Division I football for "notable achievements in the classroom, community, character, and competition."

Urschel's most prestigious honor came on April 11 when he was given the 84th James E. Sullivan Award by the Amateur Athletic Union as the nation's most outstanding amateur athlete in ceremonies at AAU headquarters in Lake Buena Vista, Florida. The award is based on character, leadership, sportsmanship, and athletic achievements. Past recipients have included Penn State Olympian Horace Ashenfelter, Olympians Mark Spitz and Jackie-Joyner-Kersee, and football's Peyton Manning and Tim Tebow.

In presenting Urschel with the award, AAU president Henry Forrest told the audience, "John characterizes all of the pillars that this award stands on. He demonstrates character and leadership both in the academic community and on the football field."

Urschel said, "Words can't describe how honored I am to be named the most outstanding amateur athlete of the year. I am honored to represent all that is good about athletics and the lessons you can learn through sports; lessons of discipline, commitment, toughness, and perseverance in the face of adversity."

While he continues to pursue his football career in the NFL, he also will work on his PhD. Who knows what else is ahead for Penn State's smartest athlete of all time?

72 The Consensus All-Americans

Since Mother Dunn in 1906, 84 Penn State players have been honored as first-team All-Americans, and 37 are acknowledged as consensus All-Americans by the NCAA.

The NCAA list of consensus All-Americans goes back to 1889 when Walter Camp, the father of college football, created the All-American team. Over the decades, various media and other sports-related organizations came up with their All-American teams, and the NCAA now accepts more than two dozen teams in compiling the annual consensus team.

Most surprising about Penn State's list is there are no defensive backs on it. This doesn't count players of the two-way era who played offense and defense. If it did, three running backs would qualify: Charlie Way (1920), Glenn Killinger (1921), and "Light Horse" Harry Wilson (1923).

It's also a surprise that only one wide receiver qualifies, O. J. McDuffie in 1992, although two-way end Bob Higgins (1915–19) and pure tight end Ted Kwalick (1967–68) are included.

One could almost have predicted that Linebacker U would have the most players on the consensus list with 10. Running backs and defensive linemen are not far behind with eight each. Five offensive linemen fit the criteria, although two-way Maxwell Award winner Glenn Ressler spent more time playing middle guard than center in 1964.

The three quarterbacks who also won the Maxwell Award given to the best player in college football made it: two-way player Richie Lucas (1959), Chuck Fusina (1978), and Kerry Collins (1994). So did Penn State's other Maxwell Awardees: defensive tackle

Mike Reid (1969) and running backs John Cappelletti (1973), the Heisman Trophy winner, and Larry Johnson (2002).

Just three of the 37 players were two-time consensus All-Americans and two were linebackers, of course, Dennis Onkotz (1968–69) and Paul Posluszny (2005–06). Defensive tackle Bruce Clark, winner of the 1978 Lombardi Award given to college football's outstanding "offensive or defensive lineman or linebacker," also was a consensus choice in 1979.

Eight other players honored by Penn State as two-time first-team All-Americans qualified for just one year as consensus choices: linebackers Shane Conlan (1986), LaVar Arrington (1999), and Dan Connor (2007); offensive linemen Keith Dorney (1978), Sean Farrell (1981), and Jeff Hartings (1995); and ends Higgins and Kwalick. But tailback Curt Warner (1981–82), flanker Kenny Jackson (1982–83), and offensive guard Steve Wisniewski (1987–88) didn't make it for either year.

The absence of a consensus defensive back and inclusion of just one wide receiver is strange. Then again, Penn State recognizes just six defensive backs and four wide receivers as first-team All-Americans.

The first defensive back was safety Neal Smith, a onetime walk-on, chosen in 1969 by United Press International (UPI) and the Newspaper Enterprise Association (NEA). He set a Penn State record of 10 interceptions that season that was tied by safety Pete Harris in 1978, when he became an All-American and led the nation in interceptions. Pete was the younger brother of the more famous Franco Harris, who never made it further than honorable mention when he played (1969–71). Coach Joe Paterno said Pete was "a great college safety who has great range and great instincts," but he was chosen only by UPI in his junior year and then dropped out of school and never returned.

Safety Mark Robinson, one of the standouts of the 1982 national championship team, was tapped by NEA, the Football

Milt Plum

Milt Plum never was more than an honorable-mention All-American but he did something only one other Penn State football player did— play more than 10 years at quarterback in the NFL.

Plum spent 13 years in the league, primarily as a starter with the Cleveland Browns (1957–61) and Detroit Lions (1962–67) and a backup for the Los Angeles Rams (1968) and New York Giants (1969). Kerry Collins surpassed Plum's longevity at quarterback with 17 years from 1995 to 2011 with six teams, and Collins' tenure is tied with place-kicker Matt Bahr's team record of 17 years in the NFL.

Plum, a No. 2 draft choice in 1957, helped lead Cleveland to a division title in 1957 in the then-12-team league before the Super Bowl when the two division winners played for the NFL championship. But Cleveland lost the title game.

Plum was a late bloomer at Penn State. A native of Westville, New Jersey, he didn't become the Lions' starting quarterback until his junior year and didn't even letter as a sophomore in 1954. He proved to be one of the best all-around players on the team. In a day of two-way players when quarterbacks called their own plays, Plum was not only a good passer but an outstanding defensive back who kicked field goals and punted, too.

Plum tied Lenny Moore in team scoring in 1955 with 30 points when he successfully kicked 12 of 14 extra points and scored three touchdowns. The next season he led the team in punting in 1956 (33 punts for a 39.3-yard average) and his 73-yard boot against Ohio State that year is still the fifth-longest in school history. Not only did that punt help Penn State upset heavily favored No. 5 Ohio State in one of the Nittany Lions' greatest games, but Plum also kicked the extra point that won the game 7–6.

"If the Cleveland Browns had cut me, I would have talked to some people about trying to play [professional] baseball," Plum wrote in *What It Means to Be a Nittany Lion*. Good thing it didn't work out that way.

Writers Association of American (FWAA), and *Sporting News*; Strong safety Michael Zordich Sr., co-captain of the 1985 team that lost the National Championship Game to Oklahoma, was selected by the FWAA and Scripps-Howard; and "hero" Darren Perry was picked by the FWAA in 1981. They weren't consensus All-Americans but they all had solid NFL careers with Robinson playing eight years, Zordich 12, and Perry eight.

One more note on defensive backs. Only three other Penn Staters were named to second-team All-American squads, safety Tim Montgomery (1967), free safety Ray Isom (1986), and cornerback Alan Zemaitis (2005), and just three to third teams, Eddie Johnson (1988) cornerback David Macklin (1998), and free safety James Boyd (2000).

Kenny Jackson was Penn State's first wide receiver to become a first-team All-American when he was the star pass catcher on the 1982 national championship team. But that year he was selected only by the Associated Press and the next season solely by NEA. McDuffie was next in 1992, followed by Bobby Engram in 1994. Although Engram won the initial Biletnikoff Award as the nation's outstanding receiver, he only made Walter Camp's first team. All three went on to successful NFL careers with Engram playing 14 years, McDuffie nine, and Jackson eight.

Not until Allen Robinson in 2013 was another Lion wide receiver picked on a first team, although Derrick Williams was a second team choice in 2008. Robinson was selected by *Sporting News* and CBSSports.com.

The age of the Internet has increased the number of bona fide All-American teams recognized by the NCAA. Whether it enables more Penn State players to become consensus All-Americans is another matter.

73 See the Football from the Great Walk-Off

When Penn State entered the Big Ten in 1990, many fans were surprised to learn that Ohio State was the first conference opponent the football team had played. The game went all the way back to 1912 and set the tone for what would be an intense rivalry that makes the Buckeyes the Nittany Lions' most detested Big Ten opponent.

The 1912 game ended with Ohio State walking off the field in Columbus in the second half, and the repercussions were so bitter the teams didn't play again until 1956. That season, another upset in Columbus caused a seven-year breach before two more upsets at Ohio State in 1963 and 1964. The Buckeyes finally won in Columbus in 1975 and at University Park in 1976. The Lions won again in Columbus in 1978 and then in the 1980 Fiesta Bowl, and that was the end of the series until Penn State's first year of Big Ten football in 1993.

Okay, Ohio State has dominated the Big Ten rivalry, winning 14 and losing seven from 1993 to 2014, with an upset here and there, and Penn State has only won twice in Columbus during that span. Still, it's the occasional upsets by Penn State that rattles the Ohio State hierarchy and fandom second only to its longtime rival Michigan.

Readers may not want to believe it, but it was a young Ohio sportswriter who would one day be the president of Penn State who started it all.

Ed Sparks was a farm boy from Licking, about 40 miles northeast of Columbus, and while earning his undergraduate degree at Ohio State in the early 1880s, he was a cub reporter covering news and sports for the *Ohio State Journal* in Worthington. Journalism was only a sideline, and after graduating in 1884 he went into education. In 1889 Sparks joined the Penn State faculty as head of the college's Preparatory Department. He left in 1904 to get his PhD at Chicago and in 1908 returned to Penn State as the school's eighth president.

Dr. Sparks is credited with breathing new life into Penn State, expanding the curriculum, increasing funding and enrollment, and enhancing the college's reputation. It was his idea to arrange a friendly football game with his alma mater in Columbus, and he bargained a $1,200 guarantee to pay for the trip.

Ohio State had dominated the pedestrian Ohio Conference but had just joined the respected Intercollegiate Conference of Faculty Representatives, which would become known as the Big Ten. With a 5–1 record, Ohio State and its usual phalanx of arrogant followers demeaned the caliber of Penn State's perennial competition. Their fans were sure Ohio State would win by at least 20 points and tackle Ollie Vogel told one newspaper, "We're ready to eat them up."

Penn State was undefeated in six games, had given up just one touchdown—against Cornell in a 29–6 win—and had averaged 35 points. In fact, the Lions were experienced and had not lost a game since the last one in 1910.

A shocked, partisan crowd of 3,500 watched on November 16 as the smaller but quicker Penn State team literally smashed its way through the bigger and beefier opponent. It was a rough game with elbows and fists flying. At one point, Ohio State's first-year coach John Richards was overheard shouting that Penn State "must have scoured the prize rings of the East to get that crowd" of players. During the halftime break, taken under a clump of trees at the edge of the field because there were no dressing rooms, police had to protect the Penn State players from an angry, rowdy mob.

The Nittany Lions took their 16–0 first-quarter lead and stretched it to 37–0 in the opening minutes of the fourth quarter.

Other Major Upsets over Ohio State

October 20, 1956, at Columbus: Penn State 7, Ohio State 6

Penn State shocked the three-touchdown-favorite defending Big Ten champions with an outstanding defense and the punting of quarterback Milt Plum, who also kicked State's winning extra point. Ohio State did not score until two minutes were left in the game, and then messed up its successful extra point with a 12-men-on-the-field penalty. Its second attempt was wide. The upset was credited with propelling Penn State to another level in recruiting and prestige.

November 7, 1964, at Columbus: Penn State 27, Ohio State 0

Once again, Penn State shocked the heavily favored No. 2 Buckeyes in the Horseshoe. The Lions had lost four of their first five games but with middle guard-center Glenn Ressler leading the charge, Penn State had won two straight and caught the Buckeyes reading their press clippings. "A breather," cited the *Chicago Sun-Times* before the game. OSU's vaunted running netted just 60 yards as the Lions recovered two fumbles and had three interceptions. "That was the soundest trouncing we've ever gotten," OSU coach Woody Hayes told sportswriters after the loss.

October 27, 2001, at University Park: Penn State 29, Ohio State 27

Joe Paterno surpassed Bear Bryant as the all-time winning coach in major college football with 324 victories as Penn State rallied from a 27–9 deficit in the third quarter. Quarterback Zack Mills sparked the comeback over the six-point-favorite Buckeyes with a 69-yard touchdown run and two touchdown passes and defensive tackle Jimmy Kennedy blocked a 32-yard field goal attempt with 2:55 left to preserve the milestone victory.

October. 8, 2005, at University Park: Penn State 17, Ohio State 10

Before a national TV audience and a frenzied, noisy nighttime crowd of 109,839 shaking Beaver Stadium in the occasionally drizzling rain, Penn State beat the three-point favorite No. 6 Buckeyes behind a conservative offensive game plan and a big-play defense. Holding on to a 14–10 lead at halftime, the Lions clinched the upset with 90 seconds left when defensive end Tamba Hali's sack of quarterback Troy Smith at midfield forced a fumble that tackle Scott Paxson recovered.

When an Ohio State blocker was wiped out with a vicious hit on the ensuing kickoff, Coach Richards stalked onto the field and shouted, "That's enough." He waved to all his players to follow him, and they walked off the field toward their distant locker room as the surprised Penn State team and the game officials watched.

Penn State players wanted to leave, too, but because of the rules they had to stay five minutes to earn the 1–0 forfeit. Police guarded the team from taunting Ohio State fans. The police also escorted them back to their hotel and then to the train station, where Ohio State officials apologized to President Sparks and the team.

The bitterness continued for decades until the captain of Penn State's 1912 team, Pete Mauthe, was president of a company in Ohio and arranged a game in 1956 with the help of his friend Dan Galbreath, a Columbus industrialist and famous horse racing owner who also owned the Pittsburgh Pirates.

In record books at each school, the final score is listed as a 37–0 Penn State victory. But as was the custom of the day, the actual football used in the game was given to the winning team captain. That football, with the score written in large ink numerals, "1–0." is on display in a large trophy case at the Penn State All-Sports Museum.

74 Iron Mike Michalske

Penn State's first player inducted into the Pro Football Hall Fame is virtually unknown to today's Nittany Lions fans.

There's a 14x14 black-and-white photo of Mike Michalske in the Penn State All-Sports Museum and a 133-word write-up about him on the "Penn Staters in Canton" page of the football media guide. But none of that tells anything about Michalske's career at Penn State in 1923–25 or how good he was as a ferocious 60-minute pulling guard, blitzing linebacker, and a fullback who could pass as well as he ran.

"He is rated along with Joe Bedenk as the best guard ever to play at Penn State," wrote historian Ridge Riley in his definitive 1975 book *Road to Number One*. After transferring from Western Reserve in his hometown of Cleveland, Michalske started at left guard as a sophomore in 1923 and paired with the senior Bedenk to help halfback Harry Wilson become a first-team All-American. Bedenk also became an All-American that season, the only time until 1962 that two Penn State players were bona fide first-team All-Americans in the same year.

Michalske seemed to be a cinch to be an All-American in his senior year of 1925. But after four games of trying to rebuild the Penn State backfield, Coach Hugo Bezdek switched the 6'0", 206-pound Michalske to fullback to add punch, passing, and pizzazz to his power-oriented single-wing offense.

Michalske proved to be the best passer on the team and he eventually led in scoring with 18 points on three touchdowns. Alas, despite tying favored defending national champion Notre Dame in the mud at Beaver Field 0–0 before a record crowd of 20,000, the 1925 team finished 4–4–1, the worst school record since the 1–2–1 mark of the 1918 team during World War I. Michalske's 23-yard run against Notre Dame was the longest by any player in that game.

Durability was Michalske's biggest asset, and he rarely missed playing time because of an injury. One of those rare times in his college and pro career was in his final Penn State game against the Lions' biggest rival, Pittsburgh. With favored Pitt leading 17–7 just before the half, Michalske went down trying to make a tackle and was carried off the field. He returned late in the game, but Pitt won 23–7.

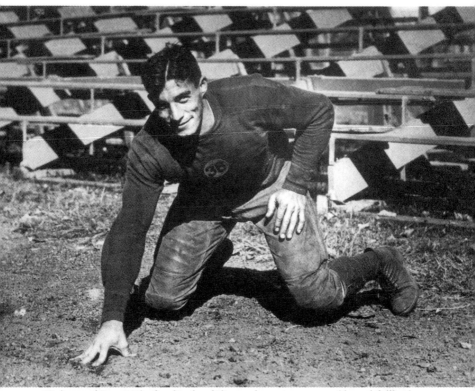

Nicknamed Iron Mike for this durability and stamina as a tackle and fullback for the Nittany Lions, Mike Michalske was Penn State's first player to be enshrined in the Pro Football Hall of Fame after a career with the Green Bay Packers.

"I just didn't get hurt," Michalske once said, and that's how August "Iron Mike" Michalske earned his lifetime nickname in college. "The players [in the pros] used to say I must have been getting paid by the minute."

Michalske's first three year as a pro were a little disconcerting. His first New York Yankees team in a different league folded after 1926 and his second Yankees team in the NFL also went out of business after 1928. But Michalske was All-Pro in 1927 and 1928, and he would be All-Pro three more times with the team that led to his enshrinement in the Pro Football Hall of Fame, the Green Bay Packers, which won three league titles with Iron Mike.

Hailed as "the Guard of the Century" in Packerland, Michalske was "fast and explosive." His page on the Hall of Fame website asserts he was "football's premier guard" for 11 years, "the toughest

Dave Cure

Ask a Penn State fan who was the school's first professional football player and it's likely few, if any, will know his name. Until reading this.

His name is Dave Cure. He was a standout fullback, punter, and placekicker who played from 1897 to 1899. He was well known for his plunges into the line, including a somersault technique he developed that enabled him to score many touchdowns.

In his junior year Cure reportedly led the country in field goals. He was the first Penn State player to kick four field goals in a game, a 45–6 win over Susquehanna in 1898, but that accomplishment is not listed in the official team record books.

Professional football traces its roots to November 1892, when William "Pudge" Heffelfinger was paid $500 from the Allegheny Athletic Association to help defeat the Pittsburgh Athletic Club 4–0. Teams were often loosely organized, and not all the players were paid. Western Pennsylvania and eastern Ohio were hot beds for teams

Cure apparently left school without graduating and began playing for a team in Canton, Ohio, in 1900, and he played there until 1907. Meanwhile, three of his Penn State teammates had joined Connie Mack's Philadelphia Athletics team—guard Brute Randolph, tackle Henny Scholl, and halfback Earl Hewitt.

In 1904 the Canton team reorganized as the Canton Athletic Club and two years later the team's name was changed and it became famous: the Canton Bulldogs. That was the same season Cure and the Canton team spent two weeks working out and scrimmaging with the Penn State team before a big game against the Deering Maroons in New York City.

According to the Pro Football Researchers Association Cure was by then "one of the best players in the land." Cure apparently quit Canton after the 1906 season, but he was the original Penn State pro.

job of all in the 1920s and 1930s." A guard in those days was expected to block the biggest opposing linemen head-on. He also had to pull from the line and lead interference for the ball carrier. When the other team had the ball, the guard was the key man in stopping the enemy run attack. But he also had to be capable of storming into the backfield to disrupt a passing play.

In a 1965 interview with the *Milwaukee Journal*, Michalske recalled his fierce blitzing from the line. "Our target was the man with the ball, especially the passer," he said, "It might not have been ethical, but it was legal in those days to rough the passer even after he got rid of the ball. We worked him over pretty good."

The most meaningful praise came from two of his Hall of Fame Green Bay teammates when Michalske died in 1983. "He was as great as any football player Green Bay ever had," said Johnny "Blood" McNally. "He was a football player's football player, and I can't say this strongly enough," end Don Hutson told the *Green Bay Press-Gazette*.

The Pro Football Hall of Fame thought so, too. After its inaugural class of 17 in 1963, the Hall of Fame included Michalske in the second group of seven in 1964.

75 Drive Around Happy Valley

If you had asked anyone 50 years ago where Happy Valley was, they probably wouldn't have known.

Perhaps they had once stayed overnight in a run-down Happy Valley Motel on some two-lane highway in Missouri. Maybe they had heard of a Happy Valley somewhere, say a small hamlet in maybe Oregon or Alaska or maybe overseas, say in someplace like

Hong Kong or Australia. (Yes, those Happy Valleys do exist.) But nowadays, thanks to television, newspapers, and magazines, Happy Valley means Penn State to millions of people.

The term characterizes the pastoral beauty, the low-key lifestyle, and the onetime serenity of the area as well as the geographical location. It's not as happy as it was before the child abuse scandal broke in 2011. Since then, many outsiders see the name Happy Valley as a community that was blind to the years of a roaming sex predator. Right or wrong, that perception will persist in many minds until the ultimate truth proves them wrong.

The valley is real. The actual name is Nittany Valley, and it lies below the Nittany and Tussey Mountains in Centre County with State College, Penn State, and numerous other smaller boroughs and unincorporated towns spread out among the farmlands, fishing streams, woods, and hills.

There's the quaint village of Boalsburg bordering on State College, with restaurants, antique shops, and the Pennsylvania Military Museum and memorial park that attracts out-of-town visitors. The town claims this was the birthplace of Memorial Day in 1868. Fisherman's Paradise, a breeding ground for all types of fish that are then thrown into various streams and lakes, is not far from the county seat, Bellefonte, and the state prison. Deer and small game still roam freely throughout the valley, and even bears are occasionally spotted.

Just where Nittany Valley begins or ends is arguable. Centre County occupies 1,122 square miles of land, and the Nittany Valley is defined generally by the central portion of the county with the Bald Eagle Mountain at the other end of the valley. But there are no marked boundaries defining Nittany Valley, and Happy Valley is more in the mind than reality.

A jovial Irish professor from the hard coal region of northeastern Pennsylvania is credited with originating the nickname. Pat O'Brien (now, isn't that a great Irish name) and his wife, Harriet, moved to State College in 1947 when Pat joined the Penn State Liberal Arts faculty. They took frequent car rides around the back roads of Centre County, and Pat began calling the Nittany Valley scenery "a happy valley."

"We were just enamored with the lovely countryside, in contrast to the city," Harriett told Nadine Kofman for her *Town & Gown* magazine cover story about Happy Valley in 2004.

Pat and Harriet became good friends with Ross and Katey Lehman, one of the town's regal couples. Ross, a 1942 graduate, was the executive director of Penn State's Alumni Association, among other things, and Katey was a columnist for the local newspaper, the *Centre Daily Times*.

The first known use of O'Brien's now-famous phrase appeared in Katey's "Open House" column on June 22, 1961, according to Kofman and research by Jan Gibeling. Lehman wrote, "'The [Nittany] mountain is better seen when viewed from the plain.' I don't know who said that, but it applies to those of us who live here in the 'happy valley' and sometimes take it for granted."

The phrase didn't catch on right away. But as waggish old Pat conversed with more friends and strangers and as Katey inserted the words more and more into her columns, residents began using the nickname, too. Another Penn State professor was so upset by what she was hearing at that time that she began to define the word in a less than complimentary manner. Dr. Ruth Silva made her "disparaging" description a formal part of her Political Science classes.

"Her definition was somewhat lengthy," recalled former student Ben Sinclair, "but basically it referred to the little universe inhabited by most Penn Staters, who pass through without serious thoughts, with parties, fun, drinking, extracurricular activities, etc., until they are forced into the real world."

Students in the late 1960s, who were unaware of either source of the nickname, thought it meant something else. "We were using the term 'Happy Valley' sarcastically to describe residents of the area who seemed oblivious to Vietnam, civil rights, the women's movement, and all the rest, and we didn't feel the residents knew anything about the outside world," said Lee Stout, the retired archivist for Penn State's libraries.

In the 1970s, sportscasters started using "Happy Valley" when broadcasting games from Beaver Stadium, often opening their telecast with video of the picturesque valley below Mt. Nittany. And that's how the Nittany Valley became nationally known as Happy Valley.

That's also why Penn State fans need to drive around the Nittany Valley on a sunny, warm, late spring, summer, or early autumn morning or afternoon and see for themselves why that grand old Irishman Pat O'Brien loved his Happy Valley.

76 History's National Champions

Penn State's great undefeated teams of 1911 and 1912 were good enough in their day to be national champions. At least one highly respected organization believes they were the champs—the National Football Foundation that oversees the College Football Hall of Fame.

In the early decades of college football, there was no such thing as a national champion. Magazines and newspapers might designate a team as its national champion and schools often tried to promote itself as the national champion, based on some type of twisted, partisan reasoning. But it was a mishmash dominated by the eastern press and teams that are now part of the Ivy League.

Not until the Associated Press began its poll in 1936 did the public come to accept a true national champion, even though it was still a mythical title based on the whim of voters with their own biases. Although other organizations also began choosing national champions, such as Dunkel in the 1930s and the Helms Athletic Foundation in the 1940s, the winner of the AP media poll was the accepted champion until the United Press created its own poll using coaches in 1950 and the International News Service started one two years later. In 1958, UP and INS merged into United Press International and until recent seasons the media and coaches polls were the final word on the national championship.

Meanwhile, several organizations began researching the past and retroactively declaring national champions. A few years ago, the NCAA combined the new research with the selections made at the actual time and produced a list of National Poll Champions dating back to 1869. Thirty-four organizations qualified for the NCAA poll. The same five were used to select the national champions from 1895 through 1916.

In 1911 and 1912, the National Football Foundation tabbed Penn State as co–national champion with Princeton in 1911 and Harvard in 1912. Since the other four polls chose Princeton and Harvard, they are regarded by historians as the mythical national champions for those two years. That's not surprising given the lack of respect for Penn State football in that era.

Four of today's Ivy League schools were considered the barometer to evaluate other teams in college football at the time. In a period from 1895 through 1908, Penn State lost every game against Pennsylvania (0–12), Yale (0–7), and Princeton (0–5) with just one win and a tie in four games vs Cornell. Not surprisingly, all the games were on the road. In that same span, of the 154 first-team All-Americans selected by the only recognized authority, legendary Walter Camp, just 16 were from outside Ivy League schools. That included Penn State's Mother Dunn in 1906, who would remain the Lions' only Camp choice until 1919.

Everything began to change for Penn State when Bill Hollenback became the head coach in 1909. Athletic director Pop Golden had

Pete, Dex, and Shorty

Pete Mauthe was such a great all-around halfback and place-kicker that he became the first Penn State player to be inducted into the College Football Hall of Fame in 1957. There wasn't another one until 14 years later, with halfback Glenn Killinger. Harry Wilson was next in 1973, followed by Eugene "Shorty" Miller (1974) and Dexter Very (1976).

Mauthe was the best fullback/halfback in school history. He and Very were the first great passing combination when the passing rules were restrictive. The 119 points he scored in 1912 on 11 touchdowns and 42 points on field goals and extra points was the school record until broken by Lydell Mitchell in 1971, and it is still sixth all-time. Mauthe's 51-yard field goal against Pitt in 1912 was Penn State's longest for 63 years.

Very was an "ironman" who started every game from his freshman year and was on the field nearly 100 percent of the time, usually playing without a helmet. In the 1912 win over Penn, a *Philadelphia North American* writer described Very's style of play: "He tackled hard enough to separate the various vertebrae in the spines of his opponents and he was glued to the ball any time it happened to get loose on a fumble."

Miller was a year behind Mauthe and Very and the last Penn State freshman to start at quarterback in 100 years. He was a 5'4", 140-pound speedster who could spin, twist, cut, and sidestep would-be tacklers in a wisp. His stunning 95-yard touchdown on the opening kickoff against Penn is one of the greatest plays in Penn State history. Shorty "squirmed through...a swarm of Penn tacklers" at the 15-yard-line, one newspaper reported, and was off "dashing, sprinting, sliding and once in a while coming to a dead stop to let the enemy overrun him before bursting in the clear near the Penn 35-yard line."

Mauthe went on to become president of an Ohio steel company and served on the Penn State board of trustees, while Very and Miller were among the top officials in college football for three decades.

already begun recruiting better players and Hollenback was just the man to turn them into a great team. Hollenback has just graduated from Penn where he was a Camp two-time All-American halfback. Hollenback was the first Penn State head coach to spend the entire season on campus. The six others since 1892 were really trainers, including Golden, or part-timers.

Hollenback's first team in 1909 was the best at the time in Penn State football's short history. It shut out five teams while scoring 166 points and tying two of the best in the East, Penn (3–3) and the Carlisle Indians (8–8). That was just the beginning. With a pair of 1909 freshman starters, halfback Pete Mauthe and end Dex Very as the backbone, the 1911 and 1912 teams won eight games each year without a defeat and only a 0–0 tie with favored Navy in 1911.

The 1911 team outscored opponents 119–15, including its first-ever victory over Penn 22–6 and a 5–0 upset over Cornell, and had seven shutouts. The 1912 team was even better, again shutting out seven foes and giving up just six points, in a 29–6 win over Cornell, while racking up 285 points. The 1912 squad not only beat Penn again 14–0 but also clobbered a well-regarded Washington & Jefferson 30–0 and Ohio State 37–0.

In comparing the 1911 record against Princeton and the 1912 mark against Harvard, one finds two common opponents in 1911 but none in 1912. Both State and Princeton tied Navy by the same 0–0 score and both beat Villanova, Penn State winning 18–0 and Princeton 31–0.

In 1911 the influential Camp chose three players from Princeton and two from Harvard as first-team All-Americans, and in 1912 he picked three from Harvard and one from Princeton. The best Penn State could do was Camp's second-team selection of Dex Very in 1911 and 1912 and quarterback Shorty Miller on his third team in 1912. Two of those Princeton All-Americans (and one more player from the 1911 team) and three from Harvard (and one more from the 1912 team) are now in the College Football Hall of Fame. So are Very, Mauthe, and Miller.

Too bad there was no college football playoff back then.

77 The Butkus Boys

Dick Butkus. If you don't know who he is, you are not a football fan. Period.

Butkus may be the greatest linebacker in history, a member of both the College and Pro Football Halls of Fame. That's one reason the only pure linebacker award in college football is named in his honor.

Linebackers are eligible for three other postseason trophies—the Bednarik, Lombardi, and Nagurski Awards—but so are other defensive players.

Winning the Butkus Award is the ultimate for college linebackers. Since the first award in 1985, only two Penn State players have received the trophy: LaVar Arrington in 1999 and Paul Posluszny in 2005. Posluszny also was a finalist in 2006 when Mississippi's Patrick Willis won and Arrington's teammate Brandon Short was a finalist in 1999.

Just three other Nittany Lions linebackers reached the normal three-man finalist stage: Shane Conlan in 1986 when Oklahoma's Brian Bosworth, the first awardee in 1985, repeated; Andre Collins in 1989 when Michigan State's Percy Snow won; and Dan Connor in 2007 when Ohio State's James Laurinaitis was the recipient.

Posluszny is one of just three of Penn State's 84 first-team All-Americans to be a two-time consensus All-American. Arrington was a consensus choice in 1999 but not in 1998 when selected

Paul Posluszny is the epitome of Joe Paterno's Grand Experiment and the poster boy for the school's reputation as Linebacker U. He won the Butkus Award in 2005 as the nation's most outstanding linebacker and was a two-time consensus All-American on the field and two-time Academic All-American off it.

by *Sporting News.* If Arrington had not left for the NFL before he graduated after his junior year he might have become Penn State's only three-time first-team All-American. His departure before 2000 is also one reason he is hardly in Penn State's record books, unlike Posluszny.

Posluszny is second in career tackles with 372 (210 solos) behind Connor's 419 (227 solos) and his 22 tackles at Northwestern in 2005 are tied for third on the all-time single-game list. Posluszny also is tied with Connor for ninth in season tackles with 116 in both 2005 and 2006 and in career tackles for a loss (36). Arrington also is on the career-tackles-for-a-loss list (39), tied at No. 7 with defensive tackle Jimmy Kennedy, and tied with defensive tackles Bruce Clark and Jay Alford at No. 8 in career quarterback sacks with 19.

"[Paul's] everything you want in a college football player," Coach Joe Paterno told Frank Fitzpatrick of the *Philadelphia*

Inquirer at the end of the 2006 season. "He's a really good athlete, loves to play football and works at it. He studies the game."

Posluszny was another of the scholar-athletes that fit into Paterno's Grand Experiment. He graduated in three and a half years with a 3.56 GPA in finance and twice was a two-time Academic All-American. He also was honored by the National Football Foundation as a Hall of Fame Scholar-Athlete with an $18,000 postgraduate fellowship.

Arrington and Paterno did not have a good relationship, and it's difficult to find Paterno saying anything about Arrington that comes close to his comments about Posluszny. "[LaVar's] a very articulate, bright kid who someday can be very, very successful," Paterno told the Associated Press as Arrington was contemplating leaving for the NFL. "But I think he's a little bit immature...."

Although both Arrington and Posluszny are from the Pittsburgh area, their personalities are quite different, with Arrington the flamboyant, independent extrovert and Posluszny the quiet, team-oriented introvert. While Arrington was making his name at North Hills High School, the younger Posluszny was hearing about him in grade school.

"When I was growing up," Posluszny said, "[Arrington] was my favorite."

Both players also won the Bednarik Award presented by the Maxwell Club since 1995 to the College Defensive Player of the Year. The award is named after another great linebacker, Chuck Bednarik, who's also in the College and Pro Football Halls of Fame. Linebackers have won it all but six times with Posluszny being the only two-time winner (2005–06). When Arrington received the award in 1999, he also finished ninth in the Heisman Trophy voting. Connor also was a recipient in 2007.

Butkus, and Bednarik 15 years before him, were two-way players who were outstanding centers as well as linebackers. Butkus was a two-time consensus All-American at Illinois and All-Pro with the Chicago Bears and Bednarik was a consensus pick at Penn and All-Pro with the Philadelphia Eagles.

The Butkus Award given by the Downtown Athletic Club of Orlando is special, and the pro linebackers know it. In 2008 the Orlando club created a similar award for the NFL, and five years later Penn State's NaVorro Bowman was the recipient as a San Francisco 49er.

When Arrington won in 1999 he not only beat out teammate Short but also Mark Simoneau of Kansas State and Raynoc Thompson of Tennessee. Posluszny beat out Ohio State's A. J. Hawk and Alabama's DeMeco Ryans in 2005, but in 2006 he and Laurinaitis finished behind Willis. (Laurinaitis won it the next year.) Like Arrington and Posluszny, all those finalists went on to NFL careers.

Asked by the *Inquirer*'s Fitzpatrick what winning the Bednarik and Butkus Awards meant to him, Posluszny spoke for all linebackers when he replied, "They're both huge honors, but I'd have to say, as a linebacker, that this one [the Butkus] means a lot more to me. Playing linebacker, to win the Butkus Award means you're the top person at your position, and that's the biggest thing you can do."

78 Hugo Bezdek and the Mystery Team

Long before Joe Paterno took Penn State to the pinnacle of college football, Hugo Bezdek almost did it.

Bezdek's teams from 1919 through 1923 were among the best in the nation, and the 1922 squad played in the Rose Bowl, which had even more prestige back then because it was the only postseason game. But that 1922 team didn't deserve the trip to Pasadena after blowing Penn State's 30-game undefeated streak by winning just one of its last five games.

The 1921 Mystery Team probably deserved an invitation the previous year, and Rose Bowl officials knew it. That's why they secretly invited the 1922 team to play in the New Year's Day game four months before the regular season began. When that agreement became known midway through the 1922 season, Rose Bowl leaders said Penn State was invited "as a tribute to past achievements."

Actually, Bezdek had manipulated the Rose Bowl invitation after missing out in 1920 and feeling snubbed in 1921. He had deep connections within the Rose Bowl hierarchy from his six years as the head football coach at Oregon and six years as the West Coast scout for baseball's Pittsburgh Pirates. Bezdek's 1916 Oregon team had won the second Rose Bowl and in the third Rose Bowl played between military teams, Bezdek had coached the winning Mare Island Marines.

Bezdek had also been the basketball and baseball coach at Oregon while scouting for the Pirates, and midway through the 1917 Major League Baseball season he took over as manager of the Pirates. Things were much different back then, and while still managing the Pirates in August 1918, Bezdek became the football coach and supervisor of athletics at Penn State. A year later he turned down a new Pirates contract and stayed with Penn State with additional academic responsibilities.

For the next four years, Penn State was one of the best teams in the country. After losing to Dartmouth in the third game of 1919, Bezdek's teams did not lose until a 14–0 upset by Navy in the seventh game of 1922. His 1919 team finished 7–1 and his following two teams were undefeated but tied in 1920 (7–0–2) and 1921 (8–0–2). Winning against not only eastern foes but also intersectional opponents such as Nebraska, North Carolina State, and Georgia Tech brought All-America honors to several players,

The 1923 Rose Bowl

The 1923 Rose Bowl is an integral part of the Tournament of Roses history but not because it was Penn State and Southern Cal's first bowl game. This was the first Rose Bowl game played in the current site in the city's Arroyo Secco section and the first bowl game ever broadcast on radio, although the audience was limited to the Los Angeles area.

It was not known as the Rose Bowl game back then, but informally as the East-West Game. Years later the name of the stadium transformed into the name of the annual game. A local newspaper reporter named Harlan "Dusty" Hall, who also was the press agent for the Tournament of Roses, came up with the stadium's name because it was similar in design to the Yale Bowl in New Haven.

The 1923 game should be known as The Game of Losers. A blunder led Penn State to be invited before the 1922 season and USC was asked to be the host team only after the three-time Pacific Coast Conference champion, California, rejected the invitation. Still, USC was the favorite after losing only to California 12–0 in 10 games.

The trip to Pasadena was enjoyable for Penn State's players, who stopped at the Grand Canyon en route, visited Hollywood while there, and toured Southern Texas and Chicago on the way back.

Because of the bad blood between Bezdek and USC's coach Elmer "Gloomy Gus" Henderson dating from Bezdek's days at Oregon, they had a shouting match and near-fistfight on the field when the State team arrived late because of a major traffic jam and the game had to be delayed 45 minutes.

The Nittany Lions took a 3–0 lead, but as the game progressed they wore down in the unfamiliar hot weather. "Their hard jaunt across the country and the week they spent in conditioning had a telling effect," wrote Mark Kelly of the Universal News Service. "Their attack lacked fire and dash. They were lethargic after the first 10 minutes..."

Penn State lost 14–3, but the game was not a total loss. A check of $21,349.64 was State's share of the Rose Bowl profits.

including first-team recognition for halfbacks Charlie Way (1920) and Glenn Killinger (1921) and guard Red Griffiths (1920).

Bezdek had positioned his 1920 team to go to the Rose Bowl but ties against surprising Lehigh (7–7) and Pitt (0–0) at the close of the season ended that maneuver. His 1921 team was supposed to be a rebuilding year. When that team opened the season with four convincing home victories, including three shutouts by 24 points or more with only seven points scored against them, eastern sportswriters began referring to them as the Mystery Team.

That's why all the big eastern city newspapers converged at Harvard's Soldiers Field on October 22 to see the Mystery Team play powerful Harvard. Harvard had not lost in three years and its 1921 team was loaded with veterans that romped over five opponents.

In what was another of the great games in Penn State history, the heavily underdog Nittany Lions shocked Harvard, the 30,000 spectators, and the sportswriters. The game appeared to be a laughter at first, with Harvard jumping off to a 14–0 first-quarter lead, but by midway in the fourth quarter Penn State was ahead 21–14. With darkness closing in fast, Harvard drove 43 yards to tie with less than three minutes remaining. Penn State quickly drove 80 yards to reach the Harvard 10-yard line, but three runs and a fourth-down pass failed and the game ended tied 21–21. Some sportswriters criticized the referee for continuing to play in the darkness, but he had followed the rules. "The Nittany Lions had trampled the Crimson," wrote one sportswriter, adding that if it was not for fumbles, State "would have beaten Harvard by a couple of touchdowns."

The following week the Mystery Team impressed the dubious sportswriters again, hammering powerful Georgia Tech 28–7 before another crowd of 30,000 in New York's Polo Grounds. Decisive wins over Carnegie Tech and Navy followed before bitter rival Pitt spoiled the season with another scoreless tie and the Lions wound up the season with Penn State's first trip to the West Coast, defeating Washington 21–7.

Bezdek's 1922 team seemed headed for another undefeated season, but after a 0–0 tie at the Polo Grounds in Penn State's first-ever game against Syracuse, they fell apart, losing to Navy, Penn, and Pitt. They also lost the Rose Bowl to USC 14–3 and finished with a 6–4–1 record. That was the beginning of the end for Bezdek and Penn State.

Penn State would not win more than six games again until 1941. Bezdek resigned as football coach after 1929 but stayed on as athletic director. He was forced out in 1936 after years of antagonizing his bosses, other administrators, and influential alumni.

The Mystery Team lives on in Penn State All-Sports Museum, where fans can see the winning football from that first trip to the West Coast.

79 The Lickliter Game

Lickliter. Just the utterance of the name sends Penn State basketball fans into a tizzy. Lickliter, first name Sam, is the referee blamed for making the worst call against Penn State in its 119-year basketball history, a wrong decision that cost the Nittany Lions an all-time upset over Indiana in 1993.

It's known forever as the Lickliter Game and is the everlasting symbol of frustration, missed opportunities, and just plain bad luck that has plagued the school's basketball team for nearly all of its existence. There have been other memorable and classic games over the decades, wins and losses, and this one with its infuriating ending is at the proverbial bottom of the barrel.

This was Penn State's first year in the Big Ten and Indiana was at Rec Hall for the first time ever on Tuesday, February 8. The Hoosiers were No. 1 in the nation and the Lions were off to their worst start in nine years with a 6–11 record and eight Big Ten defeats that included a 48-point blowout in Bloomington a month earlier.

ESPN was there to broadcast the game nationally, a rarity for Penn State in an era before the plethora of cable TV outlets saturated the country with local, regional, and national games. Rec Hall was jammed with a noisy, standing-room crowd. Indiana's flamboyant coach, Bobby Knight, was making his first appearance at Rec Hall since his coaching days at Army in 1971 and since his famous 1989 quip denigrating Penn State's entrance into the Big Ten as a "camping trip. There is nothing for about 100 miles."

Knight's latest camping trip did not go the way he intended.

Dave Jones, who covered the game for the *Harrisburg Patriot-News*, described the first half as plodding "almost like a prizefight struggling to find its rhythm" and Indiana led by just two at the intermission. The game remained close in the second half, and with 31 seconds left and Penn State leading 65–64, IU lost the ball at half-court. Penn State guard Michael Jennings grabbed it and scored on a layup just as he was fouled by Damon Bailey. Jennings made the shot giving the Lions a four-point lead as the delirious crowd seemed to make Rec Hall vibrate.

What happened in the next few seconds lives forever in Penn State basketball's court of infamy.

Penn State's Greg Bartram caught a long inbounds pass and went in for a layup amid bedlam with 17 seconds on the clock. Suddenly, the noise dissipated. A referee was waving off Bartram's points. Lickliter signaled pushing off against Bartram. He was right about that part, but Lickliter missed what everyone else and the TV cameras had seen. Indiana's Chris Reynolds had clearly yanked on

Bartram's jersey, causing the push off. The boos continued to reverberate throughout the arena as IU narrowed the lead to two with successful free throws, and the TV commentators Tim Brando and Bill Raftery complained about the call as they showed the replay.

The Freeze Games

There are several memorable games in Penn State's basketball history but the most unusual ones were the two against its then-biggest rival Pittsburgh in 1944 and 1952 known as the Freeze Games.

Basketball rules were radically different in those years and teams often held the ball for long periods of time without shooting, forcing the opponent to attack, and, frequently commit fouls in the process. This was game strategy often deployed by underdogs, but also by coaches as a psychological ploy.

Doc Carlson, who coached Pitt from 1922 to 1953, often used this tactic when playing against Penn State "sliding zone defense" created by coach John Lawther (1937–49), and it was utilized by his protégés Elmer Gros (1949–54) and John Egli (1954–1968).

The most notorious of these Pitt–Penn State battles were called Freeze Games and there were two of them that stood out. The first occurred at Pittsburgh on January 15, 1944. Pitt held the ball for most of the 40 minutes with Penn State finally winning 15–12, which is still the lowest-scoring Penn State game since 1910.

Eight years later, at Rec Hall on March 1, 1952, Doc Carlson did it again. When the two teams had played in Pittsburgh in December, Penn State had won 62–40. In the rematch at Rec Hall, the Lions led 7–3 at the end of the first 10-minute quarter and hardly touched the ball in the second quarter but still held the lead, 9–4. When one of the Pitt players sat down on the floor holding the ball, "a coed came out and offered him her knitting," according to the *Daily Collegian*.

The third quarter was a near-repeat of the second, with Pitt scoring two points to make it 9–6. With six minutes left, Pitt quit the freeze and finally played regular basketball. It was no contest as Penn State won 24–9. Three weeks later the Nittany Lions were in the NCAA postseason tournament for just the second time in school history. Doc Carlson and his "freezing" Panthers were sitting at home.

Indiana had a chance to win it with less than a second left in regulation when Greg Graham was fouled on a three-point attempt, but he missed one free throw to send the game into overtime. With the game still tied near the end of the first overtime, Penn State had the last shot but missed on an air ball. Poor foul shooting in the second overtime hurt the Lions as they missed five of eight attempts and with 6.5 second left Indiana grabbed the lead 86–84. Bailey clinched the Hoosiers' victory with two foul shots with 1.4 seconds left.

Penn State coach Bruce Parkhill said little about Lickliter's call after the game. "I was very surprised by it," he said. Knight wouldn't talk about it but said, "If I was a fan—and I'm not—I'd be rooting for Penn State. They deserved to win."

The next day Rich Falk, the Big Ten's supervisor of officials, admitted Lickliter missed the intentional foul by Reynolds. Falk said Lickliter's view had been blocked because Bartram was two full steps ahead of Reynolds. "Obviously it was a call that was blown, but it's not a call that can be made if it is not seen," Falk said. "I assure you that nobody feels worse than the official."

Baloney. Parkhill and the Penn State players felt worse, and so did their fans. They had sympathy, too, from thousands of people around the country who either saw the game or watched the repeated replay of Lickliter's mistake on ESPN and local newscasts.

"I couldn't believe how many letters I got," Parkhill told Jones years later. Somewhere close to 100. They all said something like, 'I was watching the game and I've never done this but I felt compelled to write.'"

In the still-simmering controversy, what's been almost forgotten is that another official, Gene Monje, was equally responsible for what happened.

"Monje was in back of the play and had an unobstructed view," said Steve Jones, who did the play-by-play for Penn State's radio network broadcast of the game. "He could have conferred with Lickliter, but he kept quiet."

Lickliter, a retired high school principal from Dayton, Ohio, spent 36 years as a basketball referee and then became the supervisor of officials for the Mid-American Conference and the Summit League. In 2009 he was inducted into the Ohio Basketball Hall of Fame. Sixteen years earlier he was an automatic inductee into Penn State Basketball's Hall of Shame. Monje is there, too.

80. Get Involved with the Quarterback Club and the Coaches Caravan

Interacting and socializing with the head coach is what fans enjoy most outside of going to games and tailgating. Over the decades at Penn State, that has meant being part of the State College Quarterback Club or mingling with the coach at a special event elsewhere for alumni and other fans who don't live close to State College.

The Quarterback Club traces its roots to the 1930s for its weekly in-season lunches with the head coach. Nowadays, the Coaches Caravan is an off-season alternative for meeting and talking with the head coach.

What started as a small, informal gathering of town businessmen to watch game film with head coach Bob Higgins nearly 80 years ago is now the 750-member State College Quarterback Club. Although other college coaches may have lunches with fans during the season, there is nothing elsewhere that duplicates the tradition and activities of the Penn State group, as I discovered in researching the club's history.

"I'm not aware of any clubs that meet weekly and the head coach is in attendance at each one," said Claude Felton, the senior associate athletic director for communications at Georgia, who has been in charge of sports information since 1979. "I doubt you are going to find any that have been meeting as long as ours with the head coach."

Since 1941, the State College Quarterback Club has been a nonprofit entity that not only meets for lunch but provides other funding for the football program, including sponsorship of the club's premier event, the annual end-of-season football awards banquet. The club's Academic Enhancement Fund for Football, an endowment totaling more than $100,000, helps finance academic support. When the new head coach, James Franklin, needed a new six-passenger golf cart to get around the Penn State campus, the club donated $18,000, in accordance with NCAA rules, to help pay for one.

"We exist solely to support the football program," said Pete Rohrer, who served as club president from 2012 to 2014. "Most of our members are average fans, men and women who enjoy Penn State football. The maximum we can have in the Mt. Nittany Lounge for our Wednesday luncheons is in the 470–480 range so we can only have a small number of outside guests each week. Some members show up two hours before the start to get a table up front. Many members drive at least an hour to get to the luncheons and a few travel even longer."

In the past, the head coach has been the featured speaker in the off-season at receptions and dinners around the state and in selected eastern cities, but those appearances were infrequent. Sometimes alumni chapters and other fan-based organizations had to wait years to host the head coach.

Since the spring of 2012 the Coaches Caravan has been able to fill part of that void. It's a two-to-three-week multi-stop swing through Pennsylvania and other East Coast states featuring the head football coach, but also includes the head coaches of Penn State's other varsity sports.

The Coaches Caravan was the idea of Bill O'Brien when he became the first new head coach at Penn State in nearly 50 years. "I recall his saying, 'Let's just get in a bus and go' in the winter of 2012," said Roger Williams, the Penn State Alumni Association's recently retired executive director. The Alumni Association and the Nittany Lion Club, the fund-raising arm of the athletic department, liked the idea. "We teamed up to co-sponsor and execute it," Williams said.

The coaches travel in a luxury bus decorated on the outside to attract attention. Another similar-looking bus and two vans for staff and other officials are part of the caravan. Each stop is for either a lunch, dinner, or reception. The caravan is not on the road all the time during the two-to-three-week span in May, but hits selected cities for three days in each week.

In that first year, the caravan made 18 stops in six states, including Ohio and the District of Columbia, and in the third year, when introducing Franklin as the new head coach, the caravan made 17 stops in five states. In the second season for each coach the tour was trimmed to 12 stops in fewer states. More than 20,000 have turned out for the 59 events.

"The Coaches Caravans have been extremely well received by the Penn State faithful," said Williams. "They have been the very best public-relations and alumni-relations programs the university put forward during the worst of our crisis years since November of 2011. This was an opportunity to hear from our head coaches in many varsity sports programs and see how strong the entire Intercollegiate Athletics program is, academically as well as athletically."

So if you can't get Penn State's head football coach to your tailgate before a game at Beaver Stadium, get involved with the Quarterback Club or the Coaches Caravan. They're the next-best thing.

81 Pop Golden and New Beaver Field

Pop Golden had a vision more than a century ago, and what he did transformed Penn State football from a struggling, small-time regional entity into one of the best teams east of the Mississippi River.

His name today is hardly known except by historians. But his mark and influence is still visible on campus. If not for Pop Golden, the Nittany Lion Shrine might not be located where it is today and the numerals of the 1911 and 1912 teams might not be immortalized at Beaver Stadium.

William "Pop" Golden was hired as Penn State's director of physical training in 1900. The position made him responsible for the physical health of all the students and the training regimen for the athletes, but he also was the nominal head coach of the four varsity sports teams—baseball, football, track, and basketball.

Golden was the fourth head coach of the football team. But in that early era the players ran the team with the assistance of some former players. That's the way it had been since the first trainer-coach George Hoskins in 1893, and that's the way it would remain until Golden hired Bill Hollenbeck as the seventh head coach in 1909.

Golden was in his early thirties and his warm personality soon made him one of the most popular people on campus. He brought new life to the students by devising exercise programs and encouraging their participation in indoor and outdoor games and activities. Working closely with the Alumni Association and the Athletic Board/Association that supervised sports, Golden quickly turned himself into a fund-raiser and innovator as well as an administrator and relinquished the football coaching in 1903.

He began raising funds for the first scholarships (tuition, room, and board) that would attract better athletes, and he set up a special training table to feed the football and baseball players. By the fall of 1904, 25 athletes were receiving annual stipends of $85 and Golden had funded the construction of a special three-story building for them and 10 others, called the Track House. It included living quarters, a dining room, a club room, training facilities, and locker rooms for both the home and visiting teams.

In February 1906 Golden was placed in charge of the athletic department. However, it wasn't until a bylaws change in January 1907 that he formally became the school's first director of athletics.

All the outdoor athletic facilities were then located in a small area just east of Old Main and called Beaver Field. Golden drew up plans for a new, all-encompassing athletic facility that would include new fields for football, baseball, track, lacrosse, and tennis and an outdoor basketball court, swimming pool, and an ice-skating rink for hockey. Golden's ingenious proposal also called for a new gymnasium building to supplant the Armory and a new indoor structure for baseball and track called a batting cage "with a glass roof and earth floor, 100x150 feet…surrounded by a cinder path running track…." He also planned to move the Track House to this new location and construct a second similar building for visiting teams.

Eighteen acres of woods about a quarter of a mile northwest of Old Main were designated for the project. But it wasn't until 1908 that the project began to come to fruition when the Pennsylvania legislature allocated $15,000 (more than $400,000 today) for the new athletic fields after a personal appeal by Golden. However, everything else was put on hold.

That same year, a clique of alumni within the Athletic Association led by George Meek amended the bylaws to establish a new position of "graduate manager of athletics" who would have total control over the athletic department, weakening the athletic director's authority. Not surprisingly, Meek was chosen to fill the new position.

That was the beginning of the end for Pop Golden as his power and responsibilities diminished rapidly.

By mid-spring of 1908, New Beaver Field, including a cinder track, was ready except for a grandstand. It was located about where the Nittany Parking Deck and Kern Graduate School are today, adjacent to the Nittany Lion Inn.

On May 7, 1908, New Beaver Field was used for the first time for a new scholastic track meet organized by Golden that attracted 75 teams and a baseball game against Dickinson, which Penn State won 6–4.

In March 1909 the 500-seat grandstand was moved from the old field to the new one, and on October 2, 1909, the football team played its first game there, beating Grove City 31–0. The team would not lose on New Beaver Field until 20 games later when Notre Dame won 14–7 in 1913.

By then Pop Golden was gone. He resigned in June 1912 and went into the insurance business in Pittsburgh. In time, many of his plans for Penn State athletics came true, including a new indoor facility that is still there, Recreation Hall. He was still alive to see many of them, passing away in 1949.

Pop Golden's name and what he did for Penn State athletics are hardly known by the Nittany Lions football nation. But now you know.

82 Listen to Steve and Jack on the Radio and Call In

Steve Jones and Jack Ham have been the voices of Penn State football since the 2000 season. With all the coaching changes in the last four years, they are the soul of the program, the link that binds the glorious past to the uncertain future. And listening to them is a delight for Penn State football fans.

Fran Fisher and George Paterno set the standard even though they only worked together in the last six years of the 1990s. They were "down home," like two old friends sometimes talking casually about the game while sitting on a bar stool—incisive and occasionally humorous but rather low-key. Jones and Ham are more up-tempo, two good friends anticipating each other's thoughts and words, complementing each other despite their separate roles.

"Steady Steve Jones rarely misses down-and-distance or play-by-play details and color analyst Jack Ham clearly conveys his football knowledge," wrote Steve Samspell in one of his media columns for the *Altoona Mirror*.

Ham, the Hall of Fame linebacker rated by many as the best in Penn State history, has already surpassed Paterno's 12-year tenure as the network radio analyst from 1988 to 1999. Jones already holds the record for most years involved with the radio broadcast (24 in 2015) after eight years as the third man on the team from 1983 to 1990 before his play-by-play stint began. Now he is creeping up on Fisher's combined 19 years as the play-by-play broadcaster (1970–82, 1994–99).

Mickey Bergstein is the only other broadcaster to rival the four in the decades since the first radio broadcast of a Penn State home game by the college radio station on October 1, 1927. Bergstein was an analyst for nine years (1953–55, 1959, 1964–68) and did play-by-play for three years (1956–58).

The role of the third man in the booth has changed over the years, from Fisher's first three years (1966–68) to Roger Corey today. Responsibilities have varied from doing commentary during commercial breaks for local stations to giving scores and handling pregame and postgame shows. It's too detailed to go into here.

At one time a director-producer and engineer were in the booth. That's how Corey started in 1993. Now he's involved in

Fran and George

Listening to Fran Fisher and George Paterno broadcast the football games on the radio network in the late 1990s was a little like the old Dean Martin and Jerry Lewis shows with Fran the straight man. George wasn't as funny as Jerry Lewis, but his remarks were certainly freewheeling and candid, often criticizing the coaching of his older brother.

The brothers had played together at Brown in 1948 and 1949, and George went on to be the head coach at the Merchant Marine Academy for a nine-year stretch interrupted by two years as defensive coordinator at Michigan State. Upon leaving the academy after 1975, he was hired to do the analysis for Penn State's tape-delayed two-and-a-half hour telecast of every game. In 1998 Paterno moved over to radio, working with two other play-by-play men before Fisher returned in 1994 after a 12-year absence.

"If you listened to us in the stadium, it was like getting two games for the price of one: the game you saw and the game we broadcast," Fisher joked as I was writing this book.

George was a dedicated Brooklyn guy and lived in New York City while commuting to State College for home games. He passed away on June 23, 2002, after a lingering illness.

"Working with George was a pleasure because he was so knowledgeable," Fran Fisher said. "Secondly, he knew the game and he said what he thought, and it had no bearing on his brother being the head coach. He was a good friend and a good guy to be with on the air and off it. Period."

commercials, updating scores, and covering the halftime break. Frank Giardina succeeded Jones as the third man from 1990 to 2000 and from 2012 to 2014 Loren Crispell reported from the sideline.

In 1994, Fisher and Paterno started a live pregame show before an audience in the tailgating area with Corey as the announcer. Since then, Corey has become more a part of the 90-minute program, helping to coordinate the audience questions for Jones and Ham. He does the same for the popular weekly telephone call-in show that Jones does with the head football coach in season.

"I actually was the engineer when Fran and Joe [Paterno] started doing the call-ins in 1988 from the old Greenberg building," Corey said. "I began going on the air with Steve and Jack in 2000."

For years those Thursday 6:00–7:00 PM call-in shows were the main link between Paterno and Penn State fans, with Paterno sparring verbally with some and joking with others. Some fans called so often they became well-known to listeners, such as "Judy from Muncy" or "Jerry from Philadelphia."

Judy came to represent the most loyal of Paterno and Penn State fans. Paterno could do no wrong. She never second-guessed him like other callers and even Paterno sounded embarrassed at times by all her praise. I became an acquaintance of Judy's a few years ago. Her real name was Judy Best and she was a registered nurse who did live in Muncy, which is about 10 miles east of Williamsport, home of the Little League. Unfortunately, Judy lost her battle with cancer in November 2014 at the age of 60.

"I will miss Judy's always cheerful 'hi guys' when she called in to talk with JoePa on Thursday evenings," a fan of the call-in show, A. C. Verbit of King of Prussia, posted on the funeral home's website. "I looked forward to her comments about PSU football and cheerfulness...May she rest in peace. All Penn State Fans appreciate her support. —WE ARE—"

From the beginning, the call-in shows were based in a small room at the football facility, but in 2012 new coach Bill O'Brien moved it to the main room of a local sports bar to make the show livelier. Questions from the audience are mixed in with the telephone calls, and the room is packed with fans of all ages. On home-game Thursdays, the football staff provides a blue bus to transport students camped out a half mile away at Beaver Stadium. The telephone calls continue to be entertaining and informative.

The man in charge of the game broadcast and call-in shows is Jeff Tarman, son of Penn State's former athletic director, Jim Tarman. He joined the team in 1991 when Penn State sold the network rights to the American Network Group and has continued in that role through four different network rights-holders, including Learfield since 2006.

The best way for Penn State fans to enjoy Steve and Jack's game-day broadcast is to listen to them on the radio when they are in Beaver Stadium. I've done that for years. It's just too bad we Penn State fans can't do it for away games.

83 The Hall of Fame Running Backs

Penn State has more running backs in the College Football Hall of Fame than any other position, but it's doubtful most Nittany Lions fans can name all of them.

Sure, Heisman Trophy winner John Cappelletti and All-Americans Lydell Mitchell and Curt Warner are well-known because they played for Coach Joe Paterno. How many fans have heard of the first four backs inducted into the Hall of Fame: Pete

Mauthe (1957), Glenn Killinger (1971), Harry Wilson (1973), and Shorty Miller (1974)?

Technically, Miller was a quarterback, but not typical of the modern-day quarterback. In the power-running single-wing formation age of college football until the late 1940s, all the backs carried the ball and most them passed, too. The quarterback called the signals, but as the single-wing evolved in the 1920s and 1930s, the quarterback became the prime blocking back, like fullbacks today. Miller ran the ball as much as his teammate Mauthe, who was the fullback.

Killinger also played quarterback, but he and Wilson were primarily halfbacks. Unlike Mauthe or Miller, they were consensus first-team All-Americans in the early 1920s. Charlie Way was, too, but despite being the Nittany Lions' first All-American running back (and fourth first-team All-American overall) in 1920, Way never made it into the Hall of Fame. Killinger followed Way as an All-American in 1921, and two years later Wilson was selected. After Wilson, it wasn't until 1969 that Penn State had another first team All-American back in Charlie Pittman and, like Way, he's not in the Hall of Fame either.

Way, Killinger, and Wilson played at a time when college football was second only to Major League Baseball in popularity and pro football was an afterthought. They were integral to the success of Coach Hugo Bezdek's teams that were among the best in the nation and undefeated in 30 straight games between 1919 and 1923. Their commonality is that all three had checkered high school experiences and didn't emerge as stars until their junior years.

Way, who also played quarterback as a sophomore, was a second-team All-American on the 1919 squad when sportswriters gave him several nicknames because of his breakaway speed, including Gang-Way and One-Way. He didn't play enough to even earn a freshman numeral in 1916 but cracked the starting lineup in the fifth game of 1917 before going off to World War II in 1918.

Way was a scrawny 5'7", 145-pounder who seldom started a game or played in the first half in his junior and senior years because he was not durable or rugged. That kept him fresh when the opposing defense was tiring, and he exploited that flaw with his spectacular running.

"Light Horse" Harry Wilson rivals Lenny Moore as perhaps the best all-around running back in Penn State history. He is the only Nittany Lion to be inducted into the College Football and National Lacrosse Halls of Fame.

Killinger never played high school football and didn't even make the freshman team or earn a letter as a sophomore. Before he graduated, he earned nine letters in football, basketball, and baseball—playing third base on Bezdek's 1920–21 teams, which still hold the school record for an undefeated streak of 31 games.

At 5'10" and 160 pounds, Killinger was more of a "juke" runner who could dash quickly away from would-be tacklers but also squeeze through small holes at the scrimmage line. He was also a good passer, blocker, and defensive back and the star of the 1921 Mystery Team that went 8–0–2 and almost went to the Rose Bowl.

Killinger's 85-yard kickoff return against Georgia Tech at New York's Polo Grounds in the sixth game of the year that spurred a 28–7 comeback was the key play of the 1921 season. Walter Camp was there to see it, following up after watching Killinger and the Lions outplay Harvard at Cambridge the week before in a 21–21 tie. Camp went into the Polo Grounds dressing room to congratulate Killinger, and when he selected Killinger to his All-American team, he wrote that Killinger "has the most peculiar elusiveness of any back on the field this year."

During World War II, Killinger would become famous as coach of the North Carolina Pre-Flight Team and the man who helped turn Otto Graham into a Pro Football Hall of Fame quarterback. He also became a successful football and baseball coach at West Chester and in 1970 was inducted into the College Baseball Coaches Associations Hall of Fame.

Wilson is the only Penn State athlete enshrined in both the College Football Hall of Fame and the National Lacrosse Hall of Fame, as well as the only one to also earn first-team All-American football honors with another team. That was at West Point in 1926, after he transferred following Penn State's 1923 season. Yet he originally enrolled at Penn State to play basketball.

At 5'9" and 170 pounds, Wilson may have had only one equal as the best all-around back in Penn State history: Lenny Moore.

Wilson scored 25 touchdowns in 1922–23, including the three that helped upset Navy 21–0 in 1923 in one of the greatest one-man performances ever at Beaver Field/Stadium. He returned an interception 55 yards, ran back a kickoff for 95 yards, and then dashed 72 yards off a fake reverse. That prompted sportswriters to give him the nickname Light Horse after Revolutionary War cavalry officer Light-Horse Harry Lee, who was the father of the famous Civil War general Robert E. Lee.

During World War II, Wilson commanded the 42nd bomber group in the South Pacific, flying 48 combat missions and winning the Distinguished Flying Cross and the Air Medal with six oak leaf clusters.

Now you can name Penn State's Hall of Fame running backs.

84 Penn State's Rudy and Other Walk-Ons

Recruits are the lifeblood of every college football team, and with the 85 scholarship limitations of today it's vital to have walk-ons who pay their own way to be on the team.

Penn State has had its share of walk-ons over the decades. Some became starters and set school records and one, defensive back Neal Smith, became a first-team All-American in 1969. Wide receiver Gregg Garrity scored the memorable fourth-quarter touchdown against Georgia that gave Penn State the national championship in 1982, and John Bruno's punting in the 1986 title game was crucial to the 14–10 upset over Miami. In 1999 center Joe Iorio became the first (and only) true freshman walk-on ever to start a game under Coach Joe Paterno.

Most walk-ons rarely get into enough games to earn a letter and many are simply practice fodder. But without them, teams would not have enough players each year to meet the grueling, time-consuming practice schedule from the August preseason through the January postseason.

When the NCAA reduced scholarships and encouraged transferring in the aftermath of the child abuse scandal in the summer of 2012, new coach Bill O'Brien intensified the recruiting of walk-ons and gave them a new name—run-ons—to show how valuable they were to his team.

"These guys don't walk, they run on the field, they sprint on the field, they bust their butt on the field," O'Brien explained. "[The run-on program is] something that we know is going to be important in the next few years...hopefully that resonates with kids in Pennsylvania especially."

O'Brien inherited an invited walk-on senior quarterback who had earned a scholarship and he proceeded to turn Matt McGloin from an erratic thrower of interceptions into the Big Ten's leading passer. In leading the 2012 team to a surprising 8–4 finish, McGloin set a new team record for season passing yardage (3,266 yards), tied Daryll Clark's record mark for single-season touchdowns (24), and broke Clark's record for career touchdowns (with 46) while throwing just five interceptions. McGloin was rewarded with college football's biggest walk-on prize, the Burlsworth Trophy given to "the nation's outstanding football player who started his career as a walk-on."

At the other end of the walk-on spectrum are players like Jeff Butya, who failed to make the team in 1979 but did in 1980 and 1981. He was a 5'6", 160-pound running back who was short, stocky, and slow, but he worked hard in practice. He took a physical beating on the foreign squad that scrimmaged against the starters every Tuesday, but they loved his fun-loving attitude.

Butya had one dream. All he wanted to do was play in one game, just like Rudy Ruettiger had done at Notre Dame in 1975 and become famous when a movie was made of his walk-on experience. Butya's aspiration reached fruition in the opening game of 1981 when he was in on five kickoffs, made one tackle, and ran the ball on the next-to-last play of the game for a two-yard loss. He never played in another game. "That's our Rudy," said Hall of Fame tailback Curt Warner. "He never really quit. He never gave up."

Walk-ons actually trace to the beginning of football at Penn State in 1887. Everyone walked on until scholarships were used to recruit players in the early 1900s. Penn State eliminated scholarships from 1929 until 1949. During this period some players were enticed by receiving help to find jobs, but most simply tried out of the team on their own. The walk-on program as we know it didn't accelerate until the Joe Paterno coaching era.

So when selecting the all-time walk-ons, it almost always boils down to the players since 1966. The true walk-ons earlier who became standouts are virtually unknown with the rare exception, like future All-American halfback Glenn Killinger.

In 2012, *Blue White Illustrated*, a magazine for Penn State fans, asked me to rank the five top walk-ons in history on the basis of what they did at Penn State and not later in the NFL. Here were my choices:

Top 5 Penn State Walk-Ons
1. Neal Smith, DB (1967–69)
2. Deon Butler, WR (2005–08)
3. Gregg Garrity, WR (1980–82)
4. John Bruno, P (1984–86)
5. (Tie) Troy Drayton, WR/TE (1991–92) and Joe Iorio, C (1999–2002)

Honorable Mentions (Alphabetical Order):
Jeremy Boone, P (2007–09)
Tom Bradley, ST (1977–78)
Duffy Cobbs, DB (1983–86)
Ron Coder, LB (1974–75)
Marlon Forbes, DB (1992–94)
Travis Forney, K (1997–99)
Rich Gardner, DB (2000–03
Robby Gould, K (2001–04)
Dave Kasperian, HB (1957–58)
Matt McGloin, QB (2010–12)

That year another fan magazine, *Fight On State* magazine, compiled a more extensive list of the best all-time walk-ons by position with my assistance:

- **Quarterback:** Matt McGloin (2010–12); Bobby Williams (1942–43, 1946–47)
- **Running Back:** Gerry Collins (1989–91); Ambrose Fletcher (1994–95); Dave Kasperian (1957–58); Mick Blosser (FB, 2000–01)
- **Wide Receiver:** Deon Butler (2005–08); Gregg Garrity (1980–82); Graham Zug (2008–10); Ethan Kilmer (2004–05); Rocky Washington (1982, 1984)
- **Tight End:** Troy Drayton (1991–92); Matt Kranchik (2003); Casey Williams (2002); Mike Lukac (2002–03)
- **Offensive Line:** Joe Iorio (C, 1999–2002); Kevin Conlin (1996–97); Francis Spano (C, 1999); Lance Antolick (2005); Mike Heller (1991–92)
- **Defensive Line:** Ron Coder (1974–75); Jim Shaw (2005–06)
- **Linebacker:** Josh Hull (2006–09); Gerald Filardi (1994–96); Andy Ryland (2002–03)

- **Defensive Back:** Neal Smith (1967–69); Rich Gardner (2000–03); Marlon Forbes (1992–94); Duffy Cobbs (1983–86); Paul Cronin (2002–05); Nolan McCready (2004–06)
- **Kicker:** Travis Forney (1997–99); Robbie Gould (2001–04); Collin Wagner (2009–10); Brian Franco (1979–81)
- **Punter:** John Bruno (1984–86); Jeremy Boone (2007–09)
- **Long Snapper:** Greg Truitt (1985–86, 1988)
- **Special Teams:** Tom Bradley (1977–78) and Bill Emerson (1982–83)

85 Boast About 48–14 and Root Against Pitt

The shocking score of the 1981 Pitt game still makes most older Penn State fans ecstatic, even though the once intense and fierce rivalry that was one of the best in college football is virtually nonexistent.

"This [rivalry] leaves an everlasting impression on you because, in Pennsylvania, it's the only game that counts, year-in, year-out," wrote Tim Panaccio in his detailed game-by-game book about the rivalry, *Beast of the East*, published shortly after the classic 1981 game. "Records don't mean a thing, just who wins this game."

Not anymore.

Located about 140 miles apart, the teams first met in 1893 and played 96 games until the last one in 2000. They've gone their separate ways since the shakeup in conference affiliations began with Penn State giving up its independence and joining the Big Ten in 1990. They'll battle again in early September 2016 and 2017, but the circumstances and atmosphere of those nonconference games will pale in comparison to the way it was.

The game has lost its impact and significance. Playing at the beginning of the season instead of at the end will not restore it. Meeting in early September will take away the tension, finality, and bitterness that dominated most of the late November games in the past and made the rivalry so meaningful.

Starting from the first Thanksgiving Day game in 1904, it was almost always the traditional last game of the regular season. Just like such comparable rivalries as Michigan–Ohio State, a win would gratify the victor and devastate the disconsolate loser for at least the next 12 months and sometimes for years. Penn State's only losses to Pitt in the 1940 and 1948 seasons knocked the Lions out of New Year's Day bowl games, and they reciprocated in 1956 and 1958.

Defeats by Pitt eventually cost head coaches Dick Harlow and Hugo Bezdek their jobs. A win or loss could also affect recruiting, especially in the then-talent-rich steel towns of western Pennsylvania as the schools fought over such future College Football Hall of Famers as Penn State's Richie Lucas and Pitt's Mike Ditka.

Penn State now has a comfortable lead in the series with 50 wins, 42 losses, and four ties. But from 1913 to 1938 Pitt dominated, winning every game but three during an early three-year span when Penn State won one (1919) and tied two (1920–21). The main reason for Pitt's 14-game winning streak in the 1920s and 1930s, when they claimed four national championships, was Penn State's de-emphasis on all athletics, eliminating scholarships and scouting from 1928 to 1949.

With the exception of four games (1931, 1939, 1942, and 1955), all the games from 1903 to 1963 were at Pittsburgh, a sore point that still rankles the oldest generation of Penn State fans. However, Penn State officials and the school's strong Pittsburgh alumni faction were partly to blame because they agreed to the one-sided arrangement primarily to help bolster prestige and recruiting. It started to change when Joe Paterno became the head coach. As Paterno's teams began beating Pitt on a regular basis, Paterno

Rip vs. Ben

For a 20-year period from 1950 to 1970, the Penn State–Syracuse series almost rivaled the animosity of Pitt–Penn State. The teams met annually since a 0–0 tie at New York's Polo Grounds in 1922 until Penn State entered the Big Ten in 1991 and played three games from 2008 to 2013. Penn State has a dominant 43–23–5 record, but from 1949 to 1971 the record was just 12–11 in the Lions favor.

Syracuse's greatest coach, Ben Schwartzwalder, made the difference in his tenure from 1949 to 1973, battling most of the time with Penn State's Rip Engle from 1950 to 1965. After Joe Paterno took over in 1966, Syracuse only won three more games, and two of them were 20 years later in 1987–88.

The Schwartzwalder-Engle games were a war. In 1952 Syracuse knocked Penn State out of a probable Cotton Bowl bid with a 25–7 upset at Syracuse. The next season a brawl at the Syracuse sideline ignited by an out-of-bounds attack on State's star running back Lenny Moore, with about 10 seconds left and Penn State leading 20–14, intensified the rivalry until Schwartzwalder's retirement. There were incidents and controversy almost every year. After Penn State was penalized seven times for an interpretation of illegal procedure in losing the 1958 game, Engle called it "the worst refereeing I've seen in 28 years."

Schwartzwalder's 1959 team beat Penn State at Beaver Field in a thrilling 20–18 game billed as the Battle of Unbeatens that opened the way for the school's only national title. His 1969 team almost pulled off the upset of the year at Archbold Stadium as Penn State had to battle back from a 14–0 third-quarter deficit to win 15–14 to preserve its second straight undefeated season and eventual No. 2 ranking.

The Monday after that 1969 game, Schwartzwalder told New York City sportswriters lousy officiating cost Syracuse the victory, claiming "25 or more bad calls." The ECAC investigated and found "no evidence of any laxity in officiating." The next year, Schwartzwalder's team beat Penn State for the last time 24–7 at Beaver Stadium and the Penn State–Syracuse series has never been the same.

became Pitt's most hated man—and he still is even in death, as the Internet trolls have proven.

Perhaps the biggest controversy of the series occurred in 1931. It was homecoming at New Beaver Field and Penn State's non-scholarship players were no match for Pitt's national power team. Pitt coach Jock Sutherland knew it, and he used only his backups, including third-stringers, in an easy 41–6 win. When Pitt's first team ran out on the field after the game to warm up, the home fans were insulted and booed heavily as they filed out. They held a grudge for years until they learned later that Higgins and Sutherland had agreed to Pitt's postgame warm-up.

Which brings us back to November 28, 1981, at Pitt Stadium. Pitt was No. 1 in the polls and already set for a Sugar Bowl game against No. 3 Georgia for the national championship. Penn State felt it could have been in that National Championship Game. A midseason upset loss to Miami when the Lions were No. 1 and Pitt was a close No. 2, and another defeat later at Alabama, had ruined their title aspirations. Penn State had played the second toughest schedule but Pitt was a touchdown favorite.

The feuding between Paterno and Pitt's coach, Jackie Sherill and the pre-game hostility set the tense mood for a classic Pitt-Penn State take-no-prisoners battle.

When the first quarter ended, it looked like a massacre was brewing with Penn State the victim. Pitt had overwhelmed the Lions, shutting down State's multiple offense and driving 54 and 63 yards for touchdown passes from Dan Marino to Dwight Collins, and now was poised at the Lions' 31-yard line with a second-and-7.

On the first play of the second quarter, Marino tried to hit Collins in the end zone but Roger Jackson intercepted, leading to an 80-yard touchdown drive by Penn State. Pitt roared back with a third-and-3 at the State 28, but Jackson's hard hit on the receiver caused another interception. With less than three minutes left in the half, Penn State capped a quick 80-yard drive and tied the game.

Six minutes into the second half, fiery linebacker Chet Parlarecchio, who had taunted Pitt and Sherrill in the days before the game, forced a fumble that led to Todd Blackledge's 42-yard touchdown pass to All-American Kenny Jackson. Less than three minutes later they hooked up again for a 45-yard touchdown and the game was virtually over.

"We were not your vintage Penn State team," Parlavecchio said years later. "We had an attitude. We had an anger about us."

Blackledge said beating Penn State's biggest rival 48–14 that day "was a great feeling individually, it was a great feeling as a team."

There will never be another moment like it in the history of Penn State football. To use a derogatory but not profane cheer uttered frequently during the height of the rivalry: "Under the Arm, Pitt."

 **Spider**

If Penn State fans don't know who Spider is, they surely have been living on another planet in recent years.

Brad "Spider" Caldwell is better known nowadays than most of Penn State's players going back to 1887. Until his retirement before the 2014 football season he was the equipment manager. Usually equipment managers are virtually invisible outside the program.

That's why no one knew Penn State has had more head football coaches than head equipment managers until my research and the *Blue White Illustrated* article I wrote in August 2014. James Franklin is the 16th head coach since George Hoskins in 1892. Spider's successor, Jay Takach, is the just the 11th head equipment manager.

Spider became the head man in 2002 after 15 years as the assistant for Tim Shope, who hired Caldwell fresh off his senior year as student manager of the 1986 team that played for the national championship. Spider has always been popular with the players, coaches, support staff, and media.

In fact, the 5'2" Caldwell was in his first week as a student manager in 1983 when defensive end Joe Hines gave him the nickname that has superseded his formal first name. He was born with severe scoliosis of the spine that left him with a half shoulder and long arms and legs. As he told the story in the book *What It Means*

The Trainers

Penn State's trainers are probably better known than the equipment managers. That's because the first three were also the head football coaches and three others were more notable as the head coaches of other Penn State varsity teams.

George Hoskins (1892–95), Dr. Sam Newton (1896–98), and Pop Golden (1900–10) were originally hired to be in charge of physical training for the student body, and coaching the varsity sports teams was an added responsibility. Dr. Dan Luby (1912–13), who followed Golden, was the first full-time trainer for football, and in 1937 Jack Hulme became the first trainer for all varsity teams.

In between Luby and Hulme (1937–46), five men were the team trainers but they were hired originally to coach other sports and two became Nittany Lions legends after serving as trainers for just a couple of years: boxing's Leo Houck (1926–33) and wrestling's Charlie Speidel (1934–35).

When Hulme died, his assistant Chuck Medlar was promoted and remained the head trainer (1963–77) while also being the head coach of the baseball team from 1963 to 1981. Yes, Penn State's baseball field, Medlar Field at Lubrano Park, is named after him. One of Medlar's assistant trainers, Jerry Slagle (1978–90), followed him, while another assistant, Jim Hochberg, became coordinator of sports medicine from 1980 to 1983. George Salvaterra (1991–2011) succeeded Slagle, and Tim Bream took over in 2012.

to Be a Nittany Lion, the players were in the locker room awaiting a team meeting when he "took off" across the locker room. "I was hunkered down real low, taking big, long strides, and I had my arms way out," Caldwell wrote. "Guys laughed…[and] Joe Hines said, 'He looks like Spider-Man'…I've been Spider ever since. Even my family calls me Spider."

Spider became a folk hero with the public in the aftermath of the child abuse scandal, the death of Joe Paterno, and the hiring of Bill O'Brien. When O'Brien decided before the 2012 season to end the famous tradition of not having names on game jerseys, the public learned that Spider's teacher wife, Karen, sewed the names on the jerseys, just as she had been mending the uniforms for 20 years.

Then O'Brien allowed ESPN to spend several days with the team during the 2013 preseason for a special series it aired as *All Access: Penn State Training Days*. Spider became the star.

"Caldwell wore a goofy leather football helmet and affected a Heisman pose," Mike Poorman reported for StateCollege.com. "He shared his heartfelt memories of Joe Paterno. He shared his genuine and genuinely funny interactions with the Penn State players…Caldwell became an Internet sensation, on YouTube and with some great GIFs. All feel-good stuff."

What made Spider a superstar was ESPN's *College GameDay*, one of the most watched shows in college football. When Penn State opened the 2013 season against Syracuse at New Jersey's Met Life Stadium on August 31, *College GameDay* featured a special segment on Spider. Even if you were not a Penn State fan, you couldn't help but like Spider.

"I love Spider," O'Brien frequently told the media. So did Paterno and all the other coaches, but they never said it publicly.

"Bill was a tremendous teacher," Spider told Poorman. "And so was Joe. Bill was a great teacher and loved the small details and stuff like that. I first learned that from Joe."

Equipment managers are a special breed. They do everything from ordering, cleaning, and repairing equipment and uniforms to setting up the game day locker rooms home and away. They and their assistants and student managers are the first ones and last ones at practice and at the stadiums on game day. They're up and down the sideline during the games, trying to resolve equipment issues before major problems develop.

Over the decades Penn State's equipment managers were called "stockroom attendants," since the stockroom of any athletic building was where the equipment was stored.

Ollie DeVictor was Penn State's first official equipment manager in 1919, and when he left after the 1920 season A. P. "Dean" Burrell succeeded him two years later. However, about 12 years earlier a younger Burrell was the stockroom attendant and janitor for the multipurpose athletic dormitory, the Track House. Burrell held the job until retiring in 1941, and his total 29 years makes him Penn State's longest-tenured equipment manager.

Burwell was followed by Oscar Buchenhorst (1942–57), Mel Franks (1958–64), John Tomko (1965–68), Ed O'Hara (1969–70), John Nolan (1971–78), Shope (1979–2001), Spider, and Takach in 2014.

Spider's predecessors may have been good at their jobs but, as 2012 All-American linebacker Michael Mauti told Frank Bodani of the *New York Daily News* when Spider announced his retirement, "he's basically got his own fan club. His positivity just radiated...."

In early 2015, Spider returned to Penn State as facilities coordinator at Beaver Stadium. He's not part of the football staff, but his new job means he will be more involved with the public than ever before, especially on game day. His fan club is happy.

87 Watch Hockey in the Pegula Arena

With a $90 million, state-of-the-art facility that's superior to some National Hockey League arenas, is it any wonder the hottest ticket in Penn State athletics since 2013–14 has been for the men's new varsity ice hockey team?

Thanks to the largesse of alumnus Terry Pegula, the dreams of Penn State students for more than 100 years have come true. They not only have an intercollegiate hockey team that can compete with the best programs in the country, but a home ice showplace that is the envy of their peers.

The man who made it happen was Pegula, a 1973 graduate who turned his degree in petroleum engineering into a multi-billion-dollar natural gas drilling company. The initial donation of $88 million in September 2010 he and his wife Kim made was the largest in school history, and they added $14 million more to finance the varsity program that also includes a women's team. That's why the arena is named for them.

There's nothing inside or outside the Pegula Arena named for Joe Battista, but there should be. He was the championship-winning coach of Penn State's intercollegiate club hockey team for nearly two decades and the man who convinced Pegula to fund the varsity program.

Battista grew up in Pittsburgh with ice hockey in his blood and he played on Penn State's club team, the Icers, as a fresh-man in 1978. Nine years later he became the head coach of the Icers. By the time he retired 19 years later his teams had won six championships in the American Collegiate Hockey Association, with 10 straight appearances in the title game, and accumulated a 512–120–27 record.

Battista met Pegula in 1991 at a hockey clinic in Buffalo but didn't remember until Pegula called him out of the blue in 2005 and wondered why Penn State did not have a Division I varsity team. One thing led to another, and when Pegula's donation was announced on September 17, 2010, after years of discussions, Battista said, "This was one of the happiest days of my life."

Battista continued to be the point man in the construction of the ice arena and in hiring head coach Guy Gadowski, helping to recruit the players, and administering the program. He led a committee that visited some of the best hockey facilities in college and the NHL. Melding the pluses and minuses of what the committee saw, Penn State came up with a 200,000-square-foot building with two rinks, including one for the public with a grandstand and auxiliary rooms that will be open year-round 16 to 18 hours a day.

Penn State wanted to keep the main arena's seating capacity within a reasonable number that would attempt to guarantee a packed full house for every home game and create an intimidating atmosphere for opponents. They succeeded. There are some 6,000 seats (and standing room for 250) that include suites, a private club on the upper level and loge seats and all reserved chair-back seats in the lower bowl except for the 1,000 aluminum bleacher seats for students in a section behind the south goal called "Roar Zone."

"The arena is everything we had hoped and more," Battista told me. "Terry Pegula asked us to create the loudest, most 'rockingest' arena in college hockey, and the results speak for themselves. The students sit almost on top of opposing goalies adding to one of the most intimidating atmospheres in college hockey."

Groups of Penn State students had been trying since the early 1900s to have a varsity team, and they succeeded in a short period surrounding World War II. Hockey was primarily an outdoor sport for colleges well into the 20th century.

One faction of students led by a Pittsburgh kid named Herb Baetz formed an independent team that tried to play in a college league in his hometown. That team played Penn State's first-ever intercollegiate games against Carnegie Tech on Christmas night of 1909 on an inside rink in a converted trolley barn named the Duquesne Gardens. The final score has been lost to history, and after losing to Pitt 2–1 at the Gardens a week later, the team was shut down by a vote of the entire student body.

Then, in 1940, the students voted varsity status for another two-year-old club team. On December 6, 1940, the new Nittany Lions beat Carnegie Tech 3–1 at the Shaffer Ice Palace in Johnstown. However, the lack of a home ice rink complex, indoor or outdoor, and the disruption and complications of World War II forced the athletic department to disband the team after 1946.

In the 27 games those teams played, the closest "home ice" was 80–100 miles away, in Hershey and Johnstown.

It was not until 1971 that the Icers club team began playing an intercollegiate schedule with home ice at the Ice Pavilion, which was a rink inside a Quonset hut that opened to the elements on both ends and was unheated. Over the years, the Ice Pavilion would be completely enclosed and bleachers were installed that seated 2,000. When Battista was a junior defenseman in 1981, the club team moved into a new indoor facility in the Greenberg complex that also included the football offices and field house.

Battista has come a long way since then. Pegula, who also now owns the NHL Buffalo Sabres and NFL Buffalo Bills, hired Battista in October 2013 to be the Sabres' vice president for hockey services and business administration. But Penn State fans can still see him often at the Pegula Arena sitting in Pegula's suite overlooking the Roar Zone.

In its first three years of its new varsity competition, Penn State's hockey team became one of the best in the Big Ten, and is on the verge of being one of the best in the nation. In December

2014 the team cracked the top 20 national rankings of the US College Hockey Organization, and at the end of the year Gadowski was voted the Big Ten Coach of the Year.

If you haven't been to the Pegula Arena to see them play, you need to do so—if you can buy a ticket.

88 Steve Hamas: The All-Time Letterman

Steve Hamas won more varsity letters (12) than any other Penn State male athlete, and he is one of just two who earned five letters in one season.

Hamas also was once known around the world as the No. 1 contender for the heavyweight boxing championship. If not for an elbow injury and poor guidance by his manager, he might be famous today as the Cinderella Man with a popular movie about his life.

You may have seen that 2005 movie with Russell Crowe in the title role as James Braddock, who overcame soup lines and near-homelessness to upset Max Baer for the heavyweight championship during the Depression. Hamas was not as desperate as Braddock, but if Baer had not delayed fighting Hamas as the boxing world expected, there may never have been a Cinderella Man.

Like many other Penn State athletes of the past, the only place you'll find anything about Hamas is at the Paterno-Patee sports archives and the All-Sports Museum. His photo is in the museum, alongside another forgotten boxer, Billy Soose, who is Penn State's only world boxing champion. Soose was 10 years younger than Hamas, and in 1941 he won the middleweight title. Soose is in the International Boxing Hall of Fame. So is Penn State's boxing coach

Leo Houck and James Braddock, but not Hamas, primarily because he never won a championship.

Football was Hamas' main sport at Penn State. He was a fullback who began starting during his sophomore season of 1926 and was elected captain in 1928. At 6'1" and 190 pounds, Hamas was not fast but he was a bruiser who could break tackles going up the middle.

Hamas had never boxed before but was playing basketball in the winter of 1926–27 when Houck approached him to join the boxing team three days before the Intercollegiate Boxing Association's tournament in Syracuse.

Tubby Crawford

Rowan "Tubby" Crawford, who shares the men's school record for the most letters in a single year with Steve Hamas, was a marine private from Shorewood, Wisconsin. He was among the 2,500 Army, navy, and marine recruits sent by the US War Department to Penn State in 1943 as part of the V-12 program for training and study before their assimilation into the armed forces. Crawford had already attended Dartmouth and Ohio University and he would leave Penn State after one year.

It was quite a year. He won letters in football, soccer, boxing, ice hockey, and track.

There's a photo of Tubby in the college yearbook posing with a vaulting pole to highlight his 13'3" pole vault against Cornell in August of 1943 that nearly broke the school record. That fall he played the first half of the season as goalie on the soccer team and the second half as a halfback/tailback on the football team.

After first playing hockey on the forward line or at goal in the winter of 1943–44, Tubby turned to boxing and was unbeaten at 165 pounds, but was transferred to Penn by the military before the Eastern Boxing Association tournament.

At Penn Tubby switched to the navy, but little is known about him after that. According to the Penn State Football Lettermen's Club, he is deceased and his last address was Louden, Tennessee.

"You are big enough to fight, why don't you come out for the team?" Houck said, as Hamas remembered years later. "Sure, when do I start?" Hamas replied. A few days later Hamas knocked out the hometown favorite, Dynamite Joe Livoti, and won the heavyweight championship. He won it again as a senior when he also earned letters in football, basketball, track, and lacrosse.

Hamas was a premed major from an immigrant family in Passaic, New Jersey, and he wanted to be a surgeon. He needed money to pay for medical school, and with the Depression rocking the country in 1930, Hamas turned to boxing. Over the next three years he climbed up the heavyweight ranks, earning the nickname Hurricane Hamas. After beating Max Schmeling in a 12-round decision in February 1934 and Art Lasky a few months later, he was the No. 1 contender and ready to take on Baer. His manager, Charlie Harvey, had other ideas.

Harvey wanted a big payday first, and Schmeling offered that in a rematch in Hamburg, Germany. Hamas demurred. Baer was within his grasp. But Harvey insisted. About a week before the fight fate intervened, changing Hamas' life forever.

"While training I tore a tendon in my left elbow," Hamas recalled years later. "A German osteopath said I shouldn't fight for a month...I wanted Charlie to postpone it, but he was in so deep he couldn't or wouldn't. With my left [hand] useless, I was an open target for Schmeling's right and he murdered me."

Hamas lasted nine cruel rounds on March 10, 1935, before the referee finally stopped the fight. The beating was so severe Hamas was hospitalized in Germany for nearly two weeks and his left side was temporarily paralyzed. While Hamas was recuperating back in the United States, journeyman James Braddock got the match with Baer in June that Hamas should have had. At 28 Hamas' boxing career was over. So was his dream to be a doctor, because by then he now had a wife and two children to support.

Life after boxing was erratic for Hamas, who had a couple business failures before spending 20 years as a salesman in the copper business. During World War II he became a pilot and trained other pilots how to fly stratosphere bombers, earning the rank of major. Later Hamas worked for the New Jersey Department of Vehicles and died in relative obscurity three months after his retirement in 1974.

Hamas helped make boxing king of Penn State's winter sports from the late 1920s into the late 1940s, sometimes with crowds so large spectators stood two or three deep on the running track circling above the grandstands.

"In the thirties and up until World War II, townspeople were asked to stay away [from boxing matches in Rec Hall] because there wasn't enough room for students," recalled the late Jerry Weinstein, onetime sports editor of the *Daily Collegian* and editor of the *Centre Daily Times*, in a 1985 *Town & Gown* magazine article.

Penn State eliminated boxing as a varsity sport after 1954 and in 1960 the NCAA abolished it as an official sport. It had simply become too dangerous.

In his later years, Hamas campaigned for major changes in professional boxing or for its termination. He repeatedly told sportswriters, "I never liked boxing."

89 Losing in Overtime Is Worse Than Kissing Your Sister

A tie game may be like "kissing your sister," as a couple Hall of Fame football coaches used to say, but losing in overtime is far worse. Winning in overtime is pure joy, like kissing the love of your life.

At least it seems that way for the Penn State football team.

Since the NCAA implemented overtime rules in 1996 to eliminate ties, Penn State has played in 10 overtime games as of the 2014 season and won six of them.

Think about that sixth win. It occurred in the 2014 Pinstripe Bowl at frigid Yankee Stadium 31–30 over Boston College. The players and the Nittany Lions fans celebrated like the team had just won the national championship, and why not?

The victory not only gave Penn State a satisfying win over a once-perennial eastern opponent and its third straight winning record in the aftermath of heavy NCAA sanctions; just as gratifying, it was a finger in the eye of all the critics who whined when the postseason bowl ban was lifted earlier in the season. Pure joy. Imagine how depressed the Penn State football nation would have been if those gutty 2014 Nittany Lions had lost in overtime.

Now, think back to Penn State's first overtime game. That was against Iowa on November 4, 2000, at Beaver Stadium. The Lions lost 26–23 to a 17-point underdog in double overtime. "This is going to be a tough game to rebound from," Coach Joe Paterno told the media after the game. The Lions were 4–6 at that juncture, and with a loss at Michigan and a win against Michigan State finished with the first losing season since 1988. The overtime defeat to Iowa was the difference, far worse than a tie under the old rules.

Asked about his first overtime, Paterno said, "They add a little something to the game. They're more fun, obviously, if you win." Bingo.

The next overtime game was the most controversial one. It was against Iowa again, on September 28, 2002, at Beaver Stadium. Penn State came back from a 22-point deficit in the last eight minutes to force a tie, only to lose 42–35 in overtime. Upset by some of the officiating, particularly on a pass play that led to the winning touchdown, Paterno chased after referee Dick Honig at the end of the game to complain and yanked his shirt, a no-no.

Naturally, that wouldn't have happened if Penn State had won, but Paterno's cross-field run is one of the most memorable moments in Beaver Stadium history. Maybe even worth the loss and better than kissing my sister.

Three other overtime wins before the Pinstripe Bowl were memorable and equally satisfying.

January 3, 2006, vs. Florida State at the Orange Bowl: This was the last of eight games between the two winningest coaches in major college football, Paterno and Bobby Bowden, and it took a marathon 4:39 and three overtimes to finish. Freshman kicker Kevin Kelly had a chance to win the game in regulation but missed a 29-yard field goal with 32 seconds left. After missing another field goal in the first overtime, Kelly redeemed himself with another 29-yard kick that won the game 26–23 and gave the Lions their best finish in 11 years with an 11–1 record and ranked No. 3 in the final polls. A loss would have spoiled one of the most rewarding seasons ever for the team and its fans.

November 24, 2012, vs. Wisconsin at Beaver Stadium: Most of the announced crowd of 93,505 had left because of the freezing, snowy weather when Wisconsin's 44-yard field goal was wide left, giving the Lions a 24–21 win on Sam Ficken's 37-yard field goal. It was a fitting climax to a day when the seniors were honored for leading the beleaguered team through the demoralizing NCAA sanctions to a surprising winning season. The victory gave Penn State an 8–4 record and second place in the Big Ten's Leaders Division. Even a defeat would not have altered the respect the players and coaches had earned for what they accomplished that season.

October 12, 2013, vs. Michigan at Beaver Stadium: In a Big Ten–record four overtimes, Penn State shocked undefeated No. 18 Michigan before a fired-up whiteout crowd of 107,884 and a national television audience with a 43–40 victory. A lightning five-play, 23-second drive led by Christian Hackenberg with 50 seconds left tied the game at 24–24. Spurning a tying field goal attempt in the fourth overtime, Coach Bill O'Brien went for the win on a two-yard run by Bill Belton. Whether a loss would have led to a losing season is questionable, but anytime Penn State beats Michigan it's pure joy.

In the 41 tie games Penn State played since the first tie, 6–6 with Dickinson in 1888, several were seen as moral victories or upsets. That included two with Harvard, 13–13 in 1914 and 21–21 in 1921, and the 0–0 deadlock with Notre Dame in the mud at Beaver Field in 1925. Another was the 7–7 tie at Pitt in 1956 that cost the Panthers a New Year's Day bowl game.

The most famous Penn State tie was in the 1948 Cotton Bowl against SMU 13–13. Now, that was like kissing your sister.

90 Tailgate at a Snow Bowl

Watching a Penn State football game in cold, freezing, and snowy weather is as much of a tradition as the team's blue-and-white uniforms. Certainly, such weather conditions are prevalent elsewhere across the football landscape from late October into January. The most loyal fans will turn out no matter what the weather.

Sitting in the stadium and watching the game bundled up like an Alaskan fisherman in the dead of winter is one thing. Tailgating in that horrendous weather is another thing. It's only for the hardy, or maybe the nutcases. Especially for those fans who don't tailgate inside their motor homes, vans, or heated tents.

Every fan has his or her own story. My coldest game was on November 12, 1983, when Penn State beat Notre Dame 34–30. The wind chill was so low in the blistering wind outside Beaver

Stadium that the eggs we were cooking on the stove alongside our van were cold almost before you could take one bite. True. Two years later, we tailgated under the awning of our van in our ponchos as a 24-hour steady rain pelted Beaver Stadium at another winning game against Notre Dame. Of course, winning makes it all worthwhile. Losing makes you wonder if you belong in a cell next to Hannibal Lecter.

Which brings us to the Snow Bowls. That's when it snows so much, the snow has to be removed from the field and grandstands just to play the game. Many parking lots are closed and thousands of fans are advised to forego tailgating and take buses to the stadium. In those cases, the tailgate commandos spring into action. Don't tell us we can't tailgate! And just like that, tailgating before and after a Snow Bowl is akin to a frosty winter carnival without ice skating.

Penn State played in at least three bona fide Snow Bowls and two occurred in the early 1950s before tailgating was fashionable. In all three instances, the heavy snowfall surprised everyone, including the weather forecasters. (Laugh out loud.)

Many of today's Penn State fans remember the 1995 Snow Bowl game against Michigan at Beaver Stadium because they were either among the estimated crowd of 80,000 freezing their butts off or the thousands watching the nearly nationwide ABC telecast. Four days before the November 18 game, a surprise storm dumped nearly 18 inches of snow on State College, leaving some 18,000 homes without power, some almost up to game time.

Penn State hired 300 volunteers, including 81 low-security inmates from four area prisons, to clear the field, seats, and walkways. One of their shovels is displayed at the Penn State All-Sports Museum. Snow was still underneath the seats and piled along the sidelines when the stadium gates opened for the 12:08 kickoff. With just one-third of the parking spaces available and with no motor homes allowed and nothing reserved, vehicles started lining

Students and Blue Band members help clear Beaver Field of heavy snow in 1953 before a game with Fordham, a scene that was repeated 42 years later at Beaver Stadium before another Snow Bowl game against Michigan.
(Photo courtesy of Anonymous)

up on access roads before dawn so fans like those in our family could snare a close tailgating spot.

Penn State clinched the 27–17 victory in the last two minutes on a fake field goal with holder Joe Nastasi scoring a two-yard touchdown. The postgame tailgating in the cold among snow piles around the parking lots was a blast.

Forty-two years earlier, another sudden storm hit State College overnight before Penn State's final home game of the season against Fordham at New Beaver Field, which was then located across from Rec Hall. The weather forecast in the *Daily Collegian* predicted "clear and cold" for game day. By 8:00 AM on Saturday, November 7, 13 inches of snow had fallen, and it continued to fall lightly throughout the game.

Two hundred students helped clear the field, including 98 members of the Blue Band. The scheduled 1:30 PM kickoff had to be delayed 45 minutes because the team was late. They had stayed Friday night at an isolated hunting camp 30 miles away known as Camp Hate to Leave It which had some 21 inches of snow. Every player and coach had to walk a mile through more than a foot of snow to reach a bus, with star halfback Lenny Moore going last. Moore scored two touchdowns, including a 24-yard run in the fourth quarter that won the game 28–21.

Tailgating was unknown in those years, but one can be certain snow didn't dampen the pregame lunches downtown and in the dormitories or the postgame partying at the fraternities.

The other famous Snow Bowl occurred in Pittsburgh when Penn State's scheduled game on November 25, 1950, against chief rival Pitt had to be postponed a week. Snow started falling all over western Pennsylvania the Friday after Thanksgiving and reached 26 inches by Monday. It is still the largest snowfall on record for the city. The Penn State bus made it to the hotel near Pitt Stadium Friday afternoon, but it took army trucks to get the team to the downtown train station Saturday for the return trip.

Rather than remove the snow from the stadium, the city cleared out nearby Forbes Field because the Steelers had a game there the following Sunday. Because much of the grandstand had been protected by a roof, the snow was not deep in many seating sections. On Saturday, December 2, an estimated 7,000 spectators watched the Lions almost blow a three-touchdown lead but come back for the win 21–20 after Pitt missed an extra-point attempt in the fourth quarter. Must have been great "tailgating" business in those Oakland bars.

So the next time the snowstorm of the century turns Beaver Stadium into another Snow Bowl, you definitely need to be there to tailgate. Just like us pseudo-nutcases.

91 Hinkey Haines, Babe Ruth, and the Toast of New York

Of all Penn State's star athletes in the first half of the 20th century, Hinkey Haines is the most intriguing.

It may be difficult to believe, but Henry Luther Haines is the only man in history to play on both an NFL and World Series championship team.

At one time he was one of the most popular sports celebrities in the Cast, a superstar for the New York Giants football team and recognized as the Toast of New York. In 1927 he led the Giants to their first NFL championship, four years after scoring one of the runs that helped the New York Yankees baseball team featuring Babe Ruth clinch its first World Series title.

Yet Hinkey Haines is hardly known for his exploits at Penn State except by historians. In his historical masterpiece about Penn State football, *Road to Number One*, Ridge Riley called Haines "one of the most exciting athletes of all time, equally outstanding on the [football field,] the baseball diamond, and the basketball court."

Haines was a star halfback on Coach Hugo Bezdek's undefeated (but tied) nationally rated football teams of 1920 and 1921 who helped set a school-record 30-game unbeaten streak lasting nearly 50 years. Riley called Haines one of the Three Musketeers running backs in 1920, a group that also included Charlie Way and Glenn Killinger with Harry Wilson replacing the graduated Way in 1921. Way, Killinger, and Wilson became first-team All-Americans chosen by Walter Camp, which is the reason the 5'8", 170-pound Haines only made it to Camp's third team.

Baseball was Haines' favorite sport. He was the center fielder and cleanup hitter on the 1920 and 1921 teams (and captain in 1921) that won 31 straight games (which is still the Penn State record). Haines' speed made him a superb fielder. A sportswriter covering a Penn State game at West Point wrote how Haines "pulled down a fly ball from among the branches of a tree on the outskirts of the diamond." Army's coach Hans Lobert, who had played in the major leagues from 1903 to 1917, said he had "never seen a catch equal to it in any league."

Just where the Hinkey nickname came from is buried somewhere in the Penn State archives or in his hometown of Red Lion, southeast of York, where his father was a six-term US congressman. Haines was a character and a popular campus leader who loved to play the piano. When one of the student football managers organized an orchestra for various social events, he asked Haines to be the substitute pianist. That group became the forerunner of the soon-to-be-world-famous Fred Waring and His Pennsylvanians, but by that time Hinkey was playing baseball and football in New York.

A tryout with the Yankees led to two years in the minors before Haines made the 1923 roster as a reserve outfielder and pinch runner. During the same period, he also was playing professional football with independent teams in the Philadelphia area not aligned with the struggling National Football League that had started in 1920.

The Yankees used him sparingly in 1923. He appeared in just 28 regular-season games, batting 25 times with four hits for a measly .160 average, with two doubles, three RBIs, and nine runs while making 17 put-outs and one assist without any errors.

Haines appeared in two World Series games against the New York Giants. In the eighth inning of Game 3, Hinkey replaced Babe Ruth in right field when Ruth moved to first base. He led off the ninth inning by grounding out to third base for what would be his only at-bat in the Series. With the Series on the line in Game 6 and the Giants leading 4–1 in the top of the eighth, the Yankees loaded the bases and Haines was sent in as a pinch runner at first base. Two walks narrowed the score to 4–3 and Haines scored the tying run on Bob Meusel's ground ball single to center field that gave the Yankees a 6–4 lead that eventually clinched the game and the Series.

Haines, who had been earning just $500 a month, received a full share of the Yankee payout, $6,143.49. He never played in another major league game, but drifted through the minors until 1933.

In 1925 the New York Giants football team joined the NFL and recruited Haines to be the starting tailback for the then-hefty sum of $4,000. Among his teammates that first season was an aging 38-year-old Jim Thorpe. Haines, who became the team captain, was a multiple-threat signal-caller who ran, kicked, threw and caught passes, and played defense. Sportswriters called him the Giants' "first superstar," and the Giants frequently advertised their games with this headline: "Come see Hinkey Haines and his New York Football Giants."

One writer even wrote a poem about Haines:

Oh Hinkey Haines, oh Hinkey Haines!
The New York Giants' football brains.
He never loses, always gains.
Oh Hinkey Haines, oh Hinkey Haines!

After finishing fourth in the league in 1925 and 1926, the Giants won the championship in 1927 with an 11–1–1 record when the title was given to the team with the best record. In early December, Haines was the guest of honor at a packed Testimonial Dinner at the Hotel Astor in Times Square. He played another season with the Giants and retired from pro football after 1931.

Three years later, Haines began refereeing NFL and college games and did it for the next 20 years, while also working for the government, becoming the district chief of the Philadelphia IRS and loan officer of small business administration.

You can see a photo of the intriguing Hinkey Haines with Babe Ruth in the Penn State All-Sports Museum.

92 The Big Uglies

Andy Lytle was the first loyal fan of the Penn State football team, and the Big Uglies are the most visible of today's devoted fans.

If you haven't seen the Big Uglies cavorting around the lower grandstands and firing up the crowd at Beaver Stadium or on television, then don't count yourself a loyal fan. You can't miss the Big Uglies. They're the three people dressed in full Penn State football uniforms wearing those goofy rubber masks with wide grins and some teeth missing. They have the traditional uniforms down pat, complete with plain white or blue jerseys, shoulder pads, white helmets, white socks, and black shoes.

Lytle was a farmer who worked on the construction of the original Old Main in 1863 when he was growing up, and in the 1920s old Andy was honored as the football team's No. 1 fan. The Big Uglies don't have a near-perfect attendance at home and away games as Andy did for more than three decades until his death in 1928. But no fans since Andy have been more visible than the Big Uglies.

By this time, many other fans know who the Big Uglies are because they've made so many friends with their antics in the stadium and tailgating outside.

The Big Uglies are the most visible of all the fans in the Penn State football nation because of the football uniforms they wear to lead cheers for the Nittany Lions. Underneath those ugly masks are the three Duda brothers, raised in State College within the shadows of New Beaver Field. (Photo courtesy of the Duda Brothers)

"When we take off our masks, people are surprised at how old we are and that we have grey hair," said John Duda, one of the three brothers behind those masks. "Some people who have seen us over the years think we hand this down from person to person. But we've been doing it ourselves for roughly 25 years."

They're the Duda brothers, who grew up not far from Beaver Stadium. Their late father, Larry, was the head of Penn State's Chemical Engineering department for years and their mother, Margaret, still lives in State College. People are surprised when they learn John is a neurologist and surgeon and a world-renowned authority on Parkinson's disease.

His twin brother, David, owns a bookstore/cafe in New Haven, Connecticut, called the Book Trader Cafe, and their one-year-younger brother Paul, the undisputed best dancer of the Big Uglies, owns a photo studio in New Haven called Studio Duda. "I'm just the most gung-ho and have a little bit of rhythm for dancing," Paul joked.

"Growing up in State College, we were longtime fans," John said. "When we were very young we used to run around the bleachers in the south end zone and pick up the stuff people dropped. Then as we grew older, we used to take tickets at the Beaver Stadium gates and even work the 'Booze Patrol' where we'd try to sniff out the beer the students were trying to bring into the game."

As a student, John was a little over the top. He was one of those zany students who paint their face and chest blue-and-white and go shirtless in freezing weather. He knew he couldn't do that after college, but he wanted to be different, and so did his brothers. When their mother found three of those clownish masks in a garage sale—leftovers from a car rental giveaway during Penn State's appearance in the 1986 Orange Bowl—they had their gimmick.

They started out in the late 1980s wearing the goofy masks and before 1990 they were in full uniforms, prancing around and cheering to jack up the fans. Once the television cameras began focusing on them they reached the promised land: TV face time around the nation.

Because of personal reasons and the child abuse scandal, they cut back on attending as many games as they had in the past. "We took a little time off as we decided what we were really doing and how we felt about the scandal and everything," John said.

Traveling has also become a little more problematic, especially for away games, because of their personal lives and their out-of-state residences. Sometimes a friend will substitute, and in the last couple years the prime replacement has been Todd Speck, who runs the Penn State Football Nation Facebook page. They've rarely missed a postseason bowl game and were at Yankee Stadium for the 2014 Pinstripe Bowl when the Lions were back in a bowl for the first time since the NCAA sanctions hit in 2012.

At one time the Big Uglies rarely removed their masks in the stadiums. But that's changed recently, primarily because of revised security rules caused by increased terrorist attacks. It now varies depending on the rules at different stadiums and their desire to get some fresh air without the masks.

Annie and Other Fans

Penn State has thousands of loyal fans, many of whom travel to most away games like pals Jerry Olson and Alan Brown, drive hundreds of miles for home games, or fly in from the west as far as California like Carol Pilgrim. I have met many of them in the last 30 years and some are slowing down because of health reasons, like Bob Werba and Joe Desmond.

Bob can't paint his bald head with blue and white Nittany Lion paws because of the skin cancer now in remission. Joe roamed the tailgate area for decades wearing an all-white suit including top hat passing out specially made Penn State pins, but no longer at every home game. One of the most loyal fans, Terry Todd, passed away recently after setting what may be a record of attending 282 straight games home and away before his illness.

Annie Harris is special. You'll see her motoring around Beaver Stadium in her red scooter selling programs, even in some of the coldest or rainiest weather, or asking questions of the head coach at the Quarterback Club or on radio call-in shows.

Annie has had cerebral palsy since her birth more than 65 years ago, and it hampers her movement and speech. But it hasn't stopped her from earning an undergraduate and master's degree from Penn State as well as traveling to Europe, Zimbabwe, and elsewhere and teaching and holding seminars around the country.

"It is merely the hand I was dealt," she wrote of her cerebral palsy in her recently published memoir, *It's Easier to Dance*.

Annie is a self-proclaimed outspoken woman of multicultural heritage and one of the all-time great Penn State football fans.

They've also changed jersey numbers, too. They used to have different numbers. Now, they all wear No. 12 and refer to themselves as The 12th Man, not the Big Uglies.

"We thought it was in keeping with Joe Parerno's philosophy, that it's not about the individual," John said, "and we like to think that we are just part of the greater Penn State 12th Man."

The Big Uglies rarely show up outside the football environment, but they are now committed to one special public appearance. "The last two years we have had the honor of helping support the dancers who are raising money for the kids [to fight pediatric cancer], by making an appearance on the floor at the dance marathon," said John.

You can be sure those kids laughed even harder than Penn State's football fans at those Big Uglies in the goofy masks.

93 Levi Lamb and the War Heroes

Penn State football players have been fighting and dying in wars since World War I. Their names may be unfamiliar to today's generation of fans, but what they did for the country is part of the team's legacy and more meaningful than all the victories on the playing field.

Levi Lamb and Red Bebout were the first to die in combat, in the trenches in 1918. Gil Radcliff survived the Bataan Death March and four years inside five brutal Japanese prison camps. Wayne Wolfkeil was shot down in Laos and is still officially listed as missing in action.

Some of the players were three-year starters on their Penn State teams, like Lamb, Bebout, and Bob Higgins, an All-American end in seasons before and after World War I. Others were reserves with limited playing time such as Radcliff and Wolfkeil. Others like Rick Slater, a Navy SEAL for 19 years, were walk-ons who never earned a letter.

Lamb and Bebout were starting linemen as underclassmen on Penn State's great undefeated team of 1912. Lamb was an all-around athlete who was also a standout in wrestling, losing just two of 21 matches, and track, where he finished first in 34 events ranging from dashes to the shot put. Bebout was so feared by opponents and in Penn State's first-ever game against Notre Dame in 1913, the Irish players kept hollering throughout the day, "Get Red, get Red."

Lamb was killed on the first day of the Allies' offensive that started to end World War I in July of 1918, and Bebout died two months later in the final offensive. The athletic department's fund for financial contributions is named after Lamb. Both men are honored with a large metal plaque on the wall just inside the front entrance of Rec Hall, something every Penn State fan needs to see.

Higgins saw heavy combat with the 318th infantry in the same Meuse-Argonne Offensive that killed Bebout and won a battlefield promotion to first lieutenant. He survived and became a Penn State Hall of Fame coach.

Radcliff was an end who became a starter midway through the 1938 season. He joined the army and was stationed in the Philippines when it was captured by the Japanese in April 1948. He never made it home to Norristown until the war was over but received a Silver Star for his gallantry during his ordeal. Radcliff remained in the army for 30 years, retiring as a colonel, and lived until he was 84.

Wolfkeil also was making the military his career after lettering as a left halfback for the Nittany Lions in 1953. He had just been promoted to lt. colonel when his plane was shot down. Other pilots on the same mission never saw his parachute. It was two weeks before US forces could get to the crash site, and only bits and pieces of his helmet were found.

Only one other Penn State football player has died while at war, says Frank Bodani of the *York Daily Record*, who wrote about Radcliff and Wolfkeil. Ted Shattuck was a teammate of Wolfkeil's on the 1951 team when Shattuck was a starting halfback. Shattuck left school after that season and was an air force major when his plane exploded taking off on a mission from Thailand. He died a few days later.

Many Penn State football players served in the two World Wars, but not all saw combat. Here are some who did:

Charlie Atherton, the son of college president George Atherton and one of the first players in college football to kick the first placement field goal in 1894, fought with the Czecho-Slovak Army in Austria in 1917–18.

Dutch Hermann, a backup quarterback in 1910–11 but a four-time basketball letterman who became Penn State's first basketball coach in 1915, was wounded during an attack near Toul, France, in 1918, and returned to campus in 1920 to be the head basketball coach until 1932.

Harry Wilson, one of the best two-way players in Penn State history and a first-team All-American Halfback in 1923, earned the Distinguished Flying Cross and Air Medal with six oak leaf clusters while flying 48 combat missions as commander of the 42nd bomber group in the South Pacific in World War II.

John Potsklan, a defensive end on the Lions' best-ever freshman team in 1941, was captured by the Germans after heavy combat in Europe, and returned to Penn State to be the co-captain and inspirational leader of the great undefeated 1947 Cotton Bowl team.

Joe Tepsic, who was hospitalized for a year after being severely wounded in hand-to-hand combat on Guadalcanal, became the star running back in 1945 (nicknamed Jumping Joe) and later played baseball with the Brooklyn Dodgers.

Hap Frank, a starting end on the 1922 Rose Bowl team and 1923 Mystery Team, was a major general in the army reserves and commanded an infantry division that fought in China from 1943 to 1945.

94 Monte Ward: Baseball Superstar

The man who helped start baseball at Penn State is the only Nittany Lions player enshrined in the Baseball Hall of Fame at Cooperstown, but was thrown out of school for stealing chickens before getting his degree.

John Montgomery Ward helped invent the curveball, created the intentional walk, threw the second perfect game in the major league history, was one of the highest-paid superstar pitchers and batters of his era as well as a playing manager and a team president, led a players' revolt to form the first union, and earned a law degree he used to continue fighting for players' rights.

Baseball historian Mike Attiyeh calls Ward "baseball's most interesting character." He "is perhaps the most fascinating figure in baseball history," asserts Mark Alvarez, an editor for the Society of American Baseball Research.

Ward was just a 13-year-old kid from Bellefonte in 1873 when his mother, Ruth, enrolled him at Penn State not only to get an education but to give him some discipline after the death of his father two years earlier. He flunked out because of poor grades but returned in 1874 in the wake of his mother's death and became one of the best students in his class.

Students were already playing baseball on the grass surrounding Old Main. Ward joined in, pitching and playing in the infield, but the students were loosely organized. It wasn't until the spring of 1875 that Ward and two buddies sought permission from Penn State's faculty to build a real baseball field, with a dirt infield, a pitcher's box, and three bases spread out from home plate in a 90-foot square.

"We procured the consent of the college authorities to use a field northeast of the old main building and just south of a patch of woods," Ward wrote in a 1923 letter to Penn State. They built the field. However, no longer satisfied with playing among themselves they traveled to the village of Milesburg, about 20 miles away, to play their first official game against outside opposition. Ward remembered suggesting blue-and-white uniforms: "…our regular uniforms thereafter consisted of white with light blue trimmings, the stockings being of alternate bands of blue and white." (Later, dark blue replaced the light blue.)

Milesburg won that game 28–20 on May 19, 1875, and that was the beginning of Penn State baseball, although the next official game was not played until 1882.

Ward was not a bad kid, but Penn State had many strict rules and military training was mandatory for the men. Several baseball players were punished for breaking rules and other hijinks. Ward had been lucky, according to his biographer, Bryan Di Salvatore. His luck ran out in the fall of 1876 when Ward skipped school to play a baseball game in Williamsport for another team. He was almost suspended. Just before the fall term ended, Ward and another friend were caught after stealing chickens from a college chicken coop and then lying about it. On February 17, 1877, the faculty voted to expel Ward.

"He was no longer a popular, award-winning undergraduate and mainstay of the college baseball team," wrote Di Salvatore in the book, *A Clever Base-Ballist: The Life and Times of John Montgomery Ward*. "He was a sixteen-year-old liar and chicken thief."

Ward became a salesman and started barnstorming with a series of semi-professional baseball teams before signing to pitch for the Providence Grays of the two-year-old National League. He made his major league debut on July 15 before 517 spectators at Cincinnati and it was a dud. He threw three wild pitches as Providence made 28 errors, 10 by Ward's catcher, and lost 13–9. The next day Ward was on the mound again at Indianapolis. Providence won 4–2 and Ward was on his way to Cooperstown.

Ward pitched 334 innings that first season, with a 22–13 record and a league-leading 1.51 ERA. The next season he led the league in wins with a 47–19 record and strikeouts (239) as Providence won the pennant. In his third year he threw a perfect game in beating Buffalo 5–0 on June 17, 1880.

Ward would pitch for seven seasons, once winning 47 games and pitching 18 innings in one game, in compiling a 164–103 record and 2.10 ERA before injuries in 1884 while playing for the New York Giants ended his pitching career. Sportswriters of the day called him the Champion Baseball Pitcher of America. Ward quickly transitioned into a heavy-hitting shortstop, à la Babe Ruth's transformation two decades later, and went on to play for the Giants and Brooklyn Grooms until retiring after the 1894 season. He finished with 2,107 lifetime hits, 1,410 runs, 869 RBIs, 540 stolen bases, and a .275 batting average and is the only major league player to win 100 or more games as a pitcher and to accumulate 2,000 or more hits as a batter.

"Monte Ward was the Babe Ruth of baseball before Ruth was even born," baseball writer Matthew Orso wrote in 2014 for SportsWorldNews.com.

While playing for the Giants, Ward finished his undergraduate degree and earned a law degree from Columbia. In 1886 he helped organize the first players' union, the Brotherhood of Baseball Players, and when that was beaten back by the owners, he helped create a new Players' League in 1890 but the league folded after one season.

Ward became a wealthy corporate lawyer, writer, and standout amateur golfer, but continued his fight against baseball's reserve clause and for players' rights for the rest of his life. Upon his death in 1925, one writer called Ward "the greatest competitor this country has known." Thirty-nine years later, the onetime chicken thief was enshrined in the Baseball Hall of Fame.

95 Purity in the Original Dark Years

The corruption of academics within intercollegiate athletics has been an endemic problem since the turn of the 20th century. That was one of the reasons for the 1906 creation of the NCAA, which now has its own internal dishonesty and fraud corroding the collegiate atmosphere.

It's difficult to be pure when so much money is involved. That's not just the situation today, but it's been that way almost since fans were willing to pay to watch their favorite teams.

Penn State tried complete purity once, and it led to the darkest days and years in the school's athletic history until the child abuse scandal.

In the early 1920s, college football rivaled Major League Baseball and horse racing as America's favorite sports. College presidents and faculty were deeply concerned about the overemphasis of sports in the academic environment.

That certainly was true at Penn State. As Ridge Riley described in his book *The Road to Number One,* a small faction led by powerful alumni secretary Mike Sullivan began complaining openly about "indiscriminate 'athletic scholarships' and 'overemphasis.'" Sullivan's unwritten motto was a phrase he read in a *New York World* editorial on the subject "Let the boys play their own game."

Sullivan's beliefs were shared far beyond Penn State's campus, and in January 1926, the Carnegie Foundation for the Advancement of Teaching began examining the place of athletics on all college campuses. Within a year, Penn State began restructuring the athletic department and reduced athletic scholarships from 75 to 50.

While Penn State awaited the arrival of a new reform-minded president, Ralph Hetzel, in June 1927, Sullivan and others in the administration and alumni were reorganizing the athletic department and making recommendations for the future. Supervision of athletics was placed under a new 13-man Board of Athletic Control dominated by four faculty and five alumni.

On August 10, 1927, two months after the arrival of Hetzel, the Board of Athletic Control ended all financial aid to athletics. It banned all athletic scholarships, starting with the entering class of freshmen in the fall of 1928, forbid the scouting of opponents, and reduced various other spending. A recommendation to separate sports from the academic Department of Physical Education was postponed by Hetzel for further study. That reached fruition in January 1930 with the creation of the School of Physical Education that gave all coaches academic rank and placed them under the supervision of a director who would not be a coach.

Penn State immediately reported what it had done to the Carnegie Foundation in 1927. It didn't matter to the study committee. When the foundation issued its final report, known as *Bulletin 23*, in October 1929, Penn State was cited as one of the prime culprits among the 130 schools studied. It unfairly listed Penn State, Riley wrote, "as an institution whose athletic standards were not consistent with its educational and ethical values."

Although President Hetzel had persuaded the study committee to add a footnote in *Bulletin 23*, it was ignored by everyone. Does this sound familiar, Penn State fans?

The new athletic policy began to have a major impact in the 1930 football season with the last of the scholarship players. During a 25-year period before 1930, Penn State has climbed to the elite of college football with undefeated teams in 1911, 1912, 1920, and 1921 and a Rose Bowl trip at the end of 1922.

Unfortunately, most of Penn State's opponents ignored the Carnegie Report and it showed on the field. The first year without incoming scholarship players in 1928 was Penn State's first losing season since 1918. In 1930 there was another one at 3–4–2, but it would get worse. In 1931 and 1932, Penn State would win only two games each and would not have another winning season until 1937. Those were truly dark years.

It actually started to turn around after 1932. That's when Ben "Casey" Jones, a close friend, classmate, and former teammate of Higgins in 1916, stepped in to rescue Hig and Penn State football. Jones, a businessman in western Pennsylvania and president of the alumni club in Pittsburgh, led an alumni group that began recruiting young men from the coal mines and steel towns of Pennsylvania and finding them subsidized housing and jobs to help pay their tuition. There was nothing in the NCAA rules against it and other things Jones and the alumni did. But it did circumvent official school policy and was not in keeping with the spirit of the Carnegie Foundation's final report.

So much for purity.

One of Jones' cohorts in his crusade was James Gilligan, a 1912 graduate who had not played football at State but had become a school principal in Dunmore, in the heart of the hard-coal region of northeastern Pennsylvania. The jobs in fraternities, restaurants, and rooming houses were real, and the kids did work. One bookstore loaned books to the athletes and other State College businesses did additional favors. Alumni in Pittsburgh, Philadelphia, Williamsport, and Scranton began sponsoring various fund-raising projects. One of the most successful was the Scholargram program created by Jones in Pittsburgh. It involved raffling off a car and continued well into the Paterno coaching era.

In 1940 Penn State had its best season since the Mystery Team, finishing 6–1–1 and bringing an end to the original dark years, and nine years later scholarships were reinstated.

96 The Pass

It will be known forever in Penn State football history as The Pass.

If you are one of the 96,753 who saw it happen in Beaver Stadium on November 6, 1999, or watched it on ESPN's national television broadcast, you still cannot believe what happened.

The "it" was a desperate Hail Mary pass by Minnesota with 1:22 left in the fourth quarter that led to a shocking 24–23 upset loss that cost the team a chance for the national championship. It was so demoralizing that Penn State lost its next two games and seemed cursed when the Nittany Lions spiraled into a losing tail-spin that lasted five years.

If that wasn't enough, it occurred on homecoming weekend, the annual celebration when old grads return to reminisce about their good old days on campus. They watch or march in the big Friday night parade and party with friends and family the rest of the time. A rare defeat in Saturday's football game can curtail the enthusiasm, but this one left deep scars in the soul of Penn State's loyal football fans.

The fans certainly were in a great mood before the game. The football team was once again in the thick of the hunt for the national title. The snub by the polls in 1994 when they won the Big Ten championship and Rose Bowl and the depressing end of the 1997 season when they had been the preseason No. 1 was in the past. This was the year of redemption.

The 41–7 thrashing of No. 4 Arizona in the season opener at Beaver Stadium had moved the Lions from No. 3 to No. 2 in the polls and they had been there ever since, reeling off nine straight victories. Pitt had made it close and so had Miami and Purdue. But the defense featuring three surefire All-Americans and top NFL draft choices—linebackers LaVar Arrington and Brandon Short and defensive end Courtney Brown—had come through late in the fourth quarter.

With three games remaining against seemingly weaker Big Ten opponents, Penn State looked like a shoo-in for the National Championship Game at the Millennium Sugar Bowl in New Orleans. Minnesota's 5–3 record was deceptive because all three defeats against Big Ten teams had been close. And just two years before in this same homecoming game, the 14-point underdog Gophers almost beat the then–No. 1 Lions.

Minnesota was leading 15–10 in 1997 with about four minutes left and could have run out the clock when Coach Glen Mason inexplicably called for a pitchout. The tailback fumbled and Penn State recovered at the Minnesota 10-yard line, scoring a touchdown on the next play. That '97 Lions defense stopped the Gophers' last possession cold inside their own 10-yard line to eke out the embarrassing victory. Paterno said later that Minnesota deserved to win.

Minnesota was back, and again as a 14-to-15-point underdog. The fans were wary, but the team didn't seem to be. Minnesota was in the game from the opening kickoff and had a 21–20 lead with less than 10 minutes left in the fourth quarter. A Travis Forney field goal shot Penn State ahead at the 9:12 mark and with less

Another Lost Opportunity

Eight years after underdog Minnesota knocked Penn State out of a potential National Championship Game in early November with a field goal on the last play of the game, an underdog Iowa team did it again.

Undefeated Penn State was No. 3 in the polls on November 8, 2008, and an eight-point favorite in the 20-degree chill and swirling 25 mph winds at night in Iowa City. The Nittany Lions outplayed Iowa but left too many points off the board when they settled for field goals instead of touchdowns.

Penn State led 23–21 and was driving inside Iowa's 40-yard line for a field goal with four minutes left in the fourth quarter when an unusual set of circumstances thwarted the Lions: a holding penalty, an interception, and a questionable pass-interference call. That enabled Iowa's walk-on freshman Daniel Murray to kick a 31-yard field goal with one second remaining to win the game.

The Lions went on to win their last two regular-season games and go to the Rose Bowl, but USC's convincing 38–24 victory made the last-second Iowa loss less hurtful, at least to Penn State's fans.

than two minutes left another Lions drive stalled at the Minnesota 33-yard line. Coach Joe Paterno called for a punt into the end zone. "I thought our defense would hold them," he said after the game.

Minnesota took over with 1:50 remaining. On the first play, quarterback Billy Cockerham completed a booming Hail Mary pass into a gusting wind to 6'3" Ron Johnson, who outleaped the Lions defender on the right sideline at the Penn State 34-yard line. Uh-oh. The homecoming crowd tensed. The defense stepped up and pushed Minnesota back six yards on the next three plays. It was fourth-and-16 with 1:22 remaining and the last gasp for the Gophers.

What happened next was like a nightmare. Cockerham took the snap and avoided a blitz by Arrington and threw the ball as far as he could toward the sideline. A group of players from both teams were at Penn State's 15-yard line when the ball came down. Johnson and Lions defender Derek Fox jumped for the ball and in the scramble the ball bounced off Johnson's hands and was caught by Minnesota's Arland Bruce about six inches from the ground at the 13-yard line. The groan of the fans was audible.

With one timeout remaining, the Gophers called three running plays to move the ball into position for a field goal, and then called a timeout with just two seconds left. Most of the crowd had seen Arrington block attempted field goals late in the Pitt and Purdue games. Brown had also blocked one that helped beat Minnesota in 1997. Not this time. Freshman kicker Dan Nystrom calmly booted a 32-yard field goal.

Arrington and several other players dropped to their knees with tears in their eyes. "We can't point the fingers to anyone but ourselves," Short told reporters after the game.

The heartbreaking loss took the fight out of the 1999 team. They lost to Michigan the next week at home 31–27, and then at Michigan State 35–28 before pulling together and beating Texas A&M 24–0 in the Alamo Bowl to finish with a 10–3 record.

That depressing November afternoon was like a curse. In the next five years, Penn State would have just one winning season, the worst stretch in school history since the dark days of the 1930s.

The Pass! The freaking Pass! The &$%# freaking Pass!

97 Climb Mt. Nittany, Attend THON, and Go Bowling

As I was writing this book, I asked several Penn State fans what they thought other fans should do before they die. I could write a separate chapter about many of their suggestions. With their input, here is my short list in no certain order, except my first three are equally at the top.

The fabled Mt. Nittany overlooks the Happy Valley of Penn State.

Climb Mt. Nittany to get a spectacular view of Beaver Stadium and picturesque Happy Valley from the overlook. You really don't climb up the 2,000 foot mountain. You start at 1,350 feet and take one of the two well-kept hiking trails through the woods, one about 3.5 miles round-trip that is more steep and rocky and another 4.6 miles roundtrip. You hike from two to three hours depending on which trail and you choose your pace. It may not be for people with health problems. "It is a very strenuous hike to the top but a nice walk around once you are there," states the website http://mtnittany.org/mountain/hike/ which is run by the Nittany Valley Society, which purchased most of the acreage to protect it as the Mt. Nittany Conservancy.

Attend the Penn State Dance Marathon that raises money to fight pediatric cancer. You'll get to see many of the Nittany Lions athletes performing onstage in costume during the 48 hours of dancing inside the packed Bryce Jordan Center every February. The football team goes an extra step and hosts children with cancer and their parents for several hours at the Lasch Building football facility. THON, as it is called by the students who run it, has raised more than $27 million for the Four Diamonds Fund at Penn State Milton S. Hershey Medical Center since it started in 1977. Football coach James Franklin said it best in the final hours of the 2015 event when he told those gathered, "If you want to talk about Penn State culture, look around," he said, motioning to the crowd. "This is Penn State's culture."

Go bowling whenever Penn State plays in the postseason. Sometimes it is even more fun than being at Beaver Stadium if you're in warm weather and partying for several days with old friends and new ones all wearing blue-and-white. Each bowl's atmosphere is different, from carousing on New Orleans' Bourbon Street at the Sugar Bowl to watching the Rose Bowl Parade in Pasadena to sitting in the frigid late December temperatures at fabled Yankee Stadium for the Pinstripe Bowl. Since the late 1960s, the Penn State football nation has come to expect a New Year's Day vacation in some resort city. Bowl sponsors love the Nittany Lions fans, too, because they follow their team in droves and spend their money in the host city.

See the players ring the Victory Bell, and sing the alma mater with them after a game at Beaver Stadium. Ringing the Victory Bell has been a football tradition since head coach Rip Engle started it in 1964 after an away game at Army. Engle used the bell from the battleship USS *Pennsylvania* mounted outside the nearby Wagner Building, and the tradition has morphed over the years into different bells and formats. Since 2008 the victory bell has been located outside the south end zone tunnel for the players to ring after singing the alma mater in front of the student section immediately after the game. No victory, no bell ringing.

Visit the Sports Archives in the Penn State Paterno-Patee Library, where you can watch football game videos and read other documents upon request that will give you an insight into the university's historic past. The archives are left of the main entrance lobby and are open Monday through Friday.

Read the football letter now distributed weekly via the Internet in the fall that covers every football game from the unique historical perspective of a loyal alumnus who attends every game. It's a cherished Penn State tradition dating to 1938 when Ridge Riley, then the sports information director, started it with a two-page mimeographed letter mailed to alumni and is now written by John Black since Riley's passing in 1976.

Shop for Penn State clothing and other souvenirs to show off your Penn State pride. Browsing through downtown State College on a game weekend is another must-do for fans, and among the most frequented stores are the Clothesline, the Family Clothesline, Lions Pride, Old State, McLanahan's, the Student Book Store, and Rapid Transit. Must-stops on campus are the Penn State Bookstore in the Student Union Building and its satellite store at Beaver Stadium adjacent to the All-Sports Museum.

Schedule a tour of AccuWeather and the Penn State Meteorology Department. Many of the nation's radio and TV weathermen are graduates of the university's meteorology curriculum, which dates to 1859. One graduate, Joel Myers, started his own company in 1962 and now AccuWeather, based in suburban State College, is the foremost independent weather service in the world.

See Penn State's Land-Grant Frescoes on the upper walls of Old Main's lobby above the staircase. The colorful artwork is a depiction of the university's founding and growth and one of "the largest works of their kind on any campus." The lobby is open from 8:00 AM to 5:00 PM Monday through Friday.

Talk to Mike the Mailman at the University Park Post Office on the ground floor of the McAllister Building, with a special side entrance east of the Hetzel Student Union Building. With the passing of Joe Paterno, Mike Herr is the most popular person on campus, and a big fan of Penn State's sports teams. He has worked out of the branch post office in the student union building for more than 35 years and has personally talked to more students than anyone else in school history. The students love him. Check out the story about Mike from CBS news in 2014 (http://www. cbsnews.com/news/penn-state-postman-delivers-lesson-in-happiness/). Most students cannot tell you his last name, but that's okay with him. As he told writer John Patishnock, "I'm not a big deal, but everyone thinks I am...I'm just Mike the Mailman."

98 Go Out on the Town

You can't spend a football weekend at Penn State without hitting a couple of hot-spot bars and restaurants. Like any small college town far away from big cities, there are the traditional establishments that have been here for decades and others that come and go.

Much to the dismay of the university's power structure, Penn State is usually in the top 10 in party schools. In 2009 the *Princeton Review* named it No. 1, but in 2015 it was No. 7. *Newsweek* and the *Daily Beast* ranked the school No. 2 in 2012. However, you don't need alcohol to enjoy a night or two on the town.

Most of the bars serve food of some kind but the quality can vary, so don't be upset if your hamburger is greasy or your pizza sometimes tastes like it was frozen. There are plenty of alternatives for food and music. Students often have different tastes than older folks but they usually will give you good advice, depending on what you want. What follows is not a comprehensive list of restaurants and bars but a few of the most popular.

Let's start with the Corner Room, which has been in business since 1926 as a hotel and restaurant across the street from Penn State's main gate on College Avenue in the heart of downtown State College. It's a traditional stop for old grads, especially for breakfast. The Corner Room's fine dining restaurant, the Allen Street Grill, is upstairs and its Zeno's Pub is downstairs. Around the corner is another subsidiary, Pickles, which is located in a onetime movie theater that students like me once called "the arm pit" for obvious reasons. And if you want late-night dancing, try the Indigo three doors down from Corner Room at the lower level. In fact, you'll find entertainment at many of the bars and restaurants mentioned here.

Dining at the Tavern down College Avenue is another tradition that goes back to the post–World War II era, when it opened primarily as a spaghetti restaurant. The menu is much broader these days and so are the choices in the bar, which were once limited to beer because of the borough's old, restrictive liquor laws.

There's no alcohol at the Diner, another traditional restaurant going back decades that's just a few steps away from the Corner Room. The service and food can be erratic, but the famous fresh toasted sticky buns are worth it. Or buy a package of the sticky buns and toast them yourself.

For years in the middle of the 20th century, there were just two beer joints in town. Both are still there, but only one still has its original name, the Rathskeller, which opened its doors in 1933. Enjoying pregame at "the Skeller" is a tradition, once with seven-ounce Rolling Rock ponies and now with a Yuengling. The Skeller is one block east of the Corner Room and a half block west of the Tavern. The other original bar is a block south on Beaver Avenue and downstairs. Once known as the Cave, it's now the Phyrst. Above the Phyrst is Local Whiskey, a higher-end bar that locals call Second.

One of the busiest bars even on non-football weekends is Cafe 210 West, named for its address on College Avenue. When the weather is warm, the cafe's front patio and the deck in the back are the places to be, but there's also a bar, dining room, and band room in between.

Up and down College and Beaver Avenues and the side streets there are many other hot-spot bars. Kildare's Irish Pub, with its typical Irish grub and booze, is at the far east end of College Avenue before University Drive, the road that leads to Beaver Stadium. The West Side Stadium Bar and Grill is further west on College Avenue, just past a residential area about a half mile west of Cafe 210.

Between Kildare's and the Tavern is a conglomerate of Dante's Restaurants that includes the Deli, Bar Blue, the Saloon, and Inferno. Nearby are Liberty, the Lion's Den, Rotelli's, Primanti's, and a retro diner called Baby's Burgers and Shakes that is alcohol-free.

Hotels: No Room in the Inn

Finding a room in the State College area on football weekends is easy if you reserve a year ahead or the team is not winning. It will also cost you. The standard has been a two-day minimum at $200 to $500 depending on the class of hotel or motel, but prices can change quickly. This doesn't mean you might not get a room at a respectable price if you wait even until game day; there are always cancellations. A big game will almost certainly be a sellout and so will Homecoming weekend.

Thousands of out-of-town season-ticket holders are regulars who do reserve a year in advance. Others rent or buy condominiums. Sometimes the hotels and motels in nearby towns also fill up early, such as in Lewistown (30 miles east), Altoona (50 miles south), Dubois (60 miles west), and the I-80 East corridor from Milesburg to Milton. Many fans who live the farthest distance find a hotel or motel halfway or so between Beaver Stadium and their home. Keep in mind, traffic can be a pain on game day, especially going east through Harrisburg.

Most of the best hotels are chains, including several that are owned by the international Shaner Hotel Group, which is based here. Two of the finest in State College are owned by the university: the Nittany Lion Inn, in the heart of campus, and the Penn Stater, on the eastern fringe, a mile away from the stadium. Rooms at the Inn, the Carnegie House (also near the stadium), and the Atherton in downtown are the most luxurious. You're on your own at the hotels with unfamiliar names.

Campgrounds also are available in a 50-mile radius of Penn State. If you drive an RV, you are in luck. State College's two Walmarts allow free overnight parking as early as Wednesday and RVs can also park Friday and Saturday nights at special lots at Beaver Stadium.

Sleeping in your car is a no-no. You might wind up in a jail cell. Especially if you're wearing Ohio State scarlet-and-gray.

Outside downtown, you have sports bars such as Champs and Letterman's (formerly Damon's) and restaurants with their own breweries like Otto's Pub, the Happy Valley Brewery, and Home Delivery. Alumni frequent Whiskers in the Nittany Lion Inn and Legends at the Penn Stater, both hotels operated by the university, and P. J. Harrigan's in the Ramada Inn.

The Nittany Lion Inn, which opened in 1931, is the traditional on-campus hotel. Its Friday night seafood buffet in the main dining room attracts many VIPs, as does the upscale Carnegie House, which some believe to be the best restaurant in the area. The Carnegie House is not far from Beaver Stadium in the Toftrees residential area, which also has another restaurant patronized by locals, the All-American Ale House.

Faccia Luna Pizzeria also is a hangout for locals, former football players, and university VIPs. Don't be deceived by the name. Yes, its pizza is great but so are the other items on the Italian-based menu. Among the other restaurants that attract locals and visitors are Mario's (another Dante's property), Spats Café & Speakeasy (above the Rathskeller), Gigi's, Clem's Roadside Bar and Grill in the Autoport Motel, and two in suburban Boalsburg, Kelly's Steak and Seafood (which has a life-sized bull sign outside, a holdover from its years as the Boalsburg Steak House) and Duffy's Tavern, a Victorian-style tavern that dates back to 1819 when the building was a stagecoach stop.

Naturally, there are many other restaurants in the area, including chains and several serving Asian cuisine. And no visit to State College and Penn State any time in the year is complete without breakfast, brunch, or lunch at the Waffle Shop. There are three of them, and on big weekends like football, graduation, and the arts festival, the lines are long.

Penn State may be in the middle of nowhere, but even in nowhere you can eat, drink, and be merry, even if you're from Michigan.

99 Rankings Potpourri

In choosing the 100 things to be included in this book, there were many others that had to be left out. Rather than select one more for this chapter, I'm listing several that could easily be separate chapters. Perhaps to some readers a few of these are better choices than my 99. Can't please everyone. Let's just call these quick hits.

Things to Do:

Visit Joe Paterno's grave site and drive past his home. The coach is buried in a nondescript plot at the Spring Creek Presbyterian Cemetery, not far from the State College Country Club. Parking is limited and you have to walk to the grave site. His longtime home is at the end of McKee Street, a couple blocks north of campus. Don't be obnoxious. Drive by, turn around, and move on. You might be surprised that there is nothing fancy or flamboyant about his home or the neighborhood. That was Paterno's style.

Read all the books written about Penn State football (see "Sources"), especially the ones I wrote (half kidding). Ridge Riley's *Road to Number One* is the definitive history of Penn State football from 1881 to 1975 and Ken Denlinger's *For the Glory* is the consummate inside look from the players' perspective. If you want to have a quick understanding of Paterno's philosophy try *Quotable Joe* by Budd Thalman or son Joe Paterno's book *Paterno Legacy*, while brother George Paterno's *Joe Paterno: The Coach from Byzantium* is probably the most honest and perceptive look at the late head coach and his family.

Watch the "TV Quarterbacks" show. This weekly program featuring Penn State's head coach aired statewide during the season on various public television stations from 1965 through 1984, long before the saturation of cable TV and the Internet. It started with Coach Rip Engle and was originally called *Wednesday Quarterbacks* and Paterno turned it into a popular must-watch show hosted primarily by Fran Fisher that not only included game video but off-the-cuff and sometimes humorous interviews with players. The shows are available for viewing at the sports archives in the Paterno-Patee Library.

Attend a women's volleyball game in Rec Hall. This isn't beach ball. Coach Russ Rose has made Penn State the best collegiate women's volleyball team in the country with seven national championships as of 2014. His athletes are tough and disciplined on the court and polite and amiable off it. Cheering for a winner is always easy, but once you see these ladies in action you will be hooked, win or lose. A loyal following routinely turns up at Rec Hall, but seats are almost always available.

Visit the grave of Penn State president George Atherton. Atherton was president from 1882 to 1906 and helped saved the college from the edge of oblivion. He encouraged student participation in sports and enthusiastically supported the creation of intercollegiate sports teams in baseball, football, and track that occurred under his presidency. Atherton hired the first six head football coaches and approved the expansion of athletic facilities that led to Beaver Field. Atherton's grave is not far from Old Main, alongside Schwab Auditorium, and he is the only person buried on campus and within the borough of State College.

Sing and dance to Zombie Nation's "Kernkraft 400" at Beaver Stadium, especially during a nighttime whiteout. Perhaps you are already familiar with the electronic tune by Zombie Nation. The students know the name, but the over-50 crowd sitting in the more expensive seats may not. It goes like this (without the music, of course): "Oh, oh, oh, ohoo. Oh, oh, oh, ohoo. We are, Penn State!" and repeats a couple of times. Go on YouTube and search for "Penn State Zombie Nation" and see for yourself. Then, the next time you hear "Kernkraft 400" in Beaver Stadium after a big play, jump up and join the fun.

Do the wave at Beaver Stadium. Okay, this one's old hat. The first time the Hawaiian Wave rolled around the stadium was in the opening game of 1984 against Rutgers, September 8 to be precise. We don't know how it started, but the 84,409 spectators enjoyed doing the wave several times as Penn State beat Rutgers 15–12 in a game not settled until late in the fourth quarter. And in case you didn't know it, this was the debut of Rutgers' new head coach Dick Anderson, a former Penn State player and assistant coach who returned to be an assistant again seven years later when his luck ran out in New Jersey.

Take a selfie with head football coach James Franklin. If you don't know what a selfie is you either don't use a cell phone or you are not up to date with the technological savvy of the millenials. Simply use your cell phone to take a photo of yourself and whoever is with you. Coach Franklin isn't bashful about posing for selfies, unless, of course, you try to take yours while he's strolling the sideline during a game.

Take a selfie with other head coaches of Penn State's 33 varsity teams. Or try to do it, at least. Some of them may not be as cooperative or as accessible as the football coach. And please don't tell them I sent you.

Stop by Nittanyville before home games and mingle with the students camping out. Thursday is best when the team is there. Sing the "Alma Mater" and other songs with the campers, bring them food if you can, and lead them in the "We Are—Penn State!" cheer.

See the NCAA banners for the women's basketball team in the Bryce Jordan Center. Since 1982 the Lady Lions have been to 25 postseason NCAA tournaments, including the Final Four in 2000, 13 Sweet 16s, and four Elite Eights, with such players as Susan Robinson, the Wade Trophy National Player of the Year in

1992; two-time AP first-team Kelly Mazzante (2003–04); and the Pomeroy-Naismith Award winners as the national players of the year shorter than 5'8": Suzie McConnell (1988), Helen Darling (2000), and Alex Bentley (2013).

Watch a Penn State baseball game played on Medlar Field in Lubrano Park. This is a classy, comfortable baseball stadium across the street from Beaver Stadium with another picturesque view of Mt. Nittany, especially at dusk. Built in partnership with the Altoona Curve Class AA baseball organization and opened in June 2006, Lubrano Park also serves as the home of the State College Spikes in the short-season Class A New York–Penn League, and you can even buy a beer there, just like in the major leagues. You can also be arrested if you drink too many beers, just like in the major leagues.

Things to Know:
See my next book.

100 Root for James Franklin's Football Teams

I've saved this chapter for last because it looks at the future rather than the past and present, which is what this book is all about. Besides, it also might get more attention ranked here from readers wondering why it's the last thing Penn State fans should know and do. Did I catch you?

The future of Penn State football is now in the hands of James Franklin, the 16th head coach in the school's history. Will he be there two years like the last coach, Bill O'Brien, or 46 years like Joe Paterno, or—much more likely—somewhere in between?

This is a radically different period in college football and it changed quickly since Paterno's last season in 2011.

Social media is dominant, and the old dependable print media has morphed into an Internet battleground with Twitter, Facebook, and who knows what's next influencing what happens on and off the field.

Salaries for head coaches and their assistants have taken off like rockets to outer space, making a new caste of multimillionaires. Players are now being paid thousands of dollars legally for out-of-pocket expenses beyond their tuition and housing scholarships and their numerous other perks such as training tables and academic counseling.

Facilities constantly need upgrades and modernization in an ever-increasing arms race to attract the bluest of blue-chip recruits. What was good enough just a couple years ago is now passé, because your biggest rivals just spent millions to showcase their locker rooms, indoor practice fields, and players' lounges and if you don't do it, too, it's sayonara.

Naturally, the price of tickets is also going up. Parking at the stadiums costs more and so does the food and drink at the concession stands. If you don't want to pay, you stay home and watch the games on television. There will always be someone else willing to take your place—as long as the team is winning, right?

This is not meant to be a cynical observation about college football in 2015 and beyond. It's the world we live in, and Penn State football fans *need* to know that.

Don't complain if James Franklin does things differently than Joe Paterno or Bill O'Brien did. If you don't like his play-calling, that's your problem, not his. You may not have liked some of the play-calling under Paterno, either. It's Franklin's team, and we're just fans. He wants to please us and he won't do it simply by posing for a selfie photo with you. He *needs* to win.

But he has to do it the Penn State Way: play by the rules, no cheating, no shortcuts, with the highest respect for academics.

Franklin's chances of winning are significantly better than when he took the job in early January 2014. The destructive NCAA sanctions have been lifted. All the scholarships are back and the Big Ten championships and postseason bowls are again a reality. His 25-man 2015 recruiting class was rated No. 13 in the country by Scout.com and No. 15 by Rivals.com and both scouting services had Penn State at No. 2 in the Big Ten behind Ohio State.

Many in the college football media rate Franklin as one of the best head coaches in the country. "[He's] a relentless salesman and recruiter who oozes energy and self-confidence; Franklin will get people excited about Penn State football again," wrote Stewart Mandel for SI.com before the 2014 season.

Franklin is certainly one of the highest paid. *USA Today*'s annual survey of college football salaries in November 2014 ranked Franklin's $4.3 million contract as sixth nationally and third in the Big Ten after Michigan State's Mark Dantonio ($5.64 million) and Ohio State's Urban Meyer ($4.54 million). Dantonio and Meyer are proven winners of conference titles with Meyer also having won two national championships at Florida and the 2014 crown at OSU. Since the *USA Today* survey former NFL head coach Jim Harbaugh was hired by his alma mater, Michigan, at a $5 million base salary plus incentives.

Franklin's being paid a lot of money for someone with moderate success in four years at undermanned Vanderbilt of the powerful SEC. Penn State fans will see if Franklin and his staff are up to the challenge.

That will take at least another two to three years because of the NCAA sanctions and the time needed for Franklin to get his on-field coaching style and his recruits in place and humming. Penn State fans *need* to be patient and Franklin *needs* the fans to be on his side. That doesn't mean you should not criticize and be vocal about it. Above all, cheer for the players and their success.

Super quarterback Christian Hackenberg and his teammates have been through a lot in the last few years. They have been special Penn State players, like those on the 2012 team that overcame the worst of the worst. They will be forever part of the proud Penn State football legacy, and the new players can be part of it, too.

So can all Penn State fans. Watch James Franklin's football teams and cheer, "We Are—Penn State!"

Sources

I have written about Penn State sports for 60 years, and my prime sources were either from my own work or from books, articles, and video I have used in the past. This includes hundreds of interviews over the years. I did find new sources while writing various chapters and sidebars, and where possible I have cited the source in the chapter. I also did a number of fresh interviews that are noted within the chapters.

It is impossible to go back through all my material and mention each specific source for each chapter. This is not a book with footnotes or addendums. If pressed, I would have no problems backing up the content of the chapters and sidebars. Based on my experience, there will be errors and mistakes in this book. They will not be intentional, and I apologize to readers in advance for every one of them. In fact, I hope readers will contact me with corrections. That has happened in the past, and some of the mistakes I made then have been corrected for this book.

Since researching my first Penn State book, *The Penn State Football Encyclopedia*, published in 1998, and for nearly all books and articles since, the best source for much of the team's history is Ridge Riley's *Road to Number One*, published in 1977. Ridge's seminal work is the bible of Penn State football. I like to think of it as the Old Testament, with the rest of us authors contributing to the New Testament.

I also need to mention the Penn State athletics department and three specific publications that enabled me to develop my historical expertise.

After the publication of my encyclopedia, the Nittany Lion Club hired me on a freelance basis to edit its monthly newsletter sent to season-ticket holders. About the same time, the sports information office gave me the opportunity to write historical stories for the home-game football programs, and I have continued to do that every football season. I also have contributed to two different Internet projects for the athletic department.

The Penn State Football Encyclopedia also led to my contributions to three local magazines, starting in the late 1990s: *Town & Gown* and its *Penn State Football* and *Basketball Annual*(s) subsidiaries, *Blue White Illustrated*, and *Fight On State*. I continue to write for those publications and/or their websites, particularly *Blue White Illustrated* where I do a monthly column as well as a frequent feature.

Much of what I have written for the athletic department and for those three publications are integrated throughout this book, but rarely cited specifically. For example, the background on the We Are—Penn State cheer first appeared in *Town & Gown* with an updated version a few years later in *Blue White Illustrated*. *Blue White Illustrated* also had the original story on Penn State's ice hockey program that dates to 1906 while *Fight On State* published the first article I did about the history of Linebacker U. The non-football chapters in this book about the school's pioneering women's varsity sport program and baseball coach Joe Bedenk's involvement in creating the College World Series came out of original articles for the athletic department.

In my previous books, I frequently quoted from newspaper articles written by Penn State football beat reporters. I do not believe I used any of those quotes without attribution in this book. If I did, again, it was not intentional.

What follows is a list of the selected sources.

Books

Anonymous. *Cookin' with the Lion.* University Park, PA: Penn State Alumni Association, 1988.

Bergstein, Mickey. *Penn State Stories and More.* Harrisburg, PA: RB Books, 1998.

Bezilla, Michael. *Penn State: An Illustrated History.* University Park, PA: The Pennsylvania State University Press, 1985.

Bilovsky, Frank. *Lion Country: Inside Penn State Football.* West Point, NY: Leisure Press, 1982.

Blockson, Charles L. *Damn Rare: Memoirs of an African-American Bibliophile.* Tracy, CA: Quantum Leap Publisher, Inc. 1998.

Boyles, Bob and Paul Guido. *Fifty Years of College Football.* New York: Skyhorse Publishing, 2007.

Brown, Scott. *The Lion Kings.* Greensburg, PA: Charles M. Henry Printing Co, 1996.

Brown, Scott and Sam Carchidi. *Miracle in the Making: The Adam Taliaferro Story.* Chicago: Triumph Books, 2001.

Chesworth, Jo. *Story of the Century: The Borough of State College, Pennsylvania 1886–1996.* Published by the Borough of State College in cooperation with the Barash Group, 1995.

Cope, Myron. *Double Yoi! A Revealing Memoir by the Broadcaster/Writer.* Champaign, IL: Sports Publishing LLC, 2002.

Denlinger, Ken. *For the Glory.* New York: St. Martin's Griffin, 1995.

Di Salvatore, Bryan. *A Clever Base-Ballist: The Life and Times of John Montgomery Ward.* New York: Pantheon Books, 1999.

Donnell, Rich. *The Hig.* Montgomery, AL: Owl Bay Publishers, 1994.

Dorney, Keith. *Black and Honolulu Blue: In the Trenches in the NFL.* Chicago: Triumph Books, 2003.

Esposito, Jackie R. and Steven L. Herb. *The Nittany Lion: An Illustrated Tale.* University Park, PA: The Pennsylvania State University Press, 1997.

Gallagher, Mark. *The New York Yankee Encyclopedia (Vol.3).* Champaign, IL: Sagamore Publishing, 1997.

Hyman, Jordan. *Game of My Life.* Champaign, IL: Sports Publishing LLC, 2006.

Hyman, Mervin D. & Gordon S. White, Jr. *Joe Paterno: Football My Way.* New York: Macmillan, 1971.

Maxyumk, John. *The 50 Greatest Plays in New York Giants Football History.* Chicago: Triumph Books, 2008.

Misssanelli, M. G. *The Perfect Season.* University Park, PA: The Pennsylvania State University Press, 2007.

Moore, Lenny with Jeffrey Jay Ellish. *All Things Being Equal.* Champaign, IL: Sports Publishing LLC, 2005.

Panaccio, Tim. *Beast of the East: Penn State vs Pitt.* West Point, NY: Leisure Press, 1982.

Paterno, George. *Joe Paterno: The Coach from Byzantium.* Champaign, IL: Sports Publishing, 1997.

Paterno, Jay. *Paterno Legacy: Enduring Lessons from the Life and Death of My Father*. Chicago: Triumph Books, 2014.

Paterno, Joe with Bernard Asbell. *Paterno By the Book*. New York: Random House, 1989.

Pittman, Charlie and Tony Pittman. *Playing for Paterno*. Chicago: Triumph Books, 2007.

Prato, Lou. *The Penn State Football Encyclopedia*. Champaign, IL: Sports Publishing LLC, 1998.

Prato, Lou and Scott Brown. *What It Means to Be a Nittany Lion*. Chicago: Triumph Books, 2006.

Prato, Lou. *The Penn State Football Vault*. Atlanta: Whitman Publishing, 2008.

Prato, Lou. *Game Changers: The Greatest Plays in Penn State Football History*. Chicago: Triumph Books, 2009.

Prato, Lou. *We Are PENN STATE: The Remarkable Journey of the 2012 Nittany Lions*. Triumph Books, 2013.

Radakovich, Dan with Lou Prato, *Bad Rad: Football Nomad*. Pittsburgh, PA: Touchdown Books, 2012.

Range, Thomas F. and Sean Patrick Smith. *The Penn State Blue Band*. University Park, PA: The Pennsylvania State University Press, 1999.

Rappoport, Ken. *The Nittany Lions*. Huntsville, AL: The Strode Publishers, 1973.

Rappoport, Ken. *Where Have You Gone?* Champaign, IL: Sports Publishing LLC, 2005.

Rattermann, Dale. *The Big Ten A Century of Excellence*. Champaign, IL: Sports Publishing LLC, 1996.

Richeal, Kip. *Welcome to the Big Ten*. Champaign, IL: Sagamore Publishing, 1994.

Riley, Ridge. *The Road to Number One*. New York: Doubleday, 1977.

Stout, Lee. *Ice Cream U: The Story of the Nation's Most Successful Collegiate Creamery*. University Park, PA: The Pennsylvania State University Press, 2009.

Thalman, L. Budd. *Quotable Joe*. Nashville: Tower House Publishing, 2000.

Newspapers

Altoona Mirror, *Arizona Republic*, the *Bellefonte Democratic Watchman*, *Blue White Illustrated*, *Centre Daily Times*, *Chicago Sun-Times*, *Chicago Tribune*, *Cincinnati Enquirer*, *Columbus Citizen-Journal*, *Columbus Post-Dispatch*, *Daily Collegian*, the *Dallas Morning News*, *Dallas Times-Herald*, *Dayton Daily News*, *Detroit Free Press*, *Detroit News*, *Football News*, *Green Bay Press Gazette*, *Greensburg-Pittsburgh Tribune-Review*, *Harrisburg Patriot-News*, *Huntingdon News*, *Indianapolis Star*, *Kansas City Star*, *Kansas City Times*, *Los Angeles Times*, *Miami Herald*, *Miami News*, *Milwaukee Journal*, *New Orleans Times-Picayune*, the *New Orleans State-Item*, *New York Amsterdam*, *New York Times*, *New York World Telegram*, *Philadelphia Daily News*, *Philadelphia Inquirer*, *Phoenix Gazette*, *South Bend Tribune*, *Sporting News*, *USA Today*, *Washington Post*, and *York Daily Record*.

Magazines
Blue White Illustrated, Fight On State, Newsweek, Princeton Review, PRO, Sport, Sports Illustrated, State College Town & Gown, and *Town & Gown's Penn State Football and Basketball Annuals.*

Wire Services
The Associated Press, United Press International.

Other Penn State Sources
LaVie (Penn State Annual Yearbook), *Nittany Lion Club Newsletter, The Penn State Football Letter,* Penn State Football Media Guides, Penn State Game Day Football Programs, Penn State Official Athletic Record Books, Penn State News Releases, *Penn State in the World War 1917–1919, Souvenir Program Penn State versus the University of Pittsburgh Thanksgiving 1908,* Penn State Paterno-Patee Library Sports Archives, the Penn State All-Sports Museum, Penn State postgame news conferences, personal interviews with former players, and videotapes of Penn State football games.

Other Miscellaneous Sources
Official 2006 NCAA Divisions 1-A and 1-AA Football Records Book, Official 1955 NCAA Basketball Guide, The 1994 Information Please Sports Almanac, and the *Report of Special Investigative Counsel Regarding the Actions of the Pennsylvania State University Related to the Child Sexual Abuse Committed by Gerald A. Sandusky, by Freeh, Sporkin and Sullivan, LLP, July 12, 2012.*

Websites
BigTen.org
JHowell.net
CollegeFootball.org
ESPN.com
FightOnState.com
NCAA.org
Ibhof.com
NCASports.org
Infoweb.Newsbank.com
Creamery.psu.edu
Pro-football-reference.com
Profootballhof.com
Sabr.org
Upliftingathletes.org
bryantmuseum.com
bwi.rivas.com
CBSNews.com
Cwsomaha.com
Heisman.com
Johncappelletti73heisman.com
Libraries.psu.edu
Pennstate.scout.com
PSU.edu
Gopsusports.com/
Mtnittany.org/mountain/hike/
mmqb.si.com
Roseparadeonline.com
SI.com
Sports-reference.com
Statecollege.com/news/
Talgating.com
Tournamentofroses.com
uscho.com
Washjeff.edu
Wikipedia.org
YouTube.com